1995

THE ART OF RAISING MONEY

THE ART OF RAISING MONEY

William J. Smith

American Management Association

This book is available at a special
discount when ordered in bulk quantities.
For information, contact Special Sales Department,
AMACOM, a division of American Management Association,
135 West 50th Street, New York, NY 10020.

Library of Congress Cataloging-in-Publication Data

Smith, William J., 1917–
  The art of raising money.

    Includes index.
    1. Fund raising.   I. Title.
HG177.S64   1985   658.1'5224   84-45791
ISBN 0-8144-5830-0

Printing number

10 9 8 7 6 5 4 3 2 1

To Peg,
my wife of over forty years,
whose love, understanding, support, and humor
have helped me through many a difficult time.

ACKNOWLEDGMENTS

Grateful appreciation is extended to the following individuals who have been generous with their time and talent and who have made a substantial contribution to the completion of this work.

DOERMANN, HUMPHREY   President, The Bush Foundation. St. Paul, Minnesota.

JOHNSON, HAROLD   Former Executive Director, Annual Catholic Appeal, St. Paul, Minnesota.

KAZMIERCZAK, ANN MARGARET   Administrative Assistant, St. Paul, Minnesota.

KEENAN, JAMES A.   Former Vice President, Development, College of St. Thomas, St. Paul, Minnesota.

KURTZ, HAROLD P.   Director of Development, Children's Hospital, St. Paul, Minnesota.

LaBELLE, JOSEPH E.   Executive Director, Minnesota Higher Education Facilities Commission, St. Paul, Minnesota.

MANTHY, MARK   Sands and Weinberg, Certified Public Accountants, St. Paul, Minnesota.

MARSH, KIM   Executive Director, United Jewish Fund & Council, St. Paul, Minnesota.

McCARTHY, PETER L.   Advanced Underwriting Counsel, Minnesota Mutual Life Insurance Company, St. Paul, Minnesota.

PETERSON, H. GEOFFREY   Director, Advanced Underwriting, Minnesota Mutual Life Insurance Company, St. Paul, Minnesota.

SMITH, DAVID G.   Chief Administrative Officer, St. Mary's Hospital, Decatur, Illinois.

SMITH, EDWARD B.   President, Integrated Equity Management Corporation, St. Paul, Minnesota.

SMITH, LINDA B.   Assistant Director of Development and Guaranty Fund Administrator, Minnesota Orchestra, St. Paul, Minnesota.

SMITH, MICHAEL D.   Former President, St. Paul-Ramsey Arts and Science Council, St. Paul, Minnesota.

TAYLOR, JOHN D.   Former President, Northwest Area Foundation, St. Paul, Minnesota.

THEOBALD, JON A.   Executive Vice President, First Trust Company, St. Paul, Minnesota.

VERRET, PAUL A.   President, The Saint Paul Foundation, St. Paul, Minnesota.

Although the major authority for this book has been the author's own experience, the following published works have served as valuable resources and also merit an acknowledgment of appreciation.

American Association of Fund-Raising Counsel   *Giving USA*

Arthur Andersen & Co.   *Tax Economics of Charitable Giving*

American Council for the Arts   *United Arts Fund-Raising* and *1981 Campaign Analyis*

Council for Financial Aid to Education, Inc.   *Corporate Support of Education* and other publications

Foundation Center   *Foundations Today, Facts and Figures*

Independent Sector   *Dimensions of the Independent Sector* and *Patterns of Giving by Individuals*

Dennis Murphy   *Asking Corporations for Money* (Gothic Press, 1982)

The Conference Board   *Annual Survey of Corporate Contributions, 1984*

CONTENTS

Part I: *Campaign Principles and Organization*

1	Victory or Defeat	3
2	The Nonprofit Sector	7
3	Getting Ready: Take a Look at Your Organization	13
4	The Essential Ingredients of a Successful Campaign	28
5	The Fund-Raising Marketplace	38
6	Why Do People Serve?	49
7	Determining the Campaign Structure	56
8	Goal Setting	67
9	The Promotion Program	72
10	Managing the Campaign	88
11	The Corporate Campaign	98
12	Soliciting the Wealthy	121
13	Soliciting Foundations	126
14	Special Campaign Markets: Small Business, Residential, and the Professions	136

Part II: *Specialized Campaigns*

15	Campaigning for the Arts	149
16	College and University Campaigns	160
17	Hospital Campaigns	171
18	Campaigns by Sectarian Federations	182
19	United Way Campaigns	190
20	Building Endowment Campaigns	210
21	Planned Giving: A Deferred-Gifts Program	220

Appendixes — 241

Index — 265

About the Author — 277

PART I

CAMPAIGN PRINCIPLES AND ORGANIZATION

1

VICTORY OR DEFEAT

The ballroom in Central City was filled to overflowing, abuzz with anticipation that this was going to be a good night. There was an ebullience in the air as people moved from table to table exchanging pleasantries and small talk about the recent campaign.

At the front of the ballroom was a large dais occupied by the chairman and his top leadership, both men and women. A small orchestra provided pleasant background music.

Following dinner the chairman rose, smiling and happy and flushed with victory. After some preliminary comments, he called on his major division leaders to report on the outcome of the campaign. Each person stood and acknowledged, to applause, the work of particularly outstanding campaigners in the division, asking them to stand for special recognition. Now the air of anticipation grew as everyone wondered what the final total would be with each division rolling over the top.

After the last division report was made the chairman again took the podium:

Ladies and gentlemen, once again this community has demonstrated its generosity. All of you have shown your concern for the individual and the necessity of giving each person the opportunity to make the most of his talents and abilities. Your gifts and your work will endure all year round and for many years to come. I want to thank each of you for what you have done and, more especially, the contributors for their generosity.

Ladies and gentlemen, I am happy to report tonight—on a goal of $5 million—a final total of $5.15 million, or 103 percent of goal.

The crowd rose as one and roundly applauded the chairman and his leaders. When the cheering subsided, a local minister strode to the lectern and offered a prayer of thanks, expressing the conviction that the funds raised would be meaningful in the lives of many fellow citizens. The crowd rose again as the band struck up "God Bless

America." People then began to leave, chatting and congratulating one another on the job that had been done. It was a happy night!

One hundred and fifty miles away in Middleburg there was a similar gathering for a cause that was similar in objective. The room was sparsely filled and there was a feeling of submission and defeat in the air. The head table had only a handful of people, many of them substitutes for the division personnel. The chairman rose and began his prepared speech:

> Ladies and gentlemen, when we started this campaign we knew that we faced almost insuperable odds in trying to reach our goal. I do not need to recite to you, since you have been on the front line, all the difficulties we encountered and the disappointments we have had. I do want to express my appreciation to you for the time and effort you have put forth on behalf of a good cause and only wish that our report tonight were more promising.
>
> I will not call on each of the division heads for their reports, but will summarize them for you.

The chairman then quickly commented on the results attained by the major divisions and some of the obstructions and difficulties that each had encountered. He ended by giving the dollar totals for each division, but not the percent of goal raised.

> Ladies and gentlemen, it is obvious that because of circumstances beyond our control this campaign cannot be concluded tonight and we cannot give a final total. Instead, we will extend the campaign for another three weeks and we sincerely ask that all of you continue your efforts to see any prospects who have not been solicited and obtain any gifts that have not been received. It is absolutely essential that we raise every dollar we can.

There was a somberness in the crowd and a sense of letdown within the whole group. After the minister gave a short prayer, people began to straggle out, commenting to one another on their campaign experiences and why they had not done better.

Here were two communities of roughly equal size in approximately the same geographic area with essentially the same campaign potential. One was celebrating a major victory, the other a major defeat. Why? Why did Middleburg do so poorly while its companion city had an over-the-top result? The reasons that some campaigns are successful are the focus of this book. It is my hope that the principles enunciated here will help guide institutions in direct need of funds to conduct successful, over-the-top campaigns. If that is achieved, the book will be a success.

WHY FUND RAISING IS NEEDED

Do we really have to have fund-raising campaigns at all? Why can't essential services be supported by taxes? There have been suggestions in recent years that the latter would, in fact, be a more equitable way of supporting the arts, health and human services, and education, since everyone would be participating equitably in the costs of these programs.

Anyone who has worked in a voluntary fund-raising capacity knows that there is a great deal of inequity in giving. Certain individuals and corporations are unusually generous and responsive to the needs of their communities. Other companies and individuals for one reason or another seem to have little interest in sharing their beneficence. In a very sad sense, they just don't enjoy giving. Still, for those who have been generous there is perhaps no greater sense of satisfaction than freely sharing their wealth with others and being able to see some of their dollars put into action. The joy of giving is truly one of the greatest experiences a person can have.

America more than any country has shared its resources with others. No country has been more generous to its enemies in defeat and, on a voluntary level, no country has ever shared its wealth so liberally with those who need it.

Those who sometimes question the value of private organizations need only look at what makes America uniquely different from so many other countries. The greatness of its educational institutions, the richness of its arts, the compassion of its human services organizations, the excellence of its health care system, the strength of its religious freedom—all of these represent the voluntary coming together of people to achieve a common objective without dictation by government or by laws that dictate their actions.

Imagine a country lacking the inspiration of independent churches or the richness of private organizations in the arts. Imagine an educational system supported entirely by taxes, with all policies and teaching methods dictated by government. Under these circumstances, how long would it take for freedom to be undermined and for America's educational system to become stultified? The competition for quality between private and public institutions would be gone and innovativeness and new technology might be lost.

America has been a leader in medical research—in finding new ways to treat the mentally ill, the retarded, and those with special diseases. Despite its problems, the American medical care system remains without peer. America's private institutions are sustained by our dedication to supporting them as generously as we can through voluntary gifts solicited by our friends. Contributions are the price we pay to live in a country that so many want to enter and so few want to leave.

WORKING FOR PEOPLE

It is important to realize that the organization, structure, and campaign methods involved in fund raising are only means to an end. There is only one basic reason for raising money—to help people. Whether the cause is for human services, education, environment, or health, fund raising makes life better for our fellow human beings.

I remember well the thrill of receiving a scholarship loan back in the 1930s when times were very tough. The loan made the difference between my being able to finish college and facing a future of manual labor. I'm sure that private financial assistance and scholarships are equally important to thousands of young men and women seeking a college education today.

We have all experienced in our lives the eradication of polio, the success of organ transplants, the strides made in conquering heart disease and cancer. All these were essentially the result of the work of private institutions and individuals.

Only a decade ago, a child with cystic fibrosis could expect to live two or three years; today that child may live well into adulthood. I remember the tears in the eyes of our campaign chairman when he visited a sheltered workshop for the cerebral palsied and the surprise of a campaign volunteer in visiting a rehabilitation center when he saw a friend who had suffered a stroke in therapy. Their satisfaction was complete when they recognized that their campaign efforts meant so much to people who needed the services they were asking their fellow citizens to support.

As you read the succeeding chapters, I hope that you will become an accomplished fund raiser. More than that, I hope you will gain a great sense of satisfaction in knowing that your efforts are so important to so many and that you, yourself, will become a better human being.

2

THE NONPROFIT SECTOR

The private nonprofit sector in the United States is composed of hundreds of thousands of organizations serving huge constituencies and employing thousands of people who are dependent upon the institutions' budgets for their livelihood.

Most of these organizations face the increasingly difficult task of balancing budgets in today's economy. Not only are costs increasing for salaries, maintenance, energy, and supplies; but in many cases other sources of revenue, particularly funds from government, are declining, making it difficult for administrators to meet responsibilities to their constituencies and still demonstrate fiscal integrity.

Accordingly, all organizations need to examine carefully every expenditure they make. The days of easy money are gone. However, careful control of expenditures is not enough; organizations must look for new sources of income, sources that are still undeveloped and untapped. Financial development departments in colleges and universities, churches, hospitals, social agencies, and cultural organizations will play a major role in enabling private organizations to operate successfully. Raising money both from the general public and from selected prospects will absorb more and more time and attention of top administrators, boards of directors, staff and volunteers.

A COMPREHENSIVE PROGRAM OF SUPPORT

Campaigns, in general, are organized for one or more of three reasons:

1. To raise funds for annual sustaining support for the institution—operating campaigns.
2. To raise funds for special building needs, including renovation—capital campaigns.

3. To create a corpus or endowment, the income from which is used either to supplement the general operating budget or for some restricted purpose.

In analyzing their financial needs and looking to the future, nonprofit organizations need to develop a *total* program of giving if their institutions are to continue to serve and have vitality.

Such a comprehensive program of giving can be likened to a three-legged stool—each leg is essential if the stool is to stand and if it is to have stability. The legs in this case are the different sources of income necessary to the long-range well-being of the institution. The support program must be long term and strategic, anticipating what the future needs of the organization may be, what kinds of financial problems it will have, and what the possible solutions are.

Generally speaking, alert leadership makes careful plans to sustain these "legs" by providing for:

1. Adequate annual support of the institution through fees, tuitions, purchase of services, or grants and, from a development point of view, through the *annual* fund-raising effort.

2. Future capital needs for the institution and at least a 10- to 15-year plan as to what may be required in the way of building renovation, repair, new buildings, and the sources of income available for construction from government grants, revenue bonds, and special capital fund campaigns.

3. The creation of an endowment through the adoption of a deferred-gifts program so that the income from the endowment may be used to sustain the institution and replace the loss of major individual gifts because of death.

Raising money from the public has become a more and more sophisticated task. It is not just a matter of saying, "Let's have a campaign." Careful planning and analysis are essential to the success of any fund-raising effort. Many efforts have floundered because of the lack of understanding of sound money-raising principles and techniques and inadequate preparation. But many more can succeed if the situation is carefully analyzed and sound fund-raising programs are adopted. It is toward that objective—helping more institutions successfully pursue their fund-raising efforts—that this book is directed.

HOW MUCH—AND TO WHOM?

Exact data about the giving patterns of America have become increasingly difficult to obtain since the IRS's introduction of the simplified tax form. At one time 50 percent of Americans completed the long form and identified their deductions, but today fully 75 percent of Americans use the short form and do not list contributions for the purpose of gaining a deduction. Changes in legislation to permit users of the short form to take a deduction for their charitable giving would make such data more readily available in the future.

Because of the lack of data, the Independent Sector commissioned the Gallup Organization to do a survey of the giving pattern of Americans in 1981. (The Independent Sector is a group of nonprofit organizations and businesses that have come together to improve the understanding of the nonprofit sector and increase support for it.) The

Table 2-1. Sources of contributions—1983.

Source	Amount (Billions of Dollars)	Percent of Total
Individuals	$53.85	82.9%
Bequests (individuals)	4.52	7.0
Corporations	3.10	4.8
Foundations	3.46	5.3
Total	$64.93	100.0%

Source: The American Association of Fund-Raising Counsel.

Gallup Organization interviewed a sample of American families and found that nine out of every ten Americans contributed to one or more charitable organizations. Of these, 71 percent contributed to a church or other religious organization, 32 percent to an educational group, 24 percent to a hospital, 66 percent to other health organizations, and 53 percent to all other charities.

The average contribution was $497, of which churches received $313; educational causes, $45; hospitals, $37; other health organizations, $64; all other, $38. The survey also showed a direct relationship between income and the amount contributed—higher-income families gave more both in total and as a percentage of income than those with lower incomes. This is understandable because higher-income families have more disposable income once the basic necessities of life—food, clothing, and shelter—have been cared for. The survey also found that people who itemized their deductions for tax purposes gave almost two and a half times as much as those who took the standard deduction.

The Independent Sector also reported that in 1981, 33 percent of giving came from households with incomes under $20,000, 50 percent came from households with incomes between $20,000 and $50,000, and the remaining 17 percent came from households with incomes greater than $50,000.

It is interesting to note that the largest proportion of philanthropic giving in the United States is attributable to living individuals. The next largest source of gifts comes from deceased individuals who have made provisions in their wills or through trusts of various kinds to continue their giving after death. Corporate contributions constitute a much smaller but increasing share, followed by foundation grants.

The American Association of Fund-Raising Counsel, a group of professional fund-raising firms committed to certain standards and ethical practices in raising funds for nonprofit organizations, estimated that in 1983 total contributions in the United States reached over $64 billion. This figure was derived from the various sources shown in Table 2-1.

WHERE THE MONEY GOES

The association's survey also pointed out that by far the largest beneficiaries of America's philanthropic giving were churches, followed by health and hospitals, education,

Table 2-2. Contributions by type of service—1983.

Type of Service	Amount (Billions of Dollars)	Percent of Total
Religion	$31.03	47.8%
Health and hospitals	9.16	14.1
Education	9.03	13.9
Social services	6.94	10.7
Arts and humanities	4.08	6.3
Civic/public affairs	1.80	2.8
Other	2.89	4.4
Total	$64.93	100.0%

Source: The American Association of Fund-Raising Counsel.

social service agencies, the arts, and civic affairs. The association's findings by type of service are shown in Table 2-2.

A cursory examination of these data might lead unsophisticated trustees or administrators to downplay the role of corporations and foundations in fund-raising efforts. Quite the reverse is true. Though individual giving will be paramount, corporate and foundation gifts are essential to success in many types of campaigns. It is for this reason, as well as many others, that each organization must determine its fund-raising plans only after taking a careful look at its needs and the potential contributing groups that might be called upon to support the organization's efforts. For example, corporations are not at all a prospect for churches, but they are a most important prospect for colleges and universities, United Ways, organizations in the arts, and others. Likewise, except for foundations specifically organized for the purpose of giving to religious organizations, most foundations will not make grants for religious purposes, although they may make gifts to organizations under religious sponsorship if their services are open to a broad spectrum of the community regardless of religious affiliation.

The Conference Board in its annual survey of 534 major corporations found that in 1983 these companies made contributions of over $1 billion, distributed in the proportions shown in Table 2-3. From this, the importance of corporate giving to education, health and welfare services, and the arts can be easily ascertained.

Table 2-3. Corporate contributions—1983.

	Amount (Millions)	Percent of Total
Education	$ 522.2	40.7%
Health and welfare	397.3	31.0
Civic activities	149.3	11.7
Culture and arts	145.8	11.4
Other	67.0	5.2
Total	$1,281.6	100.0%

Source: The Conference Board, *Annual Survey of Corporate Contributions*, 1984.

GIFTS BY AGE, SEX, AND INCOME

There are not a great many data available about the gifts of individuals to philanthropy and how much those gifts represent in relationship to income. It is known that of those who itemize their deductions, the average contribution is only about 5 percent of taxable income. However, this varies a great deal, and there are some wealthy individuals who give the full deductible allowance—50 percent.

A study made by the St. Paul and Minneapolis United Ways in 1976 is one of the few of its kind that gives information about the charitable contributions of employees. Nine major corporations in the Twin Cities area cooperated with the United Ways in providing data about the jobs their employees held, their salaries, and their charitable contributions. The corporations identified their employees as male or female but in no case was the name of any individual disclosed; data were collected from payroll and personnel records and were then correlated by the companies with the giving patterns of their employees to the United Way campaign.

Over 34,000 employees were studied in these nine firms. The results showed that:

1. Employees least likely to donate at all are young married or unmarried females in clerical positions earning less than $10,000 per year or blue collar workers under 25 years of age earning below $10,000 a year.

2. The least generous of the givers is likely to be a male blue collar worker, married or unmarried, below 35 years of age and earning less than $15,000 a year.

3. Among male donors, more generous giving is positively associated with increasing age.

4. Contribution performance is positively related to increased income. The level of yearly salary appears to be the one major determinant of employee giving.

5. The most generous donors are male, married, age 36 to 60, and employees in a managerial or professional position who earn $25,000 a year or more.

6. Gifts to United Ways are far below the amounts requested at all income levels.

These conclusions are perhaps not surprising, but this was the first time hard data were available to indicate which groups generally give and which represent the greatest potential for future giving to the United Way program. Obviously, young couples who are newly married and in the process of starting a family have limited resources that must be used for their primary needs—food, clothing, and housing. The amount that is available for discretionary use, such as contributions, is therefore limited.

As people advance in age and in responsibility levels within a company, their incomes also generally tend to rise. Accordingly, they arrive at a point where their major responsibility for rearing a family, educating children, and paying for the homestead are gradually decreased, leaving them more discretionary income for contributions.

The average female worker is generally just getting started and struggling to be self-sustaining, or is a supplementary wage earner in a household where the couple is relatively newly married. These people too are not generally good campaign potential. Women often feel that gifts should be made by the husband and that such gifts represent a joint contribution from both.

As couples have children and advance both in age and income, they tend to appreciate more the services that they and their children may use—whether in education, human services, youth programs, health, or the arts. Accordingly, they are more motivated to support them.

These factors are very important as organizations begin to examine and define their markets and determine where they will put major emphasis in their campaign effort, for there is no point in concentrating on groups that have limited ability to give.

3

GETTING READY: TAKE A LOOK AT YOUR ORGANIZATION

There is no point wasting time, effort, leadership, and money in directing an organization's efforts to a public that is not going to be responsive to its needs. A well-conceived and well-organized campaign directed to a very selective constituency can bring the institution an over-the-top result.

Every organization needs to take a good look at itself before embarking on a fund-raising campaign, and then it needs to employ those particular fund-raising techniques that are essential to its success. Though fund raising is an art, not a science, there are certain principles guiding its conduct that must be properly followed if defeat is to be avoided. There are other principles that can go a long way to ensuring the organization's success.

One of the problems facing many administrators and board members is that they are so close to the institution's program and needs that they are unable to make an objective appraisal of how the rest of the community, particularly those groups that might be asked to support the institution, look upon its services. In point of fact, does anyone know anything about an institution's program other than those immediately involved?

Organizations, if they are going to be successful, must meet a viable need in the community. They must also have a board of directors that commands respect and has the kind of fund-raising muscle to present the institution's cause forcefully to those in a position to give substantial amounts of money. There must be a well-defined constituency—one that has been served by the organization or believes in its purposes and is dedicated to it. These prerequisites for successful fund raising will be addressed in greater detail later.

DO YOU HAVE POOR RELATIONS WITH OTHER GROUPS?

A point often missed by many institutions is that they have "relationships" within the community whether they know it or not. These relationships may be good, mediocre, or poor.

In the course of ordinary affairs, every institution conducts its business with other groups in society—its employees, the people who use its services, its vendors, its board of directors, associated agencies, the taxpayers, the corporate community, and in certain cases the alumni of the organization. It is these relationships with groups that are so important to the success or failure of an institution in carrying out its mission.

Almost invariably, when fund-raising professionals discuss public relations, they launch into a description of what they are doing in the media—press, radio and TV, print materials, and so on. They completely lack an understanding that public relations is not media but *policy*. This mistake is made countless times, not only by staff who are responsible for interpreting needs but by boards of directors and top administrators who are responsible for determining the "manners" through which the organization carries on its business.

Before any organization can conduct a successful fund-raising campaign, it must be sure that its relationships are sound, particularly with those groups that it must approach in seeking financial support. The most important public relations officer in the corporation is its top-paid employee—the president, executive director, or whatever other title that person carries. The top executive is the one who analyzes the problems of the institution and who suggests or recommends policies to the board of directors. The board, in turn, is the group responsible for determining the policies that will govern the institution's actions in relationship to all the groups with which it comes in contact. This point cannot be emphasized enough. Too frequently, top administrators and board members immediately concentrate their fund-raising efforts in expensive media campaigns. These expenditures may be wasted unless the decision makers have first taken a good look at the institution and its relationships to its publics.

POOR POLICY: EIGHT KEY EXAMPLES

The following cases illustrate the kinds of situations that can result from ill-conceived policies or lack of policies. The issues they raise require careful thought by administrators and boards because in the long run such issues will determine an institution's relationships with major segments of its constituency.

• In World War I the American Red Cross, on the insistence of the Defense Department, charged the American doughboy for a cup of coffee. The Defense Department maintained that it did not want its soldiers to be treated as charity cases and that the doughboys would feel better about paying a small amount for the coffee served at the Red Cross canteens.

The policy was totally wrong, and all the brochures and all the explanations over subsequent years, could not compensate for the problems it created until the policy was later changed in World War II. The American Red Cross suffered severely for what was a mistake in judgment on what might have appeared to be a relatively minor policy matter; but the policy destroyed its relationships with millions of American men who had served in the armed forces in World War I and then refused to support its program.

• Recently a college approached a major corporation in a Midwestern community and asked for support of its campaign to erect new buildings and provide an endowment for the organization. It felt sure its cause was good and the reception would be positive.

The corporation had tried for a number of years to conduct recruitment interviews for potential employees on the campus of the college. The preparation by the college had been, to say the least, careless if not downright uncooperative. Notices regarding the interviews had not been properly posted, personnel résumés had not been prepared for the corporation to review, and students had not been informed about the interviews and the potential positions in which they might have an interest.

The corporation declined the campaign request flatly and the college representatives returned with their heads hanging; only then did they take a look at the way in which their preparation for students' interviews was being conducted. In other words, the college had not, as a matter of policy, determined the manner in which student interviews by 2 prospective employers would be conducted, and suddenly it found that it lacked a base to seek support from the corporation. The college was now faced with the necessity of restructuring its whole interviewing system and of being sure that a corporation's needs would be properly recognized.

• Most hospitals have the problem of determining whether patients who are admitted have the financial means, either individually or through third-party payments, to pay their bills. One such hospital introduced a policy whereby no service would be given to a prospective patient until this necessary information had been obtained. A patient suffering from a burst artery appeared suddenly at the out-patient department of the hospital. His nose was bleeding profusely and the man was in a near state of panic. Before he was given any medical attention he had to meet with the interviewer whose job it was to determine how the patient planned to pay the bill upon completion of services. The patient, bleeding as he was, had to take what seemed an inordinate amount of time to complete a form giving his name, address, and occupation and to state whether he was covered by Blue Cross/Blue Shield or another private insurer. Now, to be sure, this hospital had the same financial constraints faced by almost any medical facility and, at an appropriate time, needed to know how its services were going to be reimbursed. But the hospital lost a potential friend and supporter for many years because its policies were ill conceived and poorly administered.

• A nonprofit organization had a practice of following up very persistently on all pledges made by its contributors. One of its loyal supporters over the years passed away and a considerable balance remained on his pledge. The organization sent a statement to "The Estate of William Stewart" for the balance due.

Upon receiving the bill, the son of the contributor was deeply hurt, for his father had been not only a loyal supporter but a past campaign chairman and president. He called the executive of the organization and said, "Certainly there could have been a more personal and considerate way of doing this. My dad was a supporter of your organization for many years. I am sure he would have wanted this pledge to be honored, but it was unconscionable at a time of suffering for the whole family to send it to his 'estate.' Why didn't you call me?"

Appropriate apologies by the administrator smoothed things over, but the incident served notice to the institution that it needed to give attention to its billing policies. In this particular case, the organization adopted the policy that when a contributor passed away a sympathy card or personal letter would be sent to the family. Then a responsible member of the staff would call the family's attorney and seek directions about the pledge. Or a staff member would call a member of the family at an appropriate time, tactfully mentioning the pledge and seeking the ''advice'' of the relative. The organization's policy now assured the necessary steps to demonstrate its interest in a deceased person's family and not just in the donor's money. It also established goodwill and paved the way for good relationships with the family in the future.

• In revising its bylaws, the board of a Midwestern hospital eliminated the provision for lifetime contributing memberships. Most of these memberships were small in amount but did give the donors, many of whom were doctors, the right to vote for members of the board of directors in return for their contribution. The physicians viewed this change as the administration's attempt to eliminate their right to influence the composition of the board. A pitched battle ensued and eventually the medical staff, the board, and the administration became hopelessly split. The doctors finally sought a court order prohibiting payments of medicare and medicaid funds on the grounds that the board was not responsible. Because these funds represented 60 percent of the hospital's income, it was thrown into an extremely difficult financial situation, and had to resort to reserves to pay its bills.

Now some members of the community who had supported the hospital charged that it was no longer a community hospital, but a doctor-run institution. The situation finally ended up in court, and the court's intervention brought about a reorganization of the hospital and its board and the assumption of policies clearly delineating the role of the board, the administration, and the medical staff. Yes, the contributing memberships were reinstated!

• A sectarian federation found itself in a difficult situation when one of its agencies began to take public positions on some very controversial subjects. These were hitting the news media with increasing frequency. Quotations from the member agency's executive and staff appeared in the press. The federation often found itself unprepared to answer the questions coming from many of its supporters. The matter finally came to a head when a particularly controversial story hit the newspaper on the same day the federation announced its campaign goal—and appeared next to the announcement in the press. The situation was finally resolved when the agency established a *policy* that no positions on issues would be taken publicly by staff without prior discussion with and approval by the agency's board. Both the agency and the federation adopted policies recognizing the right of the agency to take positions on public policy issues, provided there was clearance before such positions went ''public.''

• A prestigious theater embarked on a new policy of producing an ''innovative'' series of plays that were a complete departure from its previous work and were designed to please the tastes and ambitions of the staff. The new policy, it was thought, would elevate the theater to even higher levels of prestige and professional reputation. The new productions were what might be termed ''professional theater,'' with startling new themes and subject matter and completely new methods of staging. The only problem was that the new direction was in complete opposition to the tastes and interests of those who had been a loyal audience for years. Ticket sales declined rapidly and the theater soon found itself in a very difficult financial bind. It was then that the board had to face the difficult policy question: Were the plays to be produced to give the professional director and staff the greatest opportunity for self-expression and experimentation, or were the plays to be directed toward the tastes of the audience that had loyally supported the theater for many years? Once the board answered that policy in favor of the audience, permitting only one experimental play a year, ticket sales again increased and the financial problems were solved.

• In the late 1930s a number of local Community Chests (predecessors of United Ways) included in their memberships chapters of the American Red Cross and some of the emerging national health agencies. The Community Chest was a federation of agencies concerned primarily with the support of local health and welfare agencies. These agencies made program decisions based on local needs. At the time, the country was in the middle of a depression and funds were scarce. As a result, local budget committees of Community Chests had to make some tough decisions on how funds were going to be allocated. However, when these committees were confronted with making allocations to chapters of national agencies, they began to overstep their authority. Since they were "local-minded" they did not perceive that certain programs—such as the care of victims of natural disasters—could be carried out effectively only on a national basis. These committees began to make arbitrary decisions to eliminate disaster preparedness, services to veterans, and, in some cases, research from the agencies' budgets. The committees failed to recognize that these were programs mandated nationally. Although this kind of line-by-line budgeting was not unusual in those days, it could not work effectively with national agencies.

With the advent of World War II, all the Red Cross chapters and nearly all the health agencies withdrew from local Community Chests and conducted their own campaigns. At first they experienced considerable growth, but as the number of agencies conducting campaigns increased, the public began to insist on a combined campaign because of the increasing call for campaign volunteers and the duplication of solicitation. Nearly all campaigns began to fall short of their goals. A solution was finally found when the United Foundation was formed in Detroit in 1949. This campaign successfully combined the local Community Chest agencies with the Red Cross and the major national health agencies. But the factor that made it work was that a new structure was formed that set up new policies and a new method of allocating funds to national agencies. In effect, the new combined campaign recognized on a *policy level* the difference between agencies whose programs are determined locally and those that have certain national obligations.

POLICIES FOR SPECIAL PUBLICS

Every organization should examine very carefully whether its policies are in fact the best that can be adopted in relationship to the many publics it has. These publics should be carefully identified and appropriate policies toward them determined. Obviously the larger the institution, the more people involved, and the more complex the relationship, the more important this aspect of the organization's policies becomes. The smaller the institution, the less formal the policies because the board and administrators are generally closer to their publics. But the need for thoughtful policies is still there.

A number of the groups about which policies need to be determined are described below.

1. *Board of directors.* Size, scope, representativeness, term of office, and stature need to be assessed.

2. *Employees.* They are the best public relations media an organization has because either they praise the institution or they criticize it to their friends, acquaintances, and clients. Adequate personnel policies should spell out compensation, fringe benefits, terminations, vacations and sick leave, and the handling of suggestions and grievances.

3. *Media.* Consideration must be given to openness and access to news and information, who is responsible for media contacts, and what the general policies are on dissemination of information.

4. *Clientele.* Whether directed to patients in the hospital or to opera lovers, policies should spell out the rights of such people and how the institution will deal with them. What are the rights of the patient confined within a hospital to know about his illness and the course of treatment? How are relationships with clients defined in a human services agency? Even such a small matter as ticket refunds can be important to an organization's clientele.

5. *Vendors.* Every institution buys from others. The institution performs a favor to those firms by buying from them. But they are also an important group that may in the future be asked to support the organization financially, and they can spread the word that the institution is either well or poorly run.

6. *Contributors.* Policies governing approaches to contributors need to be defined. For example, will former clients be solicited and, if so, under what conditions? Will the institution put top priority on the interests of the contributor rather than the needs of the beneficiary organization when seeking a bequest or trust? How will cancellation of pledges be handled? Will all gifts be acknowledged as nearly as possible? Will the organization be financially accountable to its contributors and meet the highest standards of fund raising? Will it guarantee that restricted or designated gifts are used for the purpose intended? Will it strive to keep fund-raising and administrative costs as low as possible?

7. *Volunteers.* Nearly all nonprofit organizations make substantial use of volunteers; many could not operate successfully without them. What is the organization's general attitude toward the use of volunteers? Will it refrain from substituting them for paid staff? Will it seek to make their experience rewarding and meaningful? How will their work be recognized?

8. *Affiliated organizations.* Relationships with members of a federation, medical staffs, special audiences, dioceses, hospital councils, and professional or technical groups are all important parts of an institution's publics.

9. *Third-party payers.* Policies must be set regarding government, private insurance companies, and other groups that purchase services from the organization. What is their right to information? Is there a commitment to high quality for the services purchased?

10. *Other financial resources.* What policy is followed regarding the organization's

bank deposits? How can the policy be as fair as possible? What about the investment of the organization's funds? What policy is followed regarding gifts of stock or property?

ASSESSING THE CLIMATE

By this time you should be getting the idea that fund raising is more than just a program of gimmicks and a blatant media campaign. Lest you believe that the public relations problem is so immense and difficult that you must spend endless efforts surveying yourself before you can satisfactorily conduct a campaign, let me put your mind at ease. Any reputable organization that has conducted its affairs with reasonable judgment will have given formal or informal attention to these matters over a period of time and will not need to spend months or years getting policies in order before a successful campaign can be conducted.

Good policies will not in themselves ensure a successful campaign, but they will create a favorable climate that will permit the campaign to be executed successfully. The main point is that an institution needs to be aware of this fundamental consideration if it is to be successful in its fund-raising efforts. The organization needs to spend some time looking at itself and making "soundings" in the community in order to determine whether its house is in order.

How do organizations go about doing this? There are a number of ways. When the campaign is an annual one or when the institution is not large enough to justify a highly structured approach, informal contacts by the administration and the board of directors with important individuals and past contributors, both close to the institution and remote from it, can give some inkling of a campaign's possibility for success or how much more might be raised over the year before.

Feasibility Studies

If it is a major new campaign rather than an annual one, and if professional fund-raising counsel is being employed, a feasibility study may be conducted. A basic first step of counsel is to make soundings for the institution among major contributors, both corporate and individual. This is generally done through a series of personal interviews by the fund-raising counsel with highly placed, knowledgeable, and influential people in the community. (A sample personal interview is given in Figure 3-1). At the conclusion of such interviews, counsel should be able to advise the institution on whether to go ahead and launch its campaign or whether to take some preparatory steps to strengthen itself. For example, a board of directors composed entirely of representatives of a religious order or religious congregations who have almost no contact in the general business community may face doubtful prospects for success.

Some boards of directors are composed of well-meaning and dedicated individuals who offer much from a technical point of view but who have little value from a fund-raising standpoint. In such a case, some of these dedicated individuals should be retained, but the board itself may need to be enlarged and strengthened with the kind of leadership that is known and respected in those segments of the community where the funds will be sought.

Figure 3-1. Sample personal interview with a potential contributor.

You were kind enough to come to our meeting last week and hear the presentation of our organization's needs and its plan to meet them. You could be very helpful to us if you would give us the benefit of your advice by answering a few questions.

1. What was your overall impression of the presentation (film, speech, and so on) that was made? Was it clear? Was it well done?

2. Do you have any suggestions about anything that was missed, needed clarification, or could be improved?

3. If we are going to undertake the campaign, how do you feel about the size of the goal? Is it too ambitious? Ambitious enough? About right? Does it reflect present economic conditions?

4. From the standpoint of timing, do you have any words of advice? Our present plans are to conduct the campaign from _____ to _____. Are there any major conflicts we would experience?
                                     (month)   (month)

5. Do you know of any people who might be good prospects for leadership positions? Do you know of others who might be interested in making a major gift to the campaign?

6. Here is an analysis (*hand sheet to potential contributor*) that shows what we will have to raise in certain categories of gifts if the campaign is to be successful. On this basis, and without making any commitment at this point, could you suggest a category or range of gifts that might be reasonable to request of your organization?

Thank you very much for your kind and generous cooperation. It has been truly helpful in assisting us in planning our campaign.

Occasionally administration needs to be strengthened or organizational policies need to be revised before the campaign can be successfully launched. If, for example, a corporation's employees have had a very poor experience with a given agency or hospital, it is doubtful that the corporation will respond generously unless conditions are improved.

Sometimes the survey can be contracted without a commitment by the institution to employ fund-raising counsel to conduct the campaign. Such services can be arranged through either professional fund-raising organizations or other reputable professional sources. The survey should assess not only the climate for the campaign but also its potential for success.

Organizational Questionnaires

Some organizations have distributed simple questionnaires to their former patients, students, clients, alumni, patrons, or contributors asking them to assess the quality of their programs. Such questionnaires generally do not need to divulge the identity of the respondent and are returned in anonymity. Sample questionnaires are given in Figures 3-2 to 3-4.

Potential Contributor Lunches

The potential contributor lunch is another device frequently used to discuss the program and financial needs of the institution, the plan for the campaign, and attitudes

Figure 3-2. Patient opinion poll.

It will take very little of your time to answer the questions below. We sincerely request your help as we are anxious to make sure that the finest patient care is provided you. Please tell us exactly what you think. We will take your answers in earnest and will do our best to correct any weaknesses shown.

You may complete the questions here and leave it with the receptionist or take it home and mail it to us.

Thank you for your help.

Floor _____ Room No. _____

		YES	NO
1.	Did you feel that your emotional, social, and spiritual needs were met?	☐	☐
2.	Were you interviewed in a courteous and efficient manner in the Admitting Office?	☐	☐
3.	Were you satisfied with the housekeeping services? (Cleanliness of your room and hospital)?	☐	☐
4.	Did you have as much nursing care as you needed?	☐	☐
5.	Did you feel the nurses and aides were interested in you as a person?	☐	☐
6.	Did you receive reasonably prompt service when you rang for the nurse?	☐	☐
7.	Did nurses, technicians, and other hospital personnel explain the nature of services they were giving you?	☐	☐
8.	Within the restrictions of diet ordered by your physician, did you enjoy your food?	☐	☐
9.	Was the area where you were a patient kept reasonably quiet?	☐	☐
10.	Can you better understand the reasons for the cost of hospital care?	☐	☐
11.	Did you find the Credit Office courteous and understanding about financial arrangements for the payment of your bill?	☐	☐
12.	Were you treated courteously and kindly by the staff when you were leaving?	☐	☐

13. Please indicate your rating in general of your satisfaction with the care and treatment you received while a patient.

Excellent	Good	Fair	Poor
☐	☐	☐	☐

Please state any improvement you believe should be made in services, facilities, or other.

_____

_____

_____

_____

Date _____   _____

(Sign here if you wish)

(Courtesy of St. Joseph's Hospital, St. Paul, Minnesota.)

Figure 3-3. Questionnaire for community groups.

Family Service of Greater St. Paul

Name of organization/agency _____

Name and position of person responding _____

Name of agency being studied _____ City and state _____

As regards the current program of services at the agency, I am:

_____ Very familiar, have regular contact with the agency, and know the service program well.
_____ Familiar, have occasional contact with the agency, and know of the service program.
_____ Unfamiliar, and have little contact with the agency or knowledge of the service program.

This organization/agency, in its contacts with the agency, is primarily a (you may check more than one):

_____ Funding source   _____ Purchaser of service
_____ Referral source (send clients)   _____ Provider of service
_____ Referral source (receive clients)   _____ Other (specify)
_____ Regulatory body   _____

Indicate below the best description of your impression of the agency. If you answer no, please indicate briefly your reason on an additional page.

	Yes	No	Don't Know
1. Agency services are provided by competent personnel at all levels.	____	____	____
2. Agency is active in and highly regarded by the local service community.	____	____	____
3. Agency facilities are adequate for the program of services it offers and clients it serves.	____	____	____
4. Agency informs the community of its services and activities.	____	____	____
5. Agency fees are reasonable and scaled to ability to pay.	____	____	____
6. Agency reports back on services to clients referred.	____	____	____
7. Agency screens all clients quickly and determines its ability to serve and makes referral if necessary.	____	____	____
8. Services are available to all socioeconomic groups.	____	____	____
9. Services are available to all ethnic groups (not applicable to agencies with a single ethnic orientation).	____	____	____

If your answer to question 8 or 9 is no, specify what groups you believe are not served.

Please include any other information, positive or negative, which you feel may affect the accreditation of this agency.

(Courtesy of Family Service of Greater St. Paul.)

Figure 3-4. Survey by the United Way.

United Way

in Minneapolis and St. Paul ask your assistance in helping United Way determine future directions for its programs. To ensure continuing success, the United Way must be abreast of how people feel about it and its agencies. You can help a great deal by completing this survey form.

It's completely confidential and we do need and appreciate your personal answers and opinions.

When you have completed the questionnaire, will you please mail it back in the enclosed envelope.

Thank you for your help.

UNITED WAY OPINION SURVEY

PART I

The following list contains 21 statements about the United Way. Please read them and check whether you strongly agree, agree, are not sure, disagree, or strongly disagree with each of them.

	strongly agree	agree	not sure	disagree	strongly disagree
1. By-and-large, the United Way is successful in combining many appeals into one annual campaign.	1	2	3	4	5
2. All United Way agency budgets are carefully reviewed and examined by experienced community volunteers.	1	2	3	4	5
3. A member agency which receives funds from the United Way campaign should be permitted to conduct its own public campaign, in addition to its support from the United Way.	1	2	3	4	5
4. The government is doing all that is necessary to provide health and social services for the under privileged. Therefore there its less need to give to the United Way.	1	2	3	4	5
5. Services of United Way agencies are available to everyone in the community.	1	2	3	4	5
6. Services of the United Way agencies are not relevant to today's major social problems.	1	2	3	4	5
7. I do not like any printed suggestions on how much I should give to the United Way.	1	2	3	4	5
8. The United Way should provide more funds for services to minority groups.	1	2	3	4	5
9. The United Way should encourage its agencies to form new programs to deal with social problems.	1	2	3	4	5

(Courtesy of the United Way of the St. Paul Area.)

Figure 3-4. (*Continued*)

10. The United Way spends too much money for administrative functions rather than for social services provided by its agencies.	1	2	3	4	5
11. The United Way agencies should charge fees for their services based upon the family's or the person's ability to pay for them.	1	2	3	4	5
12. I appreciate the United Way guide for Fair Share giving. It helps me decide how much to pledge to the campaign.	1	2	3	4	5
13. The United Way supports some agencies whose programs have become outdated.	1	2	3	4	5
14. The United Way should merge agencies that are providing the same kind of services.	1	2	3	4	5
15. The United Way agencies provide services only to the poor and disadvantaged.	1	2	3	4	5
16. The United Way campaign is the most economical way to raise money for social services.	1	2	3	4	5
17. A member agency should not be allowed to conduct a special money raising campaign without United Way approval.	1	2	3	4	5
18. Many non-employed housewives appreciate the opportunity to contribute at home even though their husbands give at work.	1	2	3	4	5
19. Out of every dollar I contributed to the United Way, more than 90¢ went to the agencies for services.	1	2	3	4	5
20. If a man and wife are both employed, both should contribute to the United Way.	1	2	3	4	5
21. The United Way campaign means I am solicited only once a year for its member agencies.	1	2	3	4	5

PART II—Check the 10 services most needed in the community which you feel should be supplied by the United Way agencies.

_____ 1. Counseling for families who have financial or marital problems.

_____ 2. Day care centers for children of working mothers.

_____ 3. Assisting immigrants and refugees to obtain housing, employment and education.

_____ 4. Counseling and residential care for unwed mothers.

_____ 5. Providing foster homes for neglected children.

_____ 6. Assisting families to adopt children.

_____ 7. Rehabilitation and vocational training of physically handicapped.

_____ 8. Providing legal services for the poor.

_____ 9. Homemakers for the sick, elderly or home bound.

_____ 10. Collection and distribution of free blood.

_____ 11. Visiting nurse services to the sick in their own homes.

_____ 12. Assist low income families in finding housing.

_____ 13. Summer camping for youth.

_____ 14. Assist residents to develop local neighborhood action programs to improve social conditions (housing, pollution, crime, etc.).

Figure 3-4. (*Continued*)

_____ 15. Community centers to provide social, health and recreational services to low income neighborhoods.

_____ 16. Free health care clinics for those unable to afford private care.

_____ 17. Youth character building services such as YMCA, YWCA and scouting programs.

_____ 18. Research and health education related to serious diseases such as arthritis, diabetes, and cerebral palsy.

_____ 19. Rehabilitation and training for the mentally handicapped.

_____ 20. Counseling, recreational and nutritional services for the elderly.

_____ 21. Supply emergency food, shelter, and financial assistance to disaster victims.

_____ 22. Vocational counseling and training of unemployed school dropouts.

_____ 23. Job finding, guidance and placement services for hard-to-place individuals.

_____ 24. Educational classes in arts, crafts, and other special interests.

_____ 25. Referring people to the services they need (hot line services).

_____ 26. Counseling and rehabilitation of alcoholics and their families.

_____ 27. Counseling and rehabilitation of drug addicts.

_____ 28. Counseling for family planning.

PART III

1. Have you ever visited a United Way agency?   YES ____ NO ____

   If yes, was it:

   ( ) A. On a "Come and See" tour   ( ) C. To receive a service

   ( ) B. As an agency member or agency volunteer   ( ) D. Other

2. Which of the following do you associate most strongly with the United Way?

   A. Torch symbol   ( )

   B. "Wear it proudly" slogan   ( )

   C. "People helping" symbol   ( )

   D. "Count your blessings" slogan   ( )

   E. Symbol with rainbow and open hand ( )

Figure 3-4. (*Continued*)

3. From which sources did you receive information about the United Way this past year? (check one or more)
   Which one impressed you the most? (check only one)

Informed by:	Impressed by:	Informed by:	Impressed by:
( ) TV commercials	( )	( ) Someone who was helped by a	( )
( ) Radio commercials	( )	United Way service	
( ) Billboards or displays	( )	( ) Agency visit	( )
( ) Newspaper articles	( )	( ) Campaign literature	( )
( ) United Way film	( )	( ) Other	( )
( ) At a meeting within your family	( )		

4. Did you receive any campaign literature?   YES _____ NO _____

5. Did the United Way volunteer in your company contact you personally?   YES _____ NO _____

6. What do you think are the combined costs of United Way fund raising and year
   around administration?
   ( ) A. Less than 10% of all money raised   ( ) C. 16–20%
   ( ) B. 10–15%   ( ) D. Over 20%

7. Do you feel it is important for a donor to be able to designate his/her gift
   to specific agencies?   YES _____   NO _____

8. What is your main reason for giving to the United Way?
   (Check only one)
   ( ) A. I think the United Way services   ( ) C. My employer expects me to give
        are worth supporting
   ( ) B. I know somebody who was helped   ( ) D. Most of my fellow employees give
        by a United Way agency

        ( ) E. Other _____

___

PART IV: For statistical purposes, tell us about yourself.

1. In which zip code area do you live? _____

2. Sex: ( ) A. Male
         ( ) B. Female

3. Age: ( ) A. Under 30
         ( ) B. 30-39
         ( ) C. 40-49
         ( ) D. 50-59
         ( ) E. 60 plus

4. Marital Status
   ( ) A. Not married (including single, widowed,
        divorced, separated)
   ( ) B. Married

5. Occupation
   ( ) A. Managerial (salaried)
   ( ) B. Professional (salaried)
   ( ) C. Supervisory, technical, sales (salaried)
   ( ) D. Clerical (salaried)
   ( ) E. Hourly wage earner

Figure 3-4. (*Continued*)

6. Salary Range   Comments: _____

    ( ) A. Under $10,000   _____
    ( ) B. $10,000–$14,999   _____
    ( ) C. $15,000–$24,999   _____
    ( ) D. $25,000–$39,999   _____
    ( ) E. $40,000 plus   _____

7. Did you contribute to the last United Way campaign?

    YES_____ NO_____   _____

    If yes, was annual contribution?

    ( ) A. $12 under ( ) E. $101–$250
    ( ) B. $13–$24   ( ) F. $251–$500
    ( ) C. $25–$50   ( ) G. $501–$1,000
    ( ) D. $51–$100 ( ) H. over $1,000

toward it. This is generally conducted through one or more small luncheon or dinner meetings at which the needs of the institution are described and the possible goals to be obtained are discussed with potential contributors. Their reactions are sought, either verbally at the meetings or later via a questionnaire asking them to assess the fund-raising effort and identify any problems or potential trouble areas that the institution needs to examine. It is important that the organization present its case positively, putting its best foot forward while leaving an opportunity for constructive reaction from contributors. Follow-up personal visits with those who were in attendance can also be quite effective.

There is one thing for certain. Nothing brings out both the positive and negative attitudes toward an institution as quickly as a campaign for funds. Whenever you start to touch a person's pocketbook, the good feelings and, more often, the bad ones have a way of surfacing. A campaign for funds can be viewed as an election in the voluntary sector: Contributors either vote yes for the organization with generous gifts or, unfortunately, vote their disapproval with no gift at all.

4

THE ESSENTIAL INGREDIENTS OF A SUCCESSFUL CAMPAIGN

Once you have determined that you are ready to go ahead and organize a campaign, you must think about the ingredients essential to its success. Careful attention must be given to certain important principles in campaign planning if high performance is to result.

CREDIBILITY

A 1982 poll indicated that 49 percent of Americans believe that only one half or less of all contributions are used for the designated purposes. This demonstrates a severe credibility gap for American philanthropy.

 To raise money successfully, an organization must be believable. Unless it has a salable service, it will have great difficulty convincing potential contributors to support it. Credibility is established primarily by demonstrating that a service is needed by, used by, and effective for the people it is intended to satisfy.

 As pointed out previously, an arts organization will have difficulty attracting support unless its productions are attractive to the contributor. A hospital must have demonstrated excellence of health care, competent staff, and concern for the financial circumstances of its patients. Colleges and universities must have curricula that are in tune with the times and meet the needs of business and industry. Social agencies must demonstrate that they offer practical solutions to the problems facing the community.

LEADERSHIP

The most important facet of any campaign is leadership. There is a truism in campaigning that "people give to people." Although the institution itself is important, very few campaigns are successful unless they have in prominent leadership roles the kinds of people who command respect from potential contributors and who can ask others to serve and to give.

Of particular importance is the role of the campaign chairperson. He or she must be highly respected by the business community or by the particular constituency that will be asked to serve and to give. The chairperson should be able to lead by example and be known for generosity in giving both time and money. Most campaigning in local communities is done by a relatively small percentage of the citizenry, and these people often call on one another when favors are exchanged. A person who has been known to give generously and to be willing to work for others has a better chance of success than one who does not have this kind of reputation.

It takes a given force to move a given object. Successful campaign chairpersons generally have this ability. They have the personal influence to move others to action. Obviously the more influence they have, the greater their ability to influence others to act and to make generous gifts.

Another truism in campaigning is that it takes a busy person to get things done. People who are extremely busy learn how to make the most of their time and how to work into their busy schedules a commitment to important civic causes. Although their own business responsibilities may be extremely demanding, they still are able to allocate a certain amount of time to important work for the community.

The ability of a chairperson to persuade others and to rally them to a cause is a most important asset. Sometimes a chairperson lacks the ability to speak fluently from the platform but is highly persuasive on an individual basis. In this situation, the ability to get individuals to respond financially and through service is much more important. Many campaign leaders start out as very poor speakers but then become quite fluent as the campaign progresses and they grow more and more immersed in its spirit.

No single person may have all the attributes that an organization would like to have in a campaign leader. It is difficult to find someone with prominence of position, personal wealth, interest in the organization, ability to motivate, personal persuasiveness, and ability to speak publicly. The best that can be hoped for is a person who has a generous portion of these characteristics; of primary importance is the ability to command respect and to get others to work. Vitality and good health are also factors to be considered.

> One businessman, well up in his seventies, had been active in civic affairs for years and chairman of many campaigns. He was the picture of health and vitality. When asked how he managed to stay so healthy, he replied: "Well, when I was first married I said to my wife, 'Soph, I love you dearly, but I want to have an understanding with you. I do not intend to get into any arguments with you. Any time you start an argument, I'm going out the door for a walk!' And you know something? It's remarkable how healthy you stay when you spend most of your life outdoors."

Like the chairperson of the campaign, those who will be heading up the major divisions should have sound leadership qualities. After all, it is they who will be enrolling section and group leaders in subordinate but responsible positions. In the recruitment of campaign personnel, it is always easier for a person in a position of economic prominence to ask another person at a similar level or lesser level to give and to work. It is difficult, on the other hand, for a person holding a subordinate position in business or industry to make the same request of those who are a number of notches higher on the economic ladder.

It is absolutely essential that the top campaign leadership be selected carefully with this thought in mind, for it will always be easy to recruit people at lower levels if the person doing the asking is in a superior economic or professional position. This is not institutional snobbery—it is just that people in financially secure positions feel more comfortable about asking others to work. It is also true that people at lower economic levels like to associate themselves with people who are successful.

In addition to the selection of top leadership, there must be a plan to recruit volunteers in sufficient numbers to ensure coverage of the prospects who are to be solicited. We will give more attention to the techniques that can be used in developing a potential cadre of workers as we go along.

ORGANIZATIONAL STRATEGY

Essential to a successful campaign is the development of an overall strategy that will ensure coverage of large, medium-size, and small gifts. The organizational strategy is the "grand design" for the campaign—for stating its objectives and defining the plan that will as nearly as possible bring it to success. This strategy will describe a plan of attack for each division and a chain of command that will operate in order to ensure recruitment and training of personnel, development of a campaign case (defined in Chapter 9), ways to approach larger givers, the promotional effort to be conducted, and the system of follow-up.

PROMOTION AND PUBLIC RELATIONS

Once an institution has taken a good look at itself to be sure that its relationships with its publics are good, it should be able to make concrete plans for publicizing its case.

The goal of the promotional campaign is to present the organization and its needs in a positive way. Promotion by itself will not raise very much money, however, unless the other essentials of good campaigning are present. What can be expected of a good promotion program is the presentation of the organization to the giving public as one that is worthy of support and the development of an understanding of the organization's needs for funds.

It is important to remember that all campaigns are competing with other demands upon individuals and corporations for funds. Contributors have to decide that the campaign request is so urgently needed that it must take priority over certain other things on which they would like to spend their money. In this respect, the request is competing with the need of a family for food, clothing, shelter, education, recreation, and many other important needs. Therefore, it is essential for the public relations campaign to dramatize the need in such a way that it develops a sense of urgency, on the part of both the campaign leadership and the givers, for the campaign to succeed.

A further role of the promotional campaign is to "open the door" for the solicitors and make possible a cordial reception for them. If a solicitor is met with a series of negative criticisms during calls, he or she will have to deal with hostile contributors before getting into the positive position of asking for generous gifts. Therefore, an important aspect of the public relations program is to anticipate the kind of questions that might arise and answer them straightforwardly through the various media, eliminating all objections *before calls are made*. There is no substitute for honesty in conducting a campaign, and if a problem arises it is better to meet it head on and get it out of the way than to try to hide it. Most people are surprisingly understanding once they are given the opportunity to know the facts, but they become suspicious and guarded if they feel that the truth is being hidden from them.

This is not to suggest that an organization should unearth all the problems it has and try to explain them. Under those circumstances, it will be starting from a negative stance and will have difficulty putting forth its case on a positive basis. If, however, previous interviews or meetings with potential contributors have pointed out a problem that seems to be of broad concern, it is best to anticipate this and resolve the problem in advance. Occasionally an organization may be able to turn this negative into a positive force. For example, an organization's inability to render the service needed because it has inadequate facilities, budget, or staff may bring forth even greater support.

A final objective of the promotional campaign is to help build in the public's mind the concept of what an adequate gift to the campaign entails. Failure to accomplish this most important objective can result in many gifts but a poor fund-raising effort overall. Just as there is a price for every commodity people purchase—cars, food, clothing, housing, and so on—there is also a price that givers must pay if the institution in which they have an interest is to continue to exist and provide the kind of service they want. Campaigners do not use the term *price*, but the fact is that gifts must be obtained that are adequate in both number and amount. Otherwise the campaign will have been poorly conceived and will have little likelihood of being successful.

TIMING

In constructing an overall campaign plan, both for professional development personnel and for volunteers, the timing of the campaign itself is an absolutely essential consideration.

A timetable needs to be drawn that establishes objectives by day and month for the overall development of the campaign organization and for the various office procedures to be carried out. (See Figure 4-1). The chairperson of the campaign and the various division and group leaders must know the absolute deadlines that have to be met in recruiting and training personnel as well as in conducting the solicitation itself. The accompanying timetable (Figure 4-1) is intended to be a general guide and outlines the functions to be performed each month. Every campaign will be scheduled differently depending on the needs of the individual institution. Planning details according to division and group, and setting specific dates, are also necessary.

Figure 4-1. Sample coordinated timetable.

Month	Public Information and Promotion	Organization	Office Preparation
Jan.		Review leadership suggestions with staff and campaign chairperson. Develop general campaign timetable. Critique last campaign. Start recruitment of top leadership.	Review records. Remove all prospects who are out of business, have moved, or are deceased.
Feb.	Initial discussion of campaign case.	Make recommendations for changes in campaign plan. Complete recruitment of division heads. Select public information chairperson.	Start census of new prospects—review of directories, membership lists, and so on. Begin changes in prospect list to reflect changes in campaign plan.
March	Meeting of public information committee. Discussion of theme and campaign slogan. Graphics planning. Industrial editors' cultivation planning. Film planning. Speakers' bureau planning.	Hold campaign cabinet meeting and finalize campaign plan. Obtain section leaders.	Finalize prospect lists. Begin preparation of division prospect lists. Order pledge cards. Determine prospect or card value (likely amount of contribution) by division and section.
April	Completion of campaign case theme and slogan. Preparation of graphics design and format for general distribution piece. Audiovisual (film) arrangements completed.	Hold meetings of section leaders and start recruiting group leaders. Organize precampaign cultivation committee (for high-potential prospects) and make assignments. Select firms for leadership gifts or pilot campaigns. Prepare special-case presentations for prospects in precampaign cultivation.	Select and list prospects for precampaign cultivation with supporting data. Begin preparation of pledge cards.
May	Contacts with newspapers. Contacts with broadcast media regarding cooperation. All print materials ordered.	Complete selection of section leaders and begin assignments. Have campaign goal approved by board. Make contacts with prospects selected for precampaign cultivation. Hold campaign cabinet meeting.	Begin establishing division goals and individual ratings. Complete all pledge cards.

Figure 4-1. (*Continued*)

Month	Public Information and Promotion	Organization	Office Preparation
June	All print materials completed.	Hold meetings with major corporate and foundation prospects. Present campaign case and ask for support. Hold campaign cabinet meeting.	
July	Plans for newspaper publicity completed. Plans for broadcast publicity formalized.	Begin contacts with major corporations to obtain their commitments. Obtain all workers in major divisions. Hold campaign cabinet meeting.	Package all supplies by division, section, and individual prospect.
August	Speakers' bureau training.	Have all assignments completed. Hold solicitor training meetings by division. Conduct bellwether or leadership solicitation and pilot campaigns. Hold campaign cabinet meeting.	Distribute supplies to workers and individual firms. Set up audit procedure.
Sept.	Promotion in full swing—radio, TV, speakers' bureau. Initial reporting on campaign results of early solicitation.	Kick off campaign. Check that all contacts are being made. Hold first report meeting.	
Oct.	Continued reporting of campaign results. Media promotion in full force.	Hold check-up meetings with division and section leaders. Analyze weak spots. Plan reapproach or reassignment where necessary. Hold second and third report meetings.	Audit campaign results. Report results to division heads by prospect. Analyze campaign results.
Nov.	Special "thank you" letter to givers and workers.	Make final report at victory dinner. Follow through on unreported accounts, out-of-town prospects, and the like.	Finalize audit report. Confirm names of givers, addresses, and amounts of gifts. Prepare billing.

Generally speaking, the shorter and more intensive the campaign, the more successful it will be. However, the timetable cannot be so unrealistic as to demand the execution of certain functions in such a short period that the proper mechanics of the campaign cannot be carried out. Therefore, the timetable has to anticipate the mechanics to be performed in the office and mesh them with the development of the campaign organization itself. There is no point, for example, in having all personnel recruited if the prospect lists and pledge cards are not ready or if a training program is not in place to instruct the solicitors on the next steps to be taken. One campaign director I know had a terrific kickoff meeting only to announce that the pledge cards were not ready and would be mailed in a week or so. It is easy to imagine what happened to the enthusiasm the meeting had built.

This is the time to identify high-potential prospects who have not given before or are capable of giving considerably larger gifts than they have in the past. Establish a competent committee to cultivate their interest well in advance of the general campaign.

Carefully geared into this timetable is a plan for conducting the promotion program itself. As previously mentioned, an important role of the promotional campaign is to develop the kind of climate that makes people receptive when they are approached for a contribution by campaign workers. A media blitz conducted after the contacts have already been made provides no support for the solicitors at all. This is rather like a corporation peaking its advertising campaign for the introduction of a new product before the commodity is on display in its retail outlets. Introduction and promotion of the product need to be carefully meshed. In the same way, the media campaign must be carefully planned to prepare the contributors for the calls of solicitors.

Another important aspect of timing a campaign is to take into account other campaigns that are being conducted in the community. It is important that a major campaign effort not conflict with another communitywide campaign. If it does, it is likely to hurt both organizations, for many of the people who would be called upon to serve in leadership positions or as campaign workers will be sought by both organizations. Not only will volunteers be frustrated, but one or both of the organizations may lose valuable campaigners whom they want to enroll. Care should be exercised to keep campaign periods sufficiently separated so that solicitations do not overlap. The degree to which duplicate campaign timing will be a factor depends on the size and scope of the campaigns themselves and the constituency to be solicited. A limited church campaign is not likely to interfere with a communitywide effort of the United Way. However, a major hospital or college capital campaign and a United Way effort may call upon many of the same volunteers.

Another matter to consider is the best time of year for recruiting volunteers and soliciting prospects. The middle of winter is generally not a good campaign season in the North—nor is the middle of summer good in the South—because climatic conditions are not favorable for the volunteers to make their calls. In some parts of the North late spring and summer are fairly good campaign periods because residents stay in those areas and wait for less moderate weather to go on vacation. Winter in the North is a poor time not only because of the severity of the temperature but because many top leaders take vacations in the South. The converse is true of certain Southern areas.

The economy too is an important factor. An organization would be foolish indeed if it embarked upon a fund-raising effort without taking into account existing economic conditions at the time of the campaign. Some communities experience routine swings in their economic life owing to the seasonal nature of their industries. More important are the unusual economic circumstances that might affect fund-raising results: Periods of recession, poor earnings of major industries, major changes in tax legislation, major layoffs or strikes—all are factors that can make for difficult campaigns. It has been said that "there's never a good time for a campaign" and to some extent that's true, for there are always some negative factors. If you keep waiting for the perfect time, your campaign will never get under way. But don't defy the odds if your major contributors are warning you that the time is not expedient to launch the campaign effort.

Also to be considered in devising a time schedule are important community events that might conflict. An organization should always consult a community calendar if it is available. Campaigns that are going to depend upon top leadership, for example, would not want to have their kickoff when the chamber of commerce is having its annual meeting or when a prominent business speaker is coming to the community. Religious holidays may be a factor if they mean that important members of the campaign organization cannot participate during that period. National holidays mean that there is no mail and some banks and federal offices are closed—both may be factors. Commencement exercises for high schools and colleges will take the time of those volunteers who have children graduating. Political campaigns make major demands on volunteers and also make it more difficult to get media attention.

No timetable is going to be perfect, of course, but an organization should not be blind and create problems for itself by failing to use a little forethought.

COMPETITION AND RECOGNITION

An important aspect of campaign success that is frequently overlooked by organizations is the necessity of devising a program of recognition for both the givers and the campaign workers. It is true that people work in a campaign for highly altruistic reasons, but there is no escaping the fact that suitable recognition enhances their response.

At the outset of the campaign it is essential that goals be established by team, group, section, or other division of the campaign. These goals have important purposes. They ensure that responsibility for the overall objective of the organization has been distributed equitably to all the workers and groups within the campaign. When the campaign objective is broken down to its finest components, the achievement of smaller objectives by most of the groups will ensure the final success of the overall campaign effort. Goals have the added value of giving each worker, captain, or chairperson an incentive to strive for and a way of gauging relative success. Goals also permit the organization to recognize outstanding work and express appreciation to those who have done it. Recognition can be accomplished by publishing campaign bulletins that indicate the amount raised by each campaign group and by awarding certificates or plaques for goal achievement.

Americans are essentially a goal-oriented people and are used to responding to challenges. But it is important that goals be reasonable and fair. If goals are unrealistic and unattainable, the worker may recognize this at the outset, become discouraged, and cease trying. A goal should make a volunteer stretch, but should not be so utterly impossible to achieve that the worker throws in the towel early in the campaign game.

A recognition system is important for the giver as well as for the campaign worker. The very least that should be expected is some means of thanking the giver for a gift. Depending upon the size and scope of the campaign, recognition can take the form of a personal letter, a poster in a conspicuous place in the company, or a thoughtfully worded receipt sent by mail. It can also take more formalized forms, such as listing major givers in a final campaign report or in the annual report of the organization.

Many successful campaigns make a listing of contributors by gift category (sponsor, benefactor, and so on), with each classification designating a certain contribution level ($5,000 and over, $1,000 to $5,000, and the like). A certificate of appreciation may be used or a formal plaque may be placed in a part of the building for which capital funds have been raised.

MOTIVATION AND TRAINING

The best-conceived campaign with the best leadership will not be successful if the leaders and the workers are not properly motivated and trained to do their jobs. Motivation comes primarily from being involved in the program of the institution or, at least, from gaining a good understanding of the needs of the institution and the reason that its support is essential.

Being motivated to do a good job and knowing how to do it correctly are two different things. Therefore, a formalized training program has to be instituted as part of the campaign strategy in order for the solicitors to translate motivation into achieving tangible results.

Critical to motivation are volunteer participation in the institution, the use of services by the individuals or their families, and exposure to the program through peers, the media, and campaign promotion to gain a feeling that the institution is important to the community. The training program must provide the kind of information that will convince the solicitor not only that the institution is a good one but that its programs are essential and must be supported. Each volunteer must be persuaded to put forth maximum effort to make the campaign a success, because failure to do so will bring about a reduction in services to people who need them. (How people become motivated is explored more fully in Chapter 6.)

A motivation and training program has to be tailor-made within the campaign organization. Each division is structured somewhat differently and may be approaching different types of prospects. Therefore, the program has to take into account the varying interests of the prospects in the division as well as the proper techniques to be used by solicitors in approaching them. A campaign among employee groups and the solicitation of wealthy individuals call for quite different instructions and approaches. Those who approach major corporations, foundations, and wealthy individuals have a particular sales story that has to be told, and it is important that training for this purpose be carefully thought out and formalized. Even within employee groups, there are substantial differences because of the kinds of employees involved—women, part-time workers, industrial employees, public employees, and so on. The work place and the conditions of work are not entirely the same for every group.

Even though training programs will differ by division, certain general principles hold. Training programs should focus on:

1. The general purpose of the campaign, the needs of the institution, the amount that has to be sought, and what is to be accomplished.
2. The rationale for the campaign itself—who is being approached, the amount of the goal, the overall strategy of the campaign.

3. The timing of the campaign and the expected achievement dates.
4. Specific divisional instructions—procedures and techniques to be followed by the solicitors in that particular division.
5. The amounts to be sought from the various prospects, how they have been determined, and guides for giving or other standards of requests.
6. Explanation of solicitation materials.
7. Recognition programs.

FOLLOW-THROUGH

Some campaigns are elaborately planned and promoted, have good leadership, and yet fail to achieve goal. In these cases, the missing ingredient is often an adequate plan of follow-through.

Once the organization is in place—all personnel recruited, all assignments made, and a promotional campaign established—the organization has to be sure that the calls are actually made. Up to this point the campaign is all on paper—no funds have yet been raised and no prospects have been solicited.

Staff and volunteers must include in their campaign planning a carefully devised system to ensure that the calls are being made and to track the status of solicitation at any point in time. This can be accomplished by setting firm deadlines for the solicitors that indicate when the call must be made. A personal follow-up by section and group chairperson, campaign chairperson, and staff will ensure the solicitor that the campaign leaders are alive and interested in his or her progress. The campaign mechanics should include the forms necessary to keep account of the weekly progress in solicitation. Campaign bulletins issued regularly will show results to date and also the achievement of each solicitor and section toward goal. They will also point out areas that may be slow or have special problems requiring attention. Report meetings are another device for tracking the status of the campaign and keeping it moving toward target. Further attention will be given to these factors as we move along in the book.

COMPETENT STAFF SERVICE

Although most campaigns depend essentially on volunteers to raise their money, very few can be successful unless staff has provided the necessary support services. I have seen some campaigns succeed because of excellent staff who compensated through hard work for mediocre volunteer leadership. But I have never seen a campaign succeed when the staff was inept or incompetent—even though the lay leadership was good. Volunteers have full-time jobs; their volunteer work is an avocation. They can do some things the staff can't do, but they simply do not have the time to plan, prepare, and execute all the meticulous details that are essential to campaign success.

5

THE FUND-RAISING MARKETPLACE

Essential to any campaign plan is an understanding of the marketplace in which funds will be raised. Such an understanding will enable the institution to devise a campaign plan that will minimize volunteer and staff time and not waste effort on the solicitation of prospects when there is little hope of response.

As pointed out previously, a church campaign is not going to be successful in approaching major corporations and many foundations. On the other hand, institutions of higher learning will not usually have much success in soliciting the *general* public, for there is not a defined and interested constituency that will respond.

Basically, campaign prospects can be divided into three broad categories, which in turn are subdivided into many separate groups, depending upon the institution involved in the fund-raising effort. These three categories are (1) business prospects, (2) foundations and trusts, and (3) individuals.

BUSINESS PROSPECTS

The ability of a business to respond to charitable solicitation and the quickness with which it responds are often determined by the kind of organization it is. The various ways in which business activity is carried on may or may not be understood by development personnel and their volunteers.

Individually Owned Enterprises

Literally millions of businesses in the United States are totally owned by individuals. These are commonly referred to as proprietorships. They are distinguished by the fact that the owner, or proprietor, transacts all the business with or without hired employees. Such businesses are not incorporated and do not issue stock. The total control of the company, the kind of product sold or manufactured, and decisions on policies, pricing, investment, and even contributions are made by one person. Usually these companies are small, with fewer than 25 employees. However, as a group they employ millions of people and, within a community, will often approximate the total employment of the large companies in that area. Because there are so many, they are difficult to campaign; the numbers involved require a substantial volunteer force and pose considerable geographic problems because they are scattered in small units over wide areas. Nonetheless, proprietorships do have the advantage of requiring agreement only from a single owner for a contribution to be made.

Partnerships

A partnership is an association of two or more people who carry on as co-owners of a business for profit. Partnerships are not incorporated entities. Basically they are unincorporated associations whose partners voluntarily contract to pool their capital, their labor, and their skills for the purpose of conducting a business for profit. Since each principal is a co-owner, business decisions must reflect agreement among the partners. From the standpoint of contributions, decisions usually are agreed upon by the general partners if the gifts are to be made in the name of the partnership. However, each partner has full authority to act for the firm within the regular scope of the business and is liable for its obligations.

Partnerships are either general or limited. In a general partnership all parties concerned devote full time to the business. In a limited partnership the general partners devote full time to the management and conduct of the business while the limited partner is, in effect, an investor. The limited partner has no direct influence in the conduct of the business, although he or she has a right to a full accounting and disclosure of its finances and activities. In effect, the general partners act as agents. The limited partner's liability in the firm is restricted to the amount of his or her investment.

Partnerships are fairly common among professionals—there are associations of doctors, lawyers, dentists, accountants, architects, and so on. Partnerships are also found in retail, wholesale, and other types of businesses. From the standpoint of soliciting contributions, both general and limited partnerships can be approached by making a request to one or more of the general partners, who will make the final decision.

Corporations

A corporation is a group of people acting together as a unit and vested with "personality by the law." In effect, it is formed by a group of incorporators—individuals—who file a certificate with the state indicating the name, place of business, type of business, and amount, number, and type of shares of stock to be issued. Upon payment of incorporation dues and proper filing of corporate papers, the company receives a charter from the state to do business. A board of directors is selected and the company begins operations.

Closely held corporations. In closely held (or private) corporations the stock is owned by a very limited number of individuals who generally are active in the management of the company. Frequently, but not always, these individuals are members of the same family. A board of directors is responsible for making decisions regarding policy, investments, products, and so on. A manager is employed to direct the enterprise and is frequently a major stockholder or member of the family. Such corporations generally need the approval of the board of directors when deciding upon major contributions, although they may designate an officer to approve contributions of limited amounts. Most closely held corporations are local rather than national in scope and, because they are locally headquartered, are often fairly generous in their giving patterns.

Publicly held corporations. Publicly held corporations are business organizations that issue stock to the general public. Most of the major national corporations, including the Fortune 500 group, fall into this category, but there are thousands of smaller publicly held companies whose stock is sold on one of the exchanges. Ownership of the stock is generally widely held by hundreds or thousands of stockholders, all of whom have an interest in the success of the company. They elect the members of the board of directors, who in turn are responsible for the final conduct of the organization. The board hires a chief executive officer who is responsible for the management of the company and who reports to the board of directors. Contributions policies and a contributions budget are decided by the board of directors. Administration of the contributions program is usually delegated to a committee operating under the policy determined by the board of directors. Major contributions may need board approval.

Many corporations have very well-defined corporation contributions policies that determine the types of programs they will support. Some may have formulas or guidelines regarding what they are willing to give in their multiple plant or branch locations. These corporations are often very sophisticated in their giving practices and have specialized staff to study the requests for gifts and make recommendations to the contributions committee. Many major corporations use corporate foundations as vehicles through which contributions are made.

Mutual companies. In a mutual company, the owners of the company are the policyholders, or depositors. Mutual companies are typically life insurance companies, savings and loans, and in some cases savings banks. In a mutual company, the members of the organization share in the profits and in the expenses. As the owners, the policyholders or depositors receive any earnings of the company in the form of either dividends or interest.

Federal law has recently changed in this respect, but for many years did not permit mutual companies to deduct charitable contributions in determining income tax liability. The effect was that any contributions made by the company cost 100 cents on the dollar since there was no tax advantage. For this reason, many mutual insurance companies, savings and loans, and savings banks chose to establish Clifford trusts (see pp. 44–45) for their charitable contributions. By using the income from the charitable trust, the companies could make contributions "outside" normal operating income and expense; hence the contribution did not have to be paid from "aftertax" dollars.

Recent legislation has made it possible for mutual insurance companies to deduct contributions in determining federal tax liability. However, the new legislation also increases the tax rate on income and introduces a new tax on the companies' surplus. Under these circumstances, it may still be advisable for a mutual company to establish a Clifford trust and transfer money from surplus to the trust, thereby reducing the tax on surplus and gaining additional tax savings.

Building or real estate corporations. Prospects frequently overlooked by soliciting organizations are building or real estate corporations. The stock of these corporations, whose function is to own land and buildings, may be either widely held or very closely held. Many of the very large office buildings and shopping centers in major cities, as well as buildings leased for manufacturing and commercial purposes, are owned by building corporations. Such corporations may also finance large residential real estate developments and frequently own apartment buildings or a series of apartment buildings.

These companies are very viable campaign prospects, although it takes considerable research to locate them. A review of the tax rolls of large downtown and other properties will often uncover building or real estate corporations. Approach them as you would any other corporation. Their giving programs tend to reflect their size and whether they are closely or widely held.

Cooperatives

Another type of business organization that is frequently overlooked is the cooperative. The cooperative is an enterprise or organization owned and operated for the benefit of those using its services. Cooperatives are widely used by farmers and other consumer groups. The typical farm cooperative may either manufacture or arrange for the manufacture of farm supplies, fertilizer, seed, and equipment and, in turn, market those products to its members. Accordingly, it is to the advantage of the members of a cooperative to buy their goods from the cooperative because the price is generally more reasonable and any earnings accrue to the members. There are very substantial cooperatives in the Midwest, some equal to the Fortune 500 companies in size. Cooperatives are permitted to make contributions to charitable activities, but since their profits are distributed to their consumer owners, their boards of directors are generally conservative with respect to contributions.

PRIVATE FOUNDATIONS AND TRUSTS

Technically a private foundation is a nongovernment, nonprofit organization whose funds are managed by its own trustees or directors. Foundations are established to maintain or aid social, educational, religious, or other charitable activities serving the common welfare, primarily through the making of grants. In a private foundation funds come from a single source—a corporation, family, or individual.

Corporate Foundations

Corporations, both privately and publicly held, often utilize foundations as vehicles for administering their corporate giving. The corporate foundation is a private foundation, but it is different from other private foundations in that it is solely an entity of the business itself. Corporate foundations are formed to permit the company to channel profits into the foundation during relatively profitable years, taking a tax deduction for such gifts and making possible grants from the foundation in both good and bad years. In this way, the corporation can stabilize its giving to charitable organizations regardless of the business cycle but still take advantage of charitable gift deductions in the years when it is best to do so. The corporate foundation is an extremely important aspect of voluntary giving because business profits are highly cyclical—good in some years and poor in others. Were corporate contributions dependent upon this profit cycle, the future of private organizations would be insecure indeed.

Some fund-raising administrators and volunteers do not differentiate between corporate foundations and other private foundations. For all intents and purposes the gifts of a corporate foundation are merely corporate gifts channeled through a special vehicle in order to stabilize giving and achieve tax savings. Although the foundation is an independent organization, the policies of the corporate foundation reflect the contributions policies and interests of the corporation itself.

Independent Foundations

Independent foundations are not associated with another organization, such as a corporation. Many independent foundations are family foundations. The better known ones include the Ford, Rockefeller, and Bush foundations. Independent foundations constitute one of the most important sources of charitable gifts. Although contributions from independent foundations represent only 5 percent of total giving, they often represent a very high percentage of the amounts received by certain kinds of institutions in their campaigns. They are, for example, the most important source of short-term demonstration money for specific projects. Institutions wishing to introduce or test innovative programs in new areas of need seek out demonstration grants. The money is used to "demonstrate" that the program works. Some foundations restrict annual giving and favor making short-term demonstration gifts. Foundation challenge grants are often used to stimulate giving from other donors by providing the incentive of matching funds. Foundations provide funds on the condition that the public responds with increased support. Each foundation distributes its charitable gifts differently.

Family foundations. Family foundations are independent private foundations formed either by an individual or by a family to support the charitable organizations in which the donor or donors have an interest. In some cases, the foundation may come into existence upon the death of a wealthy individual who has decided to have a substantial part of his or her estate set aside for charitable purposes.

These foundations give donors the opportunity to make substantial gifts at a time when it is advantageous from both an economic and a tax viewpoint to do so. They allow the donors to maximize gifts to the foundation when it is more desirable and establish greater continuity of giving by creating a source of funds that is less subject to economic cycles. The foundation is incorporated and has a board of trustees that is responsible for making decisions on gifts or grants. Large foundations have specialized professional staff to study and evaluate the requests and make recommendations to the board. Some foundations stress innovative and experimental programs in their funding. Family foundations are either general-purpose or special-purpose foundations.

Special-purpose and general-purpose foundations. Special-purpose foundations restrict the areas to which funds can be given. For example, a donor may wish funds to be given only for educational scholarships or may wish gifts to be made only to organizations of a particular religious persuasion. Some foundations give only for operating or demonstration purposes and will not contribute to capital or building campaigns; others may give to building campaigns as well. On the other hand, in general-purpose foundations the trustees may have wide latitude in deciding the areas to which grants will be made. There is no set pattern for foundation giving. Development directors and campaign leaders have to study each foundation's policies in order to know whether it is for special or general purposes and whether it has a viable contribution potential.

Private foundations must spend a specified percentage of their assets each year as determined by Congress, and their income is subject to an excise tax to cover the cost of IRS foundation audits.

In 1983 foundations in the United States had assets of over $41 billion and made gifts of $3.479 billion. These gifts represented 7.3 percent of their total assets. Independent foundations made the largest gifts—$2.5 billion—but corporate foundations gave the highest percentage of their assets (payout)—26.9 percent.

Trusts

According to its legal definition, a trust is the vesting of the legal ownership of property in a person or persons, known as trustees, for the benefit of another or others, or something committed to one's charge or care to be used for the benefit of another. It is a legal instrument for transferring property to the care of others and for defining the purposes, either specific or general, for which the funds are to be spent.

Trusts can be used for a wide variety of purposes—caring for one's loved ones, providing income for the creator of the trust and his or her family, providing education for children or grandchildren, or generating income for charitable purposes. When the purpose is charitable, property is vested in the care of others and is used by the trustees to carry out the wishes of the donor. The trust may be administered by the actual donor, by the donor's family, by a group of people selected by the donor, by the trust department of a bank, or by a community foundation.

There is no clear-cut distinction between trusts and foundations. Some foundations use the word "trust" in their names. Some organizations using the word "foundation" in their names are not really foundations at all according to IRS definitions—they are public charities since they receive their funds from many donors. Examples include the Cystic Fibrosis Foundation, the Heritage Foundation, and the Arthritis Foundation.

All this is bound to be confusing to the development director and his or her staff. From a practical fund-raising point of view, it makes little difference whether the organization is a trust or a private foundation. There are two important considerations: (1) the purpose of the trust or foundation and therefore the organizations and kinds of programs it will support, and (2) the person or persons to contact who can make the decision on a gift and its amount.

Some trusts may be created for a specific short-term purpose and then go out of existence. For example, a trust may be established with the provision that all income derived from it be used for charitable purposes for 10 years. At the end of the 10-year period, the corpus, or principal, reverts back to the donor. This permits the donor to make substantial contributions from the trust without having to consider the tax consequences of receiving the income and then making gifts from the income itself. A trust may also be created in such a way that a person receives income from the trust for life but upon his or her death the proceeds revert to a designated charity. Such trusts can provide income on the basis of a percentage of assets or a stipulated amount per year. A more detailed discussion of various types of trusts that can be used by individuals is included in Chapter 21.

Clifford Trusts

As noted earlier, some corporations do not have the benefit of a tax deduction for charitable contributions because of specific legislation that prohibits such deductions or because much of the company's income is tax-exempt. Mutual life insurance companies, mutual savings banks, savings and loans, and some banks are organizations of this type. Although such companies are expected to contribute generously, they are not always able to deduct charitable gifts when determining income tax liability. Instead, the gifts have to be made out of aftertax profits rather than pretax income. In other words, such gifts represent a 100 percent burden to the corporation and must be paid out of whatever revenues are left after the company has paid its taxes.

This situation is not confined totally to mutual companies. Certain financial institutions, for example, some large financial holding companies, also find no advantage in taking a tax deduction for contributions because much of their income comes from untaxable sources. If, for example, a corporation's income is derived principally from the investments in municipal bonds or other nontaxable government obligations, it can gain no tax advantage from its charitable contributions.

One of the ways in which corporations of this type have tried to be generous and still avoid having their charitable contributions cost them 100 cents on the dollar is to create a Clifford trust. Such a trust is established by the transfer of funds or property from the company's *surplus* rather than from current income (as in the case of a corporate foundation). The trust has a duration of only 10 years and a day, after which time the trust ceases to exist and the principal, or corpus, is returned to the company. During the life of the trust all funds received from surplus are invested and the income derived is used to fund the company's charitable contributions. Trusts of this type must have IRS approval and all gifts must be made to 501(c)(3) organizations that meet the charitable test. (According to the Internal Revenue Service, organizations defined by regulation (501)(c)(3) are nonprofit and gifts given to them are tax-deductible.) On the conclusion of the trust's life, the principal is returned to the corporation but can be transferred to another trust at that time.

Let us take a look at how this might be done. A company gains no tax advantage from making charitable contributions because of existing legislation or tax-exempt income sources. It therefore creates a Clifford trust and transfers $2,000,000 from surplus to the trust, which is then invested in commercial paper yielding 12 percent interest. This investment will bring the trust $240,000 per year, to be spent by the trustees of the trust exclusively for charitable purposes. The corpus is not touched. At the end of 10 years and a day, the trust goes out of existence and the $2,000,000 is returned to the company. The corpus is then added to surplus, or a new Clifford trust is established for similar purposes. In the meantime the company has distributed $2,400,000 of the trust's income for charitable purposes.

COMMUNITY FOUNDATIONS

Community foundations differ from private foundations in that their funds come from multiple donors rather than from a single individual or family. They represent a charitable vehicle through which many donors may continue their generosity after death to organizations representing multiple fields of service. These foundations have very broad purposes and great flexibility. The concept of the community foundation permits a donor's gift to have substantial meaning after his death.

Some donors provide in their wills for the establishment of a trust that will make grants to nonprofit organizations after the donors die. Frequently these trusts give trustees wide latitude to make grants to any nonprofit organizations that the trustees believe to be worthy. These are known as *unrestricted trusts*. Other donors provide for distribution of the trust's income for a very narrow purpose or only to a few organizations. These are called *restricted trusts*. Community foundations can accommodate both these types of trusts within their structure. They administer the trust income in accordance with the donor's instructions.

One of the problems with restricted trusts is that needs change over time, the government may assume responsibility for the program, or the beneficiary organization is no longer active. For this reason community foundations generally require that restricted trusts give the foundation the latitude to change the grants when necessary.

Direct gifts can also be made to community foundations by living donors who are permitted to suggest how they would like the money spent. These are called *donor-advised funds*. Such gift preference is advisory only, and the foundation trustees are not legally bound to follow the donor's suggestions, although they nearly always comply.

The Internal Revenue Service has designated community foundations as public charities rather than private foundations since, as noted above, their funds come from multiple sources rather than an individual or a family. This designation permits the community foundation to escape paying the current excise tax that is required of private foundations and avoid spending a stated percentage of its assets each year. However, in order to maintain this classification, community foundations must meet the "public support" test. The IRS provides that a certain amount of money must be raised each year from new sources: gifts, bequests, trusts, or funds received from *public charities* (such as United Way, a university, or an organization in the arts). The amount that must be raised is a stated percentage of the foundation's assets. Because the foundation may raise more in one year than another, these amounts can be averaged out over a number of years in order to meet this qualification. The community foundation, therefore, must be prepared to raise new income each year. Otherwise, it risks losing its designation and will have to pay the excise tax required of private foundations.

The community foundation is a very broad instrument, with considerable latitude in making gifts under some direction from its donors. It is able to respond to changing times and conditions and can make gifts to a number of service areas. There is usually only one community foundation in a given city, though there may be many private foundations.

From a fund-raising point of view, it is essential that development personnel study each community foundation and determine whether its restricted income permits it to support the type of program they represent. If not, it is still possible to qualify for support from the foundation's unrestricted income if sufficient funds are available and the foundation's policies permit it.

OPERATING FOUNDATIONS

Another but much less common type of nonprofit foundation in the United States is the operating foundation.

Whereas private foundations and community foundations make grants to other organizations for various types of service programs, operating foundations do not make grants, but actually conduct the service programs themselves. Private foundations and community foundations do not operate health, welfare, educational, or arts programs and their activity is limited to custody of the funds given them and to making direct grants. An operating foundation provides a direct program such as mental health services, services for dependent children, services for the aged, or recreational services. It might also conduct research. The kinds of programs conducted are guided by the will or foundation instrument under which the organization is created and by the policies established by its board of directors. The operating foundation, therefore, should be considered more of a direct service agency than a grant foundation.

Table 5-1. Aggregate fiscal data by foundation type—1981.

Foundation Type	Number of Foundations	Assets	Gifts Received	Total Giving*	Payout**
Independent Foundations	3,208	$41,529,140,504	$1,057,201,972	$2,583,247,421	6.2
Corporate Foundations	701	2,491,362,698	469,114,499	669,361,139	26.9
Community Foundations	98	2,084,343,615	173,222,179	175,105,717	8.4
Operating Foundations	56	1,436,429,607	42,381,470	52,186,002	3.6
Total	4,063	$47,541,276,424	$1,741,920,120	$3,479,900,279	7.3

* Total giving figures include grants, scholarships, matching gifts, and program amounts paid or authorized by the foundation in the year of record. Loan amounts are not included.
** Payout represents the percentage of assets paid out in total giving.
Source: Reprinted with permission from *The Foundation Directory*, Edition 9 (© The Foundation Center, 1984). The data cover only grantmaking foundations that have at least $1,000,000 in assets or that award at least $100,000 in grants annually.

Under these circumstances, operating foundations do not represent a major source of funds for nonprofit organizations and are not a viable campaign prospect. Occasionally an operating foundation might agree to fund, as part of its own program, some element of a social service program in cooperation with another organization. For example, it may be possible for a mental health clinic to get an operating foundation to provide a children's psychiatric program on a cooperative basis with the clinic itself. Such arrangements, however, are rare.

Table 5-1 shows the assets and total giving of various types of foundations in 1981.

INDIVIDUALS

Most of the giving in the United States comes from individuals. This fact is so fundamental that one might wonder why it is necessary to take any time discussing the importance of individual gifts in the fund-raising marketplace.

It is important to recognize, however, that individual gifts need to be classified from a fund-raising point of view. The exact classification will depend largely on the type of institution conducting the campaign. For example, churches gain all their support from parishioners. Colleges and universities gain substantial amounts from alumni, faculty, parents, and staff. Though all are individual prospects, for purposes of campaigning they have to be identified and approached on a selective basis.

Three Key Groups

Regardless of the specific fund-raising effort, at least three groups must be identified and treated separately, since they represent potentially different levels of giving.

1. *The independently wealthy.* Many people derive income from independent sources. Their livelihood is not dependent upon a salary and, in general, they are not employed on a regular basis. These people usually derive their income from property and investments. A substantially increasing number of them are widows.

2. *Management.* Many financially well-to-do people are employed in management positions in corporations or other types of business firms, or in the professions. They are fully employed and, for the most part, work for a stipulated salary and sometimes a bonus. They may also have substantial shares of stock and other investments.

3. *Other employed people.* Individuals who are in a lower income bracket than either the independently wealthy or the top management group constitute the greatest number of potential contributors. They may be classified for campaign purposes according to specialized groupings (professionals, faculty, parishioners, employee groups, and so on), depending on the organization soliciting the money and its defined market.

Types of Gifts

When considering contributions for charity, most people think of gifts of cash. By far, gifts of cash or check are the largest sources of income for charitable organizations, but there are a number of other types of gifts that should not be overlooked.

Stocks and bonds. Gifts of equities (stocks) and/or bonds represent a very large source of contributions for charitable organizations. Gifts of stocks, in particular, offer great advantages to the contributor, especially if the stock has appreciated in value since the donor purchased it. The donor obtains a tax deduction equal to the full market value of the stock at the time of the contribution, up to the limit of 30 percent of adjusted gross income. Were the donor to sell the stock in order to make a charitable contribution, he or she would have to pay a capital gains tax first and then make the contribution from the proceeds. By making a contribution of the stock itself, the donor is able to escape the capital gains tax and gain a much larger tax deduction.

Life insurance. Frequently overlooked by many charitable organizations is the possibility of receiving gifts of life insurance, either as deferred gifts or as current gifts. The way in which life insurance can be utilized by donors and philanthropic organizations is described in detail in Chapter 21.

Real property. Gifts of land, buildings, and other real property represent potential sources of income for charitable organizations—as outright gifts, bequests, or other forms of deferred giving.

Works of art. Wealthy individuals often donate works of art to art museums and other organizations. The value of these works not only enhances the reputation and the attractiveness of the institution but gives the donor a sizable tax deduction. Donors can take the fair market value of the gift, as determined by a recognized appraiser, as an income tax deduction. Campaign personnel need to be cognizant of the fact that there are penalties for "overappraisal" of contributed works of art.

In-kind gifts. Many businesses manufacture or sell products that are of considerable worth to nonprofit organizations; others have surplus products that can be donated to and used by nonprofit organizations. The tax deduction on such items is equal to the manufacturer's cost or the cost of purchase to the retailer. A well-known manufacturer of computers, for example, has made a practice of giving some of its products to high schools throughout the country. Another large manufacturer contributes medical supplies; still another donates overhead projectors to educational institutions. Some retail organizations contribute clothing and other commodities to sheltered workshops and/or to retail outlets operated by nonprofit organizations for the poor.

6

WHY DO PEOPLE SERVE?

It is remarkable how deeply volunteerism is embedded in American life. Thousands of organizations each year call upon and obtain the help of talented people who serve without pay in helping their colleges and universities, churches, arts organizations, United Ways, hospitals, and youth programs in a variety of capacities.

A substantial number of these volunteers are service volunteers—that is, their special talents are utilized to supplement the talents of staff in providing direct service to those served by the institution. Another large number are what might be called administrative volunteers who serve on the boards of directors and advisory committees of the institutions.

In addition to these, there are literally millions of people who give generously not only of their money but also of their time in soliciting the funds necessary to sustain the institution, to build new facilities, or to create an endowment. Campaigning is not exactly one of the most enjoyable ways of spending one's spare time. Why, then, do so many volunteer for what others might regard as a thankless job?

MOTIVES FOR VOLUNTEERING

The motives for volunteering are many and varied. The reasons noted below come not from formal studies but from personal observations in working with volunteers for over 40 years.

Return for Services Received

Many volunteers are deeply involved in the programs of the organization for which they serve. Over a period of time they have developed a deep emotional interest in the institution, either because of the personal relationships that have developed or because they believe the institution has made a deep and rewarding contribution to their own lives. Obvious reasons include appreciation for a good college education, for exemplary care in a hospital, for service given to a retarded child, and for help provided to elderly parents. Deep spiritual rewards may be derived from a person's involvement in a particular church. People who have these kinds of feelings and loyalties come from all classes and economic strata and are among an institution's most prized assets.

A woman reached her 102nd birthday and was interviewed by the press about the scores of volunteer activities in which she had been engaged.

One reporter asked, "Looking back, is there anything you would do differently if you were going to do it all over again?"

The woman thought for a moment and said, "Well, if I'd known I was going to live so long, I'd have taken better care of myself."

Community Obligation

A more sophisticated motive in volunteering is the sense of community obligation that people develop over a period of years. This may result from the feeling that they have been rather successful and have many reasons to be thankful. The community has helped them "get where they are" and they feel a responsibility to make some kind of contribution to the community in return for what it has done for them. This motivation is often found among top business executives.

Similarly motivated are those who, because of their position in business, feel a corporate obligation to perform certain types of volunteer tasks. Business leadership carries with it not only a responsibility for the profitable operation of the business and a responsibility to the stockholders and employees, but also a willingness to assume certain leadership positions in the community itself. A sense of corporate social responsibility is fast developing in the American business community. Some corporations have special departments devoted to an analysis of how a company may fulfill its role as a good citizen. One of the functions of such departments is to stimulate management and employees to assume volunteer responsibilities in the community at large.

Emotional Satisfaction

Volunteerism provides an outlet for many individuals that is completely different from what they experience in their day-to-day activities. Conducting a successful business puts major emphasis on profits and success in the materialistic sense. Volunteering in a nonprofit organization comes from an entirely different motivation and brings satisfaction through the free contribution of self. The measure of success is not the number of widgets or units that have been produced but the development of the human spirit in whatever way that may be expressed through the eleemosynary institution's program.

Recognition

The above motives are lofty and idealistic. There are other, less altruistic forces that compel people to volunteer and that also serve a very useful purpose. Voluntary participation is one way in which many people gain recognition for their efforts. Although the recognition may not be material, it often provides a tangible expression of appreciation from the institution and a certain status among associates.

Peer Influence

Peer influence frequently coaxes or encourages a reluctant person to do his or her first volunteer work. There is a natural reticence on the part of many to assume responsibilities in an institution with which they are not familiar and initially feel uncomfortable. Once the step has been taken, however, the individuals will often continue to serve because of the satisfaction they receive.

Business associates and valued customers can also exert influence, at least initially. Many a businessperson has been tapped by a member of his or her board of directors or by an important client for a civic responsibility. Perhaps that person responded initially because of his or her relationship to the person making the request. Very few will accept such an assignment, however, unless they can convince themselves that the institution is one that engages their interest and that has a program worthy of their time and effort.

In this connection, it has been noted previously that the higher the level of the person doing the recruitment, the better the chance of gaining the acceptance of the volunteer. It is relatively easy for those at higher economic levels or within the same level of economic status to recruit downward or laterally. But people in subordinate economic or social positions find it very difficult to ask other people in higher positions to take volunteer jobs. This is the reason that organizations should always start by getting top-level chairpersons who are as influential as possible.

WORKING WITH TOP LEADERSHIP—
THE ROLE OF STAFF AND VOLUNTEERS

Lay volunteers and staff represent a team that must work together closely and effectively if the campaign is to succeed. An organization can have a good volunteer structure but still falter because the staff is inept or has failed to provide the volunteer structure with the support systems it needs. Each organization, of course, has to work within the limits of the staff time it has available. This may range anywhere from the part-time work of one person to the full-time support of scores of people. Some volunteers may lack an understanding of the important role that is played by the staff assigned to the organization. Because volunteers perform most of the solicitation, they may think that the organization does not need much staff service. Some of the most dramatic failures in campaigning result when volunteers try to get by cheaply and do all the work themselves without providing an adequate budget for staffing the campaign effort. I have seen difficult campaigns succeed when volunteer leadership was only average but staff was excellent, but I have never seen campaigns succeed when staff was incompetent, even if the volunteer leadership was good.

Staffing a volunteer organization is one of the most pleasant but difficult tasks in any campaign effort. It is pleasant because the volunteers are genuinely interested in the organization and want it to succeed. They give generously of their own time and money and are usually highly intelligent and hard-working. The staff, however, has the task of getting these people organized and getting them to assume important responsibilities without any financial remuneration whatsoever.

The Importance of Staff

Some years ago, when I was chief executive of the United Way in St. Paul, the president of a very large corporation remarked that my job was very similar to his. He viewed the responsibilities of policymaking and working with the board, the financial planning, administration, and sales effort as being similar to what a business executive would carry on. I remarked that this was true, but there were a few differences. The executive in a nonprofit organization may have a new chairman of the board every year or two, and, although they are very civic-minded, each may have an entirely different perspective of the job, and the executive must adjust to the new point of view. The entire sales organization of the institution has to be reconstituted from top to bottom each year. What major corporate executive would relish that task within his or her own company?

Not only does the sales force of a nonprofit institution have to be reorganized every year, but the salespeople have to be willing to work without pay. Most nonprofit organizations will publicly announce their goals six months or so in advance. Very few business firms would be willing to have their success or failure measured in this way. The only product that a nonprofit organization has to sell is the services it renders. Frequently these services are provided by subordinate groups over which the administration has only remote control at best. Furthermore, the subsidiaries of a business corporation are striving to make the parent company profitable. When a nonprofit organization has subsidiaries, they are generally demanding funds.

The development director is perhaps the second most important staff person in a nonprofit organization. He or she has a major responsibility not only for raising the money but for handling many of the difficult relationships—both within and outside the institution—that surface in a campaign. When people are being asked for money, the real problems of the institution become apparent. The development director's skill in handling these problems and reporting them back to the administration with suggestions for how to resolve them is very important.

The most effective staff members in any campaign are those who make the job of volunteers easier. They will remove from the volunteers responsibility for the detailed work that has to be carried out in order to make any campaign a success. Development staff people need a rather unusual and broad set of qualifications. They must be detailed enough to be sure that not a single prospect is overlooked, that all addresses, names, and information are accurate, that all proposals are well conceived, and that the timetable is followed. They must also have the ability to speak effectively on their feet and to sell the services of the institution to prospective volunteers and givers. At the same time, they must not dominate the organization but must work effectively behind the scenes, except when it is essential for them to take a prominent role. Staff should know how to "grease the skids" for the volunteers. One of the best compliments a staff person can receive is for a volunteer to say, "You make the volunteers look good." Staff will reserve for volunteers those things that the volunteers can do best and for themselves the things that are essential for them to do. A campaign staff that uses volunteers in unnecessary detail is making poor use of the volunteers' time and may discourage them. For the most part, volunteers should be encouraged to be out front and to take prominent positions in the campaign. Staff should support them from behind the scenes, but provide them with all the information that is needed to do their job effectively.

Managing Leadership

One of the factors that is often overlooked by development personnel is the importance of having influential top leadership—*and* knowing how to manage it.

Some organizations waste their top leaders or make ineffective use of their time. I have seen campaign heads running from one relatively small business division to another for orientation purposes when that job could as easily have been done by the division or section leaders and staff. Meanwhile, important calls to top prospects that could spell victory or defeat were not being made.

Top business executives are used to having firm directions and goals and to setting priorities on the use of their time. They usually want a statement outlining what is expected of them and where they can best spend their time. One of the ways to accomplish this is to establish a timetable indicating what things are essential as opposed to possible or desirable. The campaign chairperson then knows what things must be done and what is optional. Figure 6-1 illustrates such a timetable.

Planning for Future Leadership

Too many nonprofit organizations fail to think of their leadership needs in the long term. They live with existing boards and major campaign leaders on a year-to-year basis. To be certain of success, an institution must think of its leadership as one of its most important assets—one that must be developed *first* and not last in the organization's planning.

Frequently such organizations will search rather frantically for a first-class chairperson to head a fund-raising appeal that is only a few months away. Too often the first, second, and even third choices have already committed themselves to other institutions or will have business plans that will not permit them to accept. As a result, the organization often ends up with leadership that is less knowledgeable and influential than it should be—and the campaign results show it.

Having good campaign leaders and good presidential leadership requires long-range planning. It is a good idea to keep a file of future campaign chairpersons who could fulfill the organization's requirements and who might be approached at least two years in advance of the campaign itself. Approaching a potential campaign chairperson this far ahead makes it possible for him or her to arrange schedules and commitments so as to find the time to head the campaign. One potential chairperson jokingly re-

Figure 6-1. Chairperson's timetable.

Timing	Essential	If Possible	As Desired
Nov.–Feb.	1. Confirmation of strategy and structure changes (1 meeting with staff) 2. Recruitment and confirmation of division and committee leaders 3. Basic orientation/planning meeting of campaign leadership (1 meeting)	1. Evaluation and critique meeting of preceding campaign	1. Monthly board and/or executive committee meeting
Feb.–July	1. Division progress reviews of plans and recruiting (1 to 2 meetings suggested) 2. Annual meeting (May)	1. Orientation sessions for area/section chairpersons by divisions (maximum of 5 for observation and motivation) 2. National campaign leaders conference—May	1. Monthly board and/or executive committee meeting 2. Assisting division chairpersons in recruiting of area/section chairpersons 3. Assistance with key account cultivation calls by division
July–Sept.	1. Board meeting (and perhaps 1 or 2 other meetings) to set goal—July 2. Rating of advance gift prospects—200 accounts 3. Advance gifts and/or chief executives meeting (major firms)—August 4. Selective calls on top 10 prospects 5. Progress report contacts with campaign leaders (meetings and/or personal conferences) 6. General campaign kickoff—September	1. Special gifts division kickoff—August 2. Loaned executive orientation and training—August 3. Instructional meetings for company chairpersons of employee divisions—September (2 or 3 meetings)	1. Account rating and assignment conferences (2 divisions) 2. Direct handling of selected special accounts 3. Monthly board and/or executive committee meeting
Sept.–Nov.	1. Weekly general campaign report meetings (4 in October) 2. Final report dinner—October 3. Progress report contacts with campaign leaders	1. Problem solving for divisions on troublesome accounts 2. Availability to media for public interpretation of progress	

marked when being approached so far in advance, "Well, after all, it's pretty hard for me to find an excuse this far away from the campaign."

People who are committed early have the opportunity to observe the campaigns of their predecessors and learn the things that are important to do when their turn comes. They also become acquainted with the problems of the organization and have the opportunity to think about some of the potential solutions. They can become as involved or detached as they wish. A word of caution, however. In one organization I worked for we routinely had the chairperson-elect serve as vice chairperson of the current campaign. In this role, the newcomer had major responsibility for the recruitment, training, and supervision of several major divisions. After a period of time we found that for some this amounted to serving as campaign chairperson for two successive years. Finally, we evolved a plan whereby direct responsibility was minimal but the observational responsibilities of the chairperson-elect were considerable.

If the top executive or development director of an organization has a reasonably friendly and close relationship with a potential campaign leader, he or she can suggest informally that the person serve as campaign chairperson sometime in the future. The executive can point out that he or she is not asking the person to accept—since that is not his or her job—but that the executive knows the person's name will be coming up for discussion by the selections committee. The response of the potential chairperson at that point—open-minded, "not anxious but could be sold," or very negative—can be helpful in suggesting to the committee whether the person may be a viable candidate several years down the road. When the time is appropriate, the formal approach can be made by the responsible lay leadership, but at least the seed has been planted.

If the drive is not an annual one but a special campaign, the organization can still ensure itself of top-level leadership if it recruits people of sufficient stature on the planning committee. These potential chairpersons can then become knowledgeable about the needs of the institution and the importance of making the project a success. When the point has arrived in the study and planning process to begin a campaign, the organization will have a number of fine prospects who are sold on the program and willing to play a major role in making it a success.

The important factor is that early planning and recruitment permit a high continuity of high-level leadership and a smooth transition from year to year that are critical to success.

7

DETERMINING THE CAMPAIGN STRUCTURE

Nonprofit organizations differ widely in the types of activities in which they are engaged. Just as they are essentially different in programs and objectives, so must they be different in the approach they take to fund raising.

Some institutions today solicit funds using professional development staff only. Generally these organizations do not have an abundance of good lay leadership. Frequently they direct their solicitation efforts solely to a limited number of major corporations and foundations because they do not have the volunteer leadership to go beyond that. These efforts frequently raise fair amounts of funds, but the results would be much more dramatic if time were spent in recruiting, interesting, and utilizing good volunteers who could make the whole campaign effort more successful.

For the most part, successful fund raising must rely upon certain natural constituencies of support. For example, physicians are usually a primary source of funds for a new hospital building, but as a group physicians may have only minor interest in an organization in the arts.

It is important that institutions organizing a fund-raising campaign recognize these differences and direct their attention to those markets that are likely to represent productive and responsible contributors. There is nothing gained in using the time of staff and volunteers to campaign among groups that are not likely to respond. A broad-scale mail campaign to the general community, for example, might be very expensive and result in a poor response because the institution involved has a limited and defined constituency of interest. A United Way, on the other hand, should run a saturation campaign—one directed at every individual and corporation—because it is supporting many organizations serving a very broad constituency in health, youth services, rehabilitation, and family services programs.

The different "markets" for various kinds of organizations might be viewed as shown in Figure 7-1.

As can be seen from this listing, wealthy individuals are prospects for all types of nonprofit organizations, but corporations are not. On the other hand, colleges need to approach specialized interest groups such as the faculty and parents of students. United Ways, because they are federated campaigns, will receive most of their money through the solicitation of employee groups, but this source of income is not available to other types of appeals. This limitation is due to the fact that corporations traditionally restrict approaches to their employees at the place of business to federated campaigns that represent many agencies and serve broad segments of the population.

One of the first jobs in determining the campaign plan and structure is to identify the prospects that legitimately might be approached during the campaign. A church should not spend much of its leadership's time going to foundations that are not going

Figure 7-1. Defining the market according to the type of institution.

Types of Markets	Hospitals	Colleges and Universities	United Way	Church	Arts Organizations
Trustees	Board of Trustees	Board of Trustees	Board of Trustees	Board of Trustees	Board of Trustees
Faculty and staff	Hospital staff	Faculty	Agency staff and boards	—	Agency staff
Corporations	Corporations (Special project or building needs)	Corporations	Corporations	—	Corporations
Foundations	Foundations (with health objectives)	Foundations	Foundations	Religious foundations only (very limited)	Foundations
Users and sponsors	Former patients and their families	Alumni Parents of students	Agency participants	Parishioners	Arts participants Patrons of arts
Employee groups	—	—	Employee groups	—	—
Wealthy individuals	Wealthy individuals	Wealthy individuals	Wealthy individuals	Wealthy parishioners	Wealthy individuals
Small businesses	—	Very selective small businesses	Small businesses	—	Very selective small businesses
Professional groups and staff	Medical staff	—	Professional groups	—	Professional groups

to respond, nor will colleges be given access to group solicitation of employees by business, although some may have a program wherein the corporation will match the voluntary gifts made by employees without solicitation by the company itself.

PRINCIPAL PROSPECTS

Regardless of the specific structure used, every campaign will need to recognize three important groups and have a plan for approaching them.

Top 10 Gifts

The success or failure of almost every campaign will be determined by how effectively the 10 potentially most generous gifts are identified and solicited. Depending upon the type of campaign, these gifts must be counted on to produce anywhere from 15 to 50 percent of the funds required. In a capital campaign, they usually must be counted on to produce from 33 percent to upward of 50 percent of the campaign goal. In operating campaigns they may give less as a total percentage, but they are still a primary factor in success. It is with this group that your fund-raising organization needs to use its first team—its most effective volunteers. It is with this group, too, that you will need to call upon your campaign chairperson, past chairpersons, president, and other influential leadership. Identifying, cultivating, and soliciting the top 10 prospects are the most important orders of business in the campaign.

The Next 200 Gifts

The "next 200 gifts" are the 200 largest gifts after the top 10. They are frequently referred to in campaign parlance as advanced or special gifts and, in amount, should fall at the level immediately below that of the top 10. These prospects must be carefully identified and evaluated in terms of their ability to give. The approach to such potential givers must be highly selective, and a careful assessment must be made of the individuals who can best make the calls. When dealing with these two categories of givers—the top 10 and the next 200—you should make sure that there is a reason for the assignment of every card. It is here that the adage "people give to people" is most important, for it is here that personal relationships and persuasiveness are of the greatest importance. No assignment to a prospect in these two groups should ever be made without knowing that the person who will make the call is the best person to discuss the needs of the institution with that individual, company, or foundation. The campaign worker should either know the prospect socially, have business relationships with him or her, or share a very close interest with the prospect in the institution raising the funds.

These groups are especially important because their gifts will establish the pattern for the rest of the campaign. Campaign success or failure will depend primarily on how the top givers respond to the solicitation. Givers primarily follow the leader. Individuals and corporations generally want to do what their peers are doing. There are always a few who take special pride in their generosity and will be generous regardless of what others do. Most givers, however, tend to equate their giving with that of others. Therefore, it is extremely important that this phase of the campaign be properly organized and get off on the right foot.

All Other Prospects

The campaign plan must include all the other prospects who have been identified. Their total gifts may be very significant—as in the case of employee gifts to the United Way—or they may represent a small proportion of the total. In any case, these prospects are still important because they can spell the difference between success and failure. The campaign plan must be structured to ensure that there is 100 percent coverage of such prospects and that they are organized into a sufficient number of groups to make the approach to them efficient and responsive.

PROSPECT IDENTIFICATION

Who are the prospects that might be approached in a campaign and how does an organization obtain their names? Quite obviously, this will depend to some extent on the kind of organization soliciting the funds and its natural constituencies.

A church's prospects are usually limited to its own parishioners, and their names are readily available from membership records. However, analysis is still necessary to determine relative ability to support the program. Patrons of the arts are usually members of an arts organization and constitute a natural giving public for that type of institution. In other cases, as described below, an organization must get the names of companies and individuals in the general community who represent reasonable prospects for solicitation.

Prospect identification should be performed primarily by the staff personnel charged with directing the campaign. Included in this group are the campaign or development director, staff, and the professional campaign counsel if outside help is being employed by the institution. In large compaigns, of course, subordinate staff, both professional and clerical, will be needed. In addition, a sharp development director will know how to use volunteers to supplement his or her own efforts in completing a prospect list. Development staff need to be constantly alert, keeping their eyes and ears open for information that will be helpful in developing and maintaining an up-to-date prospect list. Givers do die or leave the community; others rise in financial status and in their ability to give support to the institution. Some companies go out of business and others start up or become very profitable. Being alert to these changes is a most important staff task. In talking to the development director of an important organization that was having campaign problems, I was shocked to discover that she never read the daily paper. Reading the newspaper, particularly the business sections, should be a high-priority assignment for every campaigner.

Company Prospects

Good sources of information for developing a prospect list of companies include the local chamber of commerce, the telephone directory, the state industrial development department, manufacturers' or other types of business associations, and reports published by other nonprofit organizations that list their contributors. Having the names of such businesses is, of course, not enough in itself. The organization must also determine something about their size, number of employees, sales, profits, and patterns of contributing. This is essential information. It is also important that updated information be obtained about the top executive of each major business. Even though a company may have a foundation or contributions committee, it is the top executive who will be approached initially and who may approve or disapprove of the gift request.

Individual Prospects

Excellent sources for individual prospects include the rosters of service clubs and civic organizations (such as Rotary, Kiwanis, and Lions clubs), athletic clubs, private membership clubs (which usually have top executives in their groups), and country clubs. All these should be screened thoroughly to determine whether they represent legitimate prospects to solicit. Colleges and universities, of course, will give priority consideration to alumni.

Other sources of information about individuals of substantial wealth are the annual reports and annual meeting notices of major publicly held corporations. Such annual reports will list the chief officers of the corporation. More exact information about salaries of top officers and board members, as well as the number of shares of stock they own, can be found in a company's prospectus when it is floating a new stock issue and in the annual meeting notice of the company. This is public information and can be obtained through stockbrokers or through volunteers who have invested in such corporations.

As the prospect list begins to take shape, the development director should review the list with his or her major campaign volunteers. This process, among other things, will give the volunteers an opportunity to suggest potential prospects from their own acquaintanceship. Quite obviously, prospect identification is not something that occurs overnight; it is a procedure that has to be worked on month in and month out.

Once when I was conducting a capital campaign for an institution that had very incomplete records, I gave all the special-gifts volunteers a form and asked them to list at least 10 people they thought could give $2,500 or more. The result was a list of potential gifts ranging from $2,500 to $250,000. This procedure is especially valuable when an organization's lists are not well maintained—and the names that surface are sometimes surprising. A great deal of follow-through is needed, or course, to make sure that volunteers complete the forms and return them to campaign headquarters.

Many development directors tend to slacken off when the campaign is not in full swing. Yet in many ways this can be the most productive time of the year for the staff to identify prospects. It is useful, for example, to keep an ongoing file of information gleaned at social functions or business luncheons. Such information might include which companies do a substantial amount of business with one another and which influential people have close personal relationships. When the appropriate time comes to assign prospects to campaign solicitors, the file will yield suggestions on the best person to handle each particular contact.

Another practice worth pursuing is to ask banking friends or prominent executives in business to review a limited list of names and select those that represent substantial prospects for the campaign. There is no point in sending the busy president of a major corporation a list of 5,000 names. Such a person might, however, be able to free up an hour or two to examine a selected list with you while you make quick notations and ask for the executive's thoughts on who could best handle each call.

DETERMINING THE NUMBER OF SECTIONS AND WORKERS

Once a list of businesses and individuals has been determined, manageable groupings must be established for purposes of solicitation. The 10 largest potential gifts and the next 200 largest gifts should generally be grouped into one division and assigned to solicitors on a "best person to handle" basis. The next step is to organize the balance of the list.

An organization running a campaign directed primarily at businesses may want to divide the balance of the corporations by trade classification or type of business (all banks, all savings and loans, all manufacturing companies, and so on) according to size. Depending on the prospects involved, the business divisions might include all companies with 25 or more employees or, in larger communities, with 50 or more employees.

Determining how many groups and solicitors are needed in the campaign organization can best be accomplished by the *7/7 principle*. Experience has shown that the ideal number of solicitors in a group for efficient organization, recruitment, and management in the campaign is seven. And the best number of accounts for each solicitor to handle is seven. Five accounts might be better, but this will increase dramatically the number of workers needed and the number of group and section chairpersons who otherwise could serve as very effective solicitors. Ten prospects for each solicitor slows down the solicitation process and can become too heavy a burden for certain workers.

Assume that a prospect list of 500 companies has been defined. The number of companies of each type is as follows:

Type of Company	Number of Companies
Retail stores	100
Wholesale	50
Distributing	150
Light manufacturing	125
Heavy industry	40
Major insurance	14
Banks	21
Total	500

The next step is to divide each of these groupings by 7 to obtain the ideal number of campaign workers to handle each group:

Type of Company	Number of Solicitors
Retail stores	14
Wholesale	7
Distributing	21
Light manufacturing	18
Heavy industry	6
Major insurance	2
Banks	3
Total	71

As shown above, a total of 71 solicitors will be needed to cover this segment of the campaign. These are the people who will be doing the actual soliciting and making direct contact with potential contributors.

Quite obviously, no division leader can recruit, train, and supervise 71 workers all alone. Here again the 7/7 principle comes into play to determine how many section chairpersons or team captains—whatever parlance is used—are needed to recruit and follow up on the campaign solicitors. In this case, the optimum number of team captains or section chairpersons required is 10 (71 workers divided by 7).

Let us assume a general business division has 1,372 corporate prospects to be solicited. The number of workers, teams, and section chairpersons needed can be determined as follows:

$$\frac{\text{Prospects}}{7} = \text{Workers} \qquad \frac{1,372}{7} = 196$$

$$\frac{\text{Workers}}{7} = \text{Teams} \qquad \frac{196}{7} = 28$$

$$\frac{\text{Teams}}{7} = \text{Sections} \qquad \frac{28}{7} = 4$$

Once this procedure has been followed for the total prospect list, a campaign organization chart can be completed showing, for each division, the sections and teams needed in the campaign. (See Figure 7-2). Next, the number of personnel required in the campaign organization can be broken down for use by the various chairpersons, as shown in Table 7-1. These data can later be used to develop a timetable showing the dates when each task should be completed. Sample timetable and organization charts are shown in the chapters dealing with campaigns in the various fields.

Any nonprofit organization with a campaign plan that calls for direct, personal solicitation can use this system to break down its prospect list into manageable groups. A church can divide the number of parishioners to be solicited by 7 to determine the number of solicitors required. A college can tally faculty, alumni, and parents of students and divide by 7 to determine the number of solicitors required. In addition to the soliciting personnel, the organization may need several nonsoliciting committees (public information and promotion, auditing, and so on).

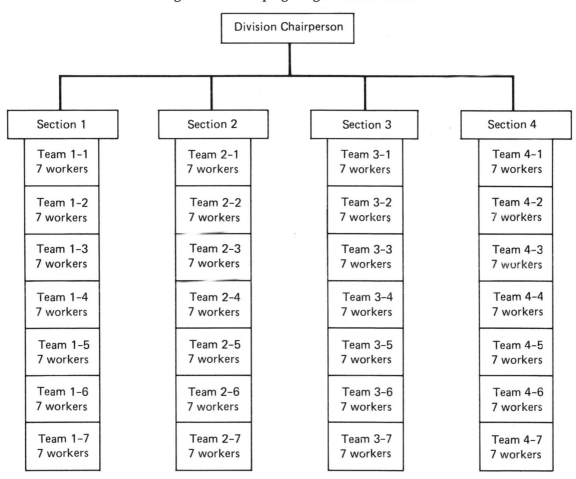

Figure 7-2. Campaign organization chart.

Table 7-1. Estimates of required personnel.

Division	Prospects	Division Heads	Section Chairpersons	Group Chairpersons	Workers
General business	1,372	1	4	28	196
Major corporations	350	1	0	7	50
Major individual gifts	175	1	0	4	25
Employees					
Industrial	270	1	0	6	39
Commercial	480	1	2	10	68
Public service	123	1	0	2	17
Schools	210	1	0	4	30
Total	2,980	7	6	61	425

THE CAMPAIGN PLAN

Once the number of workers, the timetable, and the general strategy are known, all must be put together in a campaign plan for use by the campaign chairperson and his or her division heads. The campaign plan will consist of the following:

1. A brief description of the need for funds, the fund-raising goal, and, in a broad way, how the funds will be spent.

2. The theme of the campaign and the slogan to be used.

3. The overall strategy required in the campaign to raise the necessary funds. Emphasis should be placed on the basic philosophy of the campaign and how the funds will be raised. In a capital campaign, for example, more substantial amounts will have to come from the top 10 and the next 200 prospects than would be the case in an operating campaign. How does the organization hope to accomplish this? In a college campaign, an approach to wealthy individuals and corporations must be developed, and the role that alumni, faculty, and parents might play in the campaign must be defined. What particular problems confront such a campaign and how are they to be overcome?

4. The structure of the campaign organization required to accomplish these objectives.

5. The number of personnel required to complete the volunteer component of each division, as determined previously by the 7/7 principle.

6. A timetable indicating when each step in the process (including promotion) must be accomplished in order for the campaign to be successful. In addition, a timetable for internal use should be prepared meshing the necessary office procedures into the campaign organization.

7. A list of suggestions from the staff as to candidates for leaders of the various divisions. A similar list should later be obtained for division and section heads as to those who might best serve as group chairpersons and solicitors.

RECRUITING VOLUNTEER LEADERSHIP

A valuable first step in obtaining volunteer leadership is developing brief job descriptions for the campaign chairperson and the division and section heads. Businesspeople, in particular, are used to thinking in terms of responsibilities, and job descriptions clarify what will be expected of them.

The most important job that has to be filled is, or course, that of campaign chairperson. As mentioned previously, the organization needs to look for certain leadership characteristics that will ensure the chair's ability to organize others and to solicit some of the top prospects. A list of potential chairpersons should be prepared by the staff and presented to the organization's president or whoever is responsible for recruitment.

During the recruitment process, it is extremely important that any candidate for this position be approached by peers whom he or she knows and respects. As the saying goes in campaign circles, these are people who "can put their feet on the potential chairperson's desk." Such people should not go out with hat in hand, but should have an easy approach to the prospect and be able to deal with that person on an equal basis.

The meeting with the candidate should be limited to two or three people, generally including the top staff person or development director, who can answer any technical questions about the campaign. The group should describe the reason for the campaign, the needs of the institution, and what steps must be taken to make the campaign successful. It is important to make the candidate realize why a sacrifice of his or her time and money is essential. Otherwise, the candidate may well say, "Why do you need me?" or "Why can't somebody else do it?"

Once the campaign chairperson has been recruited, he or she should be supplied with the names of other volunteers who might head the various divisions. A careful search of the organization's records—board members, alumni, current contributors, top business leaders—should be made by the staff and suggested names should be supplied to the campaign chairperson for consideration.

Throughout the recruitment process, it is important to keep descriptions of the campaign plan brief and general. The interviewing committee should not go into such great detail that a potential chairperson is overwhelmed from the very beginning.

Many years ago I had a division director who was quite anxious to get moving with his campaign organization. We had been delayed in obtaining some of our leadership because of poor business conditions in the community which caused a great deal of negative feeling.

When we made a call on a prospective volunteer division chairperson he readily accepted. Approximately two hours later, however, the campaign chairperson got a frantic call from the new volunteer indicating that the division director had already been over to see him with "all sorts of graphs, charts, and timetables" and he wanted to resign. It took some persuasion on the part of the campaign chairperson to keep him in the fold. The development director, in his anxiety to get started, had not used good judgment and had overwhelmed the volunteer too soon after his acceptance. In justice, I should add that this man later became one of the most effective campaigners in the country; only his enthusiasm for the job had created a problem.

THE ASSIGNMENT PROCESS

Once the campaign plan has been completed and the number of volunteers, groups, and sections are known, prospects must be assigned to solicitors.

In many ways, the assignment process is the most important function to be carried out. In all probability, it will determine the success or failure of the campaign in attaining goal and the amount received in each gift. The old saying "Don't send a boy to do a man's job" applies strongly here. The person calling on the prospect must be comfortable in making the presentation for the organization. If he or she approaches the person in awe or is overwhelmed by the prospect's position, the chances of success are remote. Accordingly, all the information previously gathered by the staff and volunteers—information about a prospect's business associates and friends—should now be brought into play to ensure appropriate campaign assignments.

Preassignments by Campaign Leaders

A good way to start the assignment process is to make an alphabetical listing of prospects in a particular section or division for review by the top volunteers. This should be accompanied by a staff-prepared list of suggested volunteers for the section. As each prospect is reviewed by the division head and section chairperson, a determination

Figure 7-3. Assignment sheet for special-gifts prospects.

Name of Prospect	Last Year's Gift	Suggested Gift This Year	Assignment
Abraham's	$ 1,000	$ 1,200	*Smith*
Atomic Motors	5,000	6,000	*Blake*
Barr, Inc.	10,000	12,000	*Powers*
Berg Corporation	1,500	3,000	*Campbell*
Bower-Jones, Inc.	7,000	8,500	*MacFarlane*

should be made as to who the best person is to call on that particular prospect. The section chairperson then builds a suggested roster of campaign assignments for the section, with the knowledge that every assignment has been carefully considered and the best possible person has been obtained to make the call. If, of course, a prospective volunteer declines to work, an alternate must be suggested.

This "preassignment" method eliminates the problem of having volunteers select accounts that they are not really equipped to handle. One section chairperson I knew worked on the theory that each of his workers should be given "one big account." Although this approach may have made the workers happy, it was a disaster from a fund-raising point of view. After the preassignment process has been completed, a list of unassigned accounts can be circulated among the volunteers, permitting them to select those they wish to solicit. A sample assignment sheet, with suggested goals, is shown in Figure 7-3.

It is helpful to supply each volunteer with information concerning the giving levels of companies comparable to those on his or her assignment list. For example, a volunteer may be assigned a bank, a retail store, and a manufacturing company because he or she is the best person to make those calls. The sales presentation can be fortified by providing the volunteer with information about what other banks, other retail stores, and other manufacturing companies are giving. Comparing contributions records of generous firms often stimulates the performance of those whose giving is lower.

Group Assignments

An alternative assignment method is to divide all prospects into groups—for example, all banks, all savings and loans, all department stores—and get the best possible people to handle each group. The advantage here is that solicitors will be dealing only with comparable kinds of firms. Again volunteers should be encouraged to point out what other companies of the same type are giving, since this will often stimulate the gift giving of a prospect. The only problem with this approach is that it is often difficult to find a single person (or even several people) with the kind of working relationship required for all companies in the group.

8

GOAL SETTING

Once an institution has decided to embark on a fund-raising effort, the actual goal to be reached becomes a matter of paramount importance. The budget of a philanthropic organization is basically a financial expression of its program. In other words, it involves reducing to arithmetic terms what is necessary to ensure that the program will be carried out. The budget includes all the estimated sources of income, including voluntary contributions, and all expenditures necessary to conduct the institution's program.

Budgets and goals are not identical. The budget generally represents the estimates that department heads, administrators, and budget committees have assembled. It combines their best thinking about what is desirable in financial resources and expenditures in order to conduct the program of the institution. The campaign goal is the amount of the budget that must be raised from voluntary contributions. The goal may represent the optimum the organization wishes to raise, or it may have to be a compromise figure.

A goal is not only a financial objective in the campaign; it is an integral part of campaign strategy. The established goal tells the community that it is going to be challenged materially to reach an objective and suggests the corresponding commitments that will be necessary to accomplish this end. Or the goal may represent a more modest challenge based on economic conditions and a detailed study of the giving potential available.

HIGH GOALS VERSUS MODERATE GOALS

For years the fund-raising fraternity has been arguing over whether it is better to set very high goals that may or may not be attainable but that really make the givers stretch in an attempt to achieve them, or whether it is better to accept a compromise figure between actual budget needs and an achievable amount related to campaign potential.

There are positive and negative factors in both situations. If a goal is too high, it may completely discourage the volunteers and the contributors, who may be lost to the institution in the future. Repeated failures to achieve goal can, as a matter of fact, cause a loss of credibility. Contributors soon begin to say, "Look, your goal was much higher last year; you didn't make it but you got along." When this begins to happen, the chances of getting significantly larger gifts is greatly reduced.

Repeated failures can also cause a loss of volunteer enthusiasm and participation. Most top businesspeople do not want to be associated with a failure, for they are not failures in their own activities. Little is gained in embarrassing a top executive by convincing him or her to accept a goal that everyone knows cannot be reached merely so the institution can say it attempted to raise "the need." *Remember, success has many fathers; failure is an orphan.*

On the other hand, an institution occasionally needs to challenge its constituency to rise substantially above the normal levels of giving so that it can take a major step forward in advancing new programs. Failure to seek such a challenge may make the institution stodgy, lacking the vibrancy to be attractive and to meet changing needs. The very least that an organization should attempt is to keep up with inflation; otherwise, it will retrogress.

Many institutions have found that a satisfactory approach is to take into consideration both the needs of the institution as the budget committee and campaign committee see them and the potential that can be tapped from former givers and new campaign sources. In this situation, the budget committee will make a detailed study of program requirements and recommend what it considers to be needed to the board of directors of the institution. Concurrently, the campaign committee will conduct a thorough examination of economic conditions, profits, trends, possible new sources of income, major losses in potential, and so on. The goal it recommends to the board may be less than that submitted by the budget committee. Under this circumstance, the board of directors will have to determine what the goal should be. Frequently, it will set a figure somewhere between what the budget committee would like to have and what the campaign committee believes can be raised. This compromise will make the campaign group work hard to reach a "stretch" goal without feeling it has been given an impossible task.

DETERMINING CARD VALUE

In studying campaign potential, each institution will need to establish a basic funding base for determining what amount might reasonably be expected. Organizations that have conducted campaigns in the past can do this by taking the list of all the prior year's gifts and then reducing from the total amount raised those gifts that cannot be counted on in the current year's campaign. Such gifts might include those of donors who have passed away during the year or of companies that have moved out of the community; nonrecurring gifts, such as foundation grants or specially designated gifts; and gifts lost because of major employee layoffs.

After subtracting these known losses from the prior year's campaign total, the resulting figure represents the potential for the current year's campaign if every prospect

Figure 8-1. Computation of card value.

Amount raised prior year		$1,500,000
Less: Termination of restricted gifts:		
Do Good Foundation	$10,000	
Myers Scholarship Fund	5,000	
Dunlap Research Project	7,500	
Less: Deaths of donors:		
A. J. Smith	2,500	
W. Cronin	700	
James Hawkins	1,200	
Less: Loss of corporate gifts:		
Squeeze Easy Corporation	700	
W. Haskell, Inc.	1,000	
Excellent Manufacturing Company	5,000	
Total lost prospect or card value		33,600
New beginning card value		$1,466,400

gave the same amount as the year before. This figure is the basis for planning the new campaign, and is known as its card value or prospect value. Figure 8-1 shows, as a simple example, the computation of card value for an organization that raised $1,500,000 the year before. As the data indicate, in conducting the new campaign, the institution must raise an additional $33,600, or 2.3 percent more, merely to stay at the prior year's level without seeking any new funds for additional programs, salary increases, or other increases in operating costs. Frequently, the loss in card value for an institution will run considerably higher—in the neighborhood of 5 to 8 percent—and when this occurs the campaign organization faces a major challenge.

In the situation described, if the board of directors believes that the organization must have 10 percent more in net funds in order to operate effectively, then the institution will actually have to seek a 12.3 percent increase in order to make up for the loss in card value as well as meet additional needs.

Goals reflect both the short-term and long-term plans of the institution. Annual goals are generally modest increases that reflect the short-term program objectives of the institution and the effects of inflation. The dramatically higher goals sought every five or ten years obviously reflect the organization's long-term plans—the direction it sees itself going in subsequent decades.

DIVISION GOALS

Once an overall goal has been established, the campaign organization needs to spread it among the various divisions of the campaign. Computing card value for each division and conducting a study of potential are helpful in determining how the division goals are to be set. Basically it is possible to give each division a 12.3 percent increase (as in our example), but practically this is not desirable. Certain divisions within a campaign

Table 8-1. Schedule of gifts required to raise $3,400,000.

Number of Gifts	Range	Total
1 gift at	$500,000	$ 500,000
1 gift at	350,000	350,000
1 gift at	250,000	250,000
1 gift at	200,000	200,000
3 gifts at	100,000	300,000
8 gifts at	50,000	400,000
<u>12</u> gifts at	25,000	300,000
27 gifts totaling		$2,300,000
25 gifts at	10,000	250,000
50 gifts at	5,000	250,000
<u>300</u> gifts at	1,000	300,000
375 gifts totaling		$ 800,000
<u>3,598</u> gifts under	1,000	$ 300,000
4,000 gifts totaling		$3,400,000

organization do not have the potential of others. The residential and small business divisions are examples, as is the general alumni division for certain colleges. If, however, major new corporations have moved into the community or if a special cultivation program has been conducted among wealthy alumni and individuals, these divisions may well be expected to carry substantially higher loads. Past experience of the divisions is a helpful guideline, but efforts should still be made to upgrade the giving in those divisions that have performed poorly in the past and that have substantial potential. The best approach is to have each division chairperson and staff review the individual prospects in that division and make an estimate as to how much more might be expected in the current year.

Once the division goals are set, campaign objectives must be spread formally among the prospects in each division. For example, corporate giving may be increased on a percentage basis for most companies that are doing reasonably well by the institution, but substantially more may be requested of those companies that are not. New prospects will be rated and request figures established for them. Once prospects are rated, the goal can be further broken down by sections and even extended to individual solicitors.

It is important that the total "asking" be substantially higher than the amount needed to ensure attainment of the goal because no campaign achieves 100 percent compliance of its requests. Amounts requested of companies, foundations, and corporations should be a minimum of 10 to 20 percent more than is needed, and in major challenge campaigns the figure should be 25 to 50 percent more.

Campaigns for Major Increases

In campaigns for major funds for capital needs and endowment, a schedule can be developed indicating what is needed from the top 10 or 20 givers and from others. Table 8-1 is an example from a small college that was seeking major funds. Such a

Table 8-2. Breakdown of division goals.

Division	Goal	Card Value	Percent Increase Over Card Value	Total of Prospect Goals or Askings	Margin or Loading
I—Special gifts	$1,000,000	$ 850,000	17.6	$1,100,000	$ 250,000
II—Major firms	2,500,000	2,200,000	13.6	2,750,000	550,000
III—Individual gifts	500,000	450,000	11.1	525,000	75,000
IV—Alumni	375,000	340,000	10.2	420,000	80,000
V—Foundations	400,000	330,000	21.2	440,000	110,000
Total	$4,775,000	$4,170,000	14.5	$5,235,000	$1,065,000

schedule informs potential contributors of the kinds of giving levels that are necessary to ensure the campaign's success and of what might be expected of them.

Breakdown of Goals

The division, section, and group goals that are publicized among volunteers and the general community must, of course, add up to the total that needs to be raised in the campaign. Again, however, the amounts sought from individual prospects within each division should be considerably higher than what the actual goals are.

In the example shown in Table 8-2, the goal increase over the prior year's card value is 14.5 percent. Total ratings or askings are $5,235,000, up 25.5 percent. Therefore, the campaign has a margin of 11 percent over and above the amount needed to reach goal.

The degree to which goals can be broken down to group chairpersons, team captains, and even solicitors is an important factor in stimulating competition and letting individuals know how much they need to raise. Periodic bulletins showing the goals of each campaign group and the amount and percentage raised also help stimulate competition and keep the campaign moving along.

9

THE PROMOTION PROGRAM

Conducting a campaign for a philanthropic organization is basically a sales effort. As such, the campaign must rely on the same promotional methods that are used in selling commercial products. The major difference here is that the products being sold are intangible services.

The purpose of the promotional campaign is to present the requirements of the institution in a favorable light and to convince people that the need is important enough for them to give a contribution priority over other things they may desire. The promotional campaign should also create a sense of ugency, a feeling among contributors and workers that the goal must be met. To accomplish this, the campaign must use all the media available to it. These will differ, of course, from institution to institution. A church with a limited number of parishioners will not have access to some of the public media—particularly press and TV—that are available to campaigns of a more communitywide nature.

When the organization's relationships in the community and among its constituencies are good (see Chapter 3), the organization should capitalize on those good relationships by putting its best foot forward. A campaign for funds in this sense is an extension of the year-round policy and public relations program of the institution and not something completely separate and apart. A major thrust is the dramatization of the need in such a way as to motivate people both to work and to give.

CAMPAIGN PROMOTION COMMITTEE

An essential step in planning and implementing the promotion program is the appointment of a promotion committee. The size of the committee depends on the organization and the media available to it. In a small organization, it may have only two

72

Figure 9-1. Campaign promotion committee.

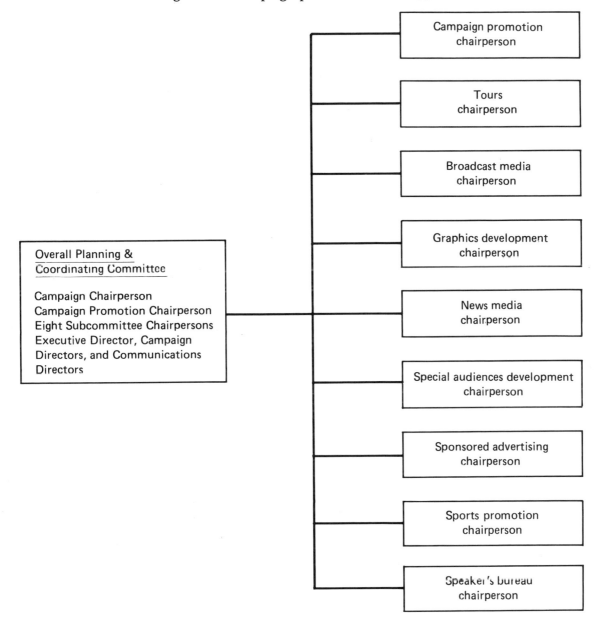

or three members; in a larger organization with multiple media opportunities, it may have 10 or 15. Volunteer chairpersons with a knowledge of promotion are recruited. When promotion is directed to a number of media, a chairperson and committee members will be recruited to work with each medium. The chairpersons and all staff members with input are members of the overall planning committee. An example of a well-developed campaign promotion committee is shown in Figure 9-1.

CAMPAIGN THEME, CASE, AND SLOGAN

Careful campaign planning should attempt to summarize the campaign's purpose in a theme that is dramatic and understandable from a public relations point of view. It is often extended into a campaign case. The campaign slogan then becomes the center of the whole promotional effort. It is designed to get the initial attention of potential contributors and leads into a fuller explanation of what the campaign is about. Let us look more closely at these three concepts.

Campaign theme—the basic story line that is to be told, including a brief summary of the problems to be met and the programs that are needed to meet them.

Campaign case—an extension of the campaign theme, presenting in detail the extent of the needs, the objectives to be accomplished, the steps necessary for their achievement, the funds necessary for the objectives to be met, and what contributors must do to accomplish those ends.

Campaign slogan—a brief attention-getting phrase expressing the aim of the campaign. The slogan reduces the theme to the smallest number of words possible consistent with dramatizing the message.

Below are some excellent examples of the way in which campaign themes are abbreviated into slogans for attention-getting purposes.

United Negro College Fund

Theme: A vast number of young minority people are seriously undereducated and, because of this, cannot make their maximum contribution to society. Lack of funds for education means that the potential contribution these people could make is being wasted, and sometimes they become a charge to society rather than taxpaying, contributing citizens.

Slogan: "A Mind Is a Terrible Thing to Waste"

Red Cross

Theme: The nation is at war and our boys are overseas making the maximum contribution to our country by offering their lives. As mothers and fathers, brothers and sisters, we all wish we could do everything possible to give them comfort and help and to make their mission as bearable as possible. The Red Cross serves this purpose by collecting and distributing blood to the military, by operating canteens and service centers, by providing a bridge of communication between the serviceman and his family, and by inspecting prisoner-of-war camps.

Slogan: "Your Red Cross Is at His Side"

Theme: The purpose of the Red Cross is to provide succor and understanding to people in need: the military and their families, victims of disaster (winds, floods, and earthquakes), patients in need of blood and nursing services.

Slogan: "The Greatest Mother of Them All"

United Ways

Theme: Every family in the community has the need for services at some time, and studies show that six out of every ten families use United Way-supported community services in any given year. These services include family counseling, nursing care, aid to disaster victims, research on major health problems, citizenship training, day care, and rehabilitation. The families that use community services make them possible by their generous contributions through a single campaign for many organizations.

Slogans:
"Everybody Benefits—Everybody Gives"
"One Gift Works Many Wonders"
"Thanks to You It Works for All of Us"

United Arts Funds

Theme: The country is in a recession and money for all philanthropic services is hard to raise. Profits are low, unemployment is high, and every individual and corporation is taking a hard look at contributions requests. The arts are particularly vulnerable, since many donors give priority to human services organizations. Nevertheless, the arts are an essential service in the community and must have continuing support. In poor times the arts are not just a luxury; they are essential to maintain morale and to provide release from the anxieties of life. As such they perform an essential and important function.

Slogan:
"We Can't Afford a Recession of the Human Spirit"

PERSONALIZING THE APPEAL

The more that needs can be personalized, the easier it is for people to relate to them.

Many years ago when I was executive of the Community Chest in Peoria, Illinois, we were convinced that one of the problems confronting the organization was that it represented a barrier between the givers and the agencies that were providing the services. We discovered that many people who actually used the services did not understand how their support of the Community Chest made these services possible. Thousands of parents who had children in scouting, in the Ys, and in neighborhood centers did not see the importance of their contribution to the Community Chest in providing those services to their children. Our public relations committee thought that if we could better personalize the appeal in some way, the response would be better.

After much thought and planning the Community Chest came up with an entirely novel approach to its fund-raising effort, one that had never been used before. A 13-year-old boy, a typically American-looking youngster with red hair and freckles, was located in the Boy Scout organization. He and his family agreed to lend his services as a symbol of all the youngsters receiving service in the community through Community Chest agencies. For publicity purposes this youngster was called Pete.

The drive started with a teaser campaign two weeks in advance of the campaign kickoff. Arrangements were made for spot announcements on all radio stations during station breaks which merely said, "For Pete's Sake." Street stencils were used on all the corners of the downtown area declaring "For Pete's Sake," as were 24-sheet billboards and "drop-ins" for department store ads.

The teaser campaign brought immediate interest and reaction from the community at large, with everyone saying, "What is this 'For Pete's Sake'?" On the day of the campaign kickoff the rest of the campaign slogan and theme were broken: "For Pete's Sake Give to Your Community Chest." There followed newspaper articles about Pete's involvement in scouting and how he symbolized the many youth who received services. He met the mayor and was taken on trips to day care centers, institutions for dependent children, and other facilities. Pete also attended every report meeting, said a few words to the volunteers, and was used extensively in any number of promotional activities. His personal charm was extremely helpful in personalizing the campaign and interpreting the services supported by the Chest. The campaign was generously oversubscribed.

The use of one person as a symbol, though unusual, does show how a campaign appeal can be personalized and how people will respond to individuals when they do not always respond to institutions. Therefore, to the degree that campaign promotion can point out the services received through case histories and actual experiences, it can be better understood by potential contributors.

When I first started fund raising, I used to hear many employees say, "We want to know where our money is going." After several years of sending financial statements to the newspapers and to the various companies, I discovered that this was not what they really meant at all. The average contributor was really saying, "Tell me about somebody you have really helped."

This point is illustrated nicely in the personalized way the Minnesota Literacy Council tells its story:

Linda was stunned by the news. She was being "let go" from her clerical job with a small industrial firm.

Why? She could not read well enough to handle the job effectively.

Linda's initial duties did not require a great deal of reading skill, so for a while she was able to hide the fact that she was only marginally literate. But as a diligent, hardworking employee she soon earned a promotion.

The promotion took Linda beyond her reading level and the job became increasingly difficult. She knew she was turning in a poor performance, yet was devastated when the ax finally fell.

After sharing her experience with a friend, Linda was referred to the Minnesota Literacy Council Incorporated (MLCI) for reading help. She was matched with an MLCI volunteer who tutored her on a one-to-one basis.

About a year later, Linda's reading and writing skills had improved dramatically. With renewed confidence, she quickly found another job.

Illiteracy Is Costly

For Linda, illiteracy is a thing of the past. For many others, it continues as a severe handicap which limits lives and plagues society.

Studies show that over half the nation's prisoners are considered illiterate. Half the chronically unemployed and a third of those on welfare are similarly afflicted.

In Minnesota, up to 30 percent of the adult population is functionally illiterate. This means many are unable to read simple product labels, read a phone directory, or fill out a job application.

The Minnesota Literacy Council, a private, nonprofit organization, has been providing tutoring services to illiterate adults since 1972. MLCI directs over 63 literacy projects throughout the state.

You Make It Happen

MLCI owes its success to the many people who volunteer their time for tutoring. In the past year, nearly 2,000 volunteers helped tutor 4,000 adults enrolled in various MLCI programs.

Your continued financial support is also needed. If you are already an MLCI member, we urge you to renew your affiliation for the coming year. If you are receiving our appeal for the first time, we ask that you join us in a most worthwhile cause—the defeat of illiteracy in Minnesota.

DIFFERING AUDIENCES

In planning a promotion program, it is important to recognize that even though all potential contributors have a common interest in the institution, their specific interests may differ. These differences need to be considered in the approach to various audiences. The common concern and interest should be supported by variations in the promotion used. For example, promotion among employees, corporations, alumni, consumers, and staff may have different emphases.

Generally speaking, employees and people in lower to middle income brackets will respond more to emotional appeals or to the demonstration of direct services that they and their families might use.

Corporate executives, though certainly motivated in the same way, are also interested in cost efficiency, the ability of the institution to have qualified staff, the track record of the institution in developing other sources of income, and the services provided to employees. Executives are also interested in knowing what other corporations may be doing. An example of a summary form that may be given to corporate executives is shown in Figure 9-2.

The alumni or past users of the service, because of their former association with the institution, may focus more on pride in the past record of the institution and the desire to preserve and enlarge it. This kind of loyalty is particularly keen at certain colleges and universities.

Figure 9-2. Sample résumé of a campaign case.

The Case for Increased Support

When the United Way was formed, it committed itself to being as inclusive a fund-raising organization as possible. Immediately it eliminated 15 communitywide campaigns and since then it has added 34 agencies to its membership. During the same period, it has closed out support to 24 organizations where needs have changed. The United Way has tried diligently to live up to its commitment and to recognize new and changing needs and requirements.

During the same period, the United Way merged or discontinued support of 15 agencies, indicating that the program is a consistently changing one and United Way support does not become permanent from year to year.

What are some of the current agency programs?

Red Cross Regional Blood Center—Recruits volunteer blood donors and provides all St. Paul area hospitals with as pure and reliable a source of blood as it is possible to obtain. Every patient using a St. Paul area hospital who requires blood receives it through the Red Cross program. Many other cities have experienced major problems of hepatitis infection.

Urban League—Through its specialized programs, trained 330 minority persons, making them self-supporting, tax-paying citizens rather than dependent on welfare.

Heart Association—Undertook to train key industrial and other personnel in pulmonary resuscitation methods, thereby permitting many to survive the attack crisis and reach hospitals for intensive care.

Arthritis Foundation—Has funded research in new surgery techniques for the replacement of fingers and joints affected by arthritis.

St. Paul Rehabilitation Center—Gave vocational training to many handicapped persons and placed 44 in private employment, thereby making them self-sustaining.

Mental Health Association—Is planning new ways for the mentally ill to remain in the local community and be self-productive rather than to require long term care in state institutions. This agency also has stimulated funds for research in mental depression.

St. Paul Drug Rehabilitation Center—Through its methadone program, is identifying and enabling drug addicts to become self-employed, rather than dependent upon criminal activities in order to support their habit; many others helped are sons and daughters of middle and upper class families.

United Way services are relevant to changing times and conditions. They not only benefit each family in the community through medical research programs, but also deal with major social problems.

What efforts are made to improve efficiency and effectiveness?

Evaluation—United Way agencies are continually evaluated in terms of changing times and conditions and program effectiveness. The withdrawal of support from 34 agencies is an indication of this function.

Cost accounting—A new United Way program requires all agencies to report on the actual cost of conducting each individual program.

Administrative and campaign costs combined—Are approximately 9 percent, the lowest of any major fund-raising group.

Centralized payroll and accounting for agencies—Are now being performed on a combined basis for the United Ways in St. Paul and Minneapolis in order to permit agencies to meet increased reporting requirements and keep costs as low as possible.

The United Way is the business of helping people as efficiently and effectively as possible.

Figure 9-2. (*Continued*)

What are its problems?

While the United Way has added 39 agencies, there is a limit to its ability to do so within the present availability of funds.

The cost of living has increased 38.5 percent and campaign results an identical amount, leaving almost no room to fund new or additional services. An additional 7 percent inflation rate is projected for next year.

During the same period, the agencies served 20 percent more people.

While some of the budget slack can be taken up by discontinuing support of other programs, there is a practical limit to what can be accomplished in a given period of time.

Although the United Way has funded some new agencies, it has been able to do nothing in expanding or improving the quality of existing services.

The United Way is the principal provider of human services in the private sector and it requires additional support unless in the future all human services are to be provided by government.

What would the United Way like to do?

The United Way would like to have sufficient uncommitted funds after meeting the inescapable, increased inflationary costs to respond to new needs in the community. Some general areas of concern are:

The aged—The United Way is providing a minimum of services to this rapidly expanding portion of our population. It would like to be able to assist aged persons to remain in their own homes rather than being forced to seek more expensive care in nursing homes.

Mobilize for community services the volunteer manpower of many aged persons who have skills to contribute.

Fatherless boys—Consider expanding services to fatherless boys who have no male parental supervision. This problem is increasing with the growth in divorce and separation.

Cardiac patients—Expand the program of cardiac pulmonary resuscitation. Heart attacks kill more persons in the United States each year than any other single disease.

Youth—There is great need to expand character-building activities. This is the one single area where government funds are nonexistent and the need is greatest.

Juvenile delinquents—Develop new programs aimed at reducing the school drop-out rate and corresponding delinquency by working with youngsters in developing positive attitudes toward their social responsibilities.

What does the United Way need?

In order to continue to be an effective force in the human services field, the United Way needs a commitment from each potential contributor—corporate, foundation, or individual—to make a gift consistent with the "guidelines for giving" program.

Consumers—clients, patients, and parents of young children, for example—are more interested in the immediate quality and availability of the service and how the campaign will make this possible. They are also interested in knowing what new programs will be offered and how they will help meet their needs.

Faculty and staff are, of course, interested in how the campaign will help retain and improve the quality of personnel, the level of program, and the opportunities for growth.

As the promotional campaign takes shape, these variations in interest need to be taken into account in developing the specific materials that will be directed to each audience, even though all materials will revolve around a central theme.

Although it is important to present the organization's services as forthrightly and positively as possible, it is important not to oversell. If an institution promises unrealistic results, this can lead only to disillusionment on the part of the giver.

A Catholic girl was going with a Protestant boy and they both wanted to get married, but the girl's father objected because the boy was not Catholic.

In an effort to resolve the impasse within the family, the girl began to tell the young man on every occasion about the values of the Catholic Church, hoping he would decide to convert.

One night after a date, the young woman came home almost hysterical.

When the father asked her what the trouble was, she said, "I've been talking to Jim about the wonders of the Catholic Church, hoping he would convert."

"Yes," said the father, "so why the tears?"

"He's—he's decided to become a priest."

DIVISIONAL STRATEGY

The variations in audience interest, and the corresponding promotional needs, must be taken into account within the various campaign divisions. The campaign staff and committee members have to ask themselves, "Who needs to be reached and how? What is the story to be told? What media are available to tell the story best?"

As the campaign structure begins to take shape, the promotion program should be geared so that it tells the overall story, but also recognizes certain facets that are of particular interest to a given division. In a college campaign, for example, the alumni division will hear a slightly different appeal than the corporate division. See Figure 9-3 for an example of how a campaign can reach out to different divisions.

In order to accomplish its objectives, the program must have an overall strategy for implementation. Included should be a timetable geared to build interest up to a crescendo as the campaign kicks off, and then to sustain that interest throughout the campaign period. Along with the timetable a plan of implementation is needed to ensure that the promotion program is carried out. A sample timetable for a corporate division is shown in Figure 9-4. (A timetable coordinating organization, promotion, and office activities was shown in Figure 4-1 in Chapter 4.)

MEDIA TECHNIQUES

There are a number of specific media techniques that can be used for promotion purposes. Of course, all of them won't be practical for a single organization. Each organization must select those most applicable—and available—to it. The following are some techniques that may prove useful.

Figure 9-3. Individualizing a university campaign case to appeal to different divisions.

A university is undertaking a $10 million campaign to expand its curricula, build new buildings, and develop an endowment. Included in the plans are an expansion of the business school and the development of a technology institute. The following points are included in the case presentation together with the adaptations made for the various divisions.

General Points

1. Trends in enrollment.
    Number of students—growth rate, trend of students by sex, increase in number of women and minorities.
    Number of entering freshmen from top 10 percent, 25 percent, and 50 percent of high school graduating classes.
2. Standing of university compared with other universities.
    Size.
    Number of students graduating—percentage completing four years.
    SAT scores of entering freshmen.
    Number going on to graduate school.
    Awards and special recognition.
3. Need.
    Changing society—changing need; reduction in heavy industry, growth of high technology and service industries.
    Growing demand for business courses.
    Need to develop institute for technology, increase supply of trained engineers.
    Requirement for renovation of physical plant and major new buildings for technology.
    New equipment needs.
    Buildings without adequate faculty are useless; need to upgrade faculty and improve salary structure.
    Reduction in federal funds means less money is available for grants, loans, and physical improvement of facilities.
    University must move ahead and meet educational needs or decline.

Alumni Division

    Repeat general points above.

In Addition:
    Alumni received good education at the university and most have been successful.
    They can be proud to be graduates of this university and obtain satisfaction from its growth, progress, and contributions. They can be proud to say "I am a graduate."
    Generous gifts are needed to complete the program; this is an opportunity to show their appreciation and support.
    Need in particular for scholarships and grants for worthy students who require annual aid.
    Suggested levels of gifts needed from alumni.

Corporate Division

    Repeat general points above.

In Addition:
    Campaign serves corporations by providing them with a resource for recruiting future employees.
    Particular areas of help will be the strengthening of curricula in business administration and the new school of technology.
    School of technology will work cooperatively with business in developing new products and processes.

Figure 9-3. (*Continued*)

Business will be asked to provide an advisory committee to guide development of high-tech school, so that it can serve their needs.

Engineers will help high-tech business maintain superiority over competitors.

Business students will be offered basic engineering courses; engineers, business courses, so they will be more rounded individuals.

New school will strengthen local economy.

Amount needed from corporate community specified.

Parents of Students (division)

Repeat general points above.

In Addition:

Their sons and daughters chose this school because they thought it met their educational needs best.

University can maintain standards and develop curriculum opportunities only if there is a major increase in new funding.

The business world is increasingly competitive—here is an opportunity to give their sons and daughters the best education possible in order to meet the competition.

A contribution is an additional investment on behalf of their children.

Studies show a direct relationship between income and educational attainment.

Even though tuition is high, gifts from parents are needed if the university is to make a major step forward and ensure a better education for their children.

Wealthy Individuals

Repeat general points above.

Repeat points made to corporate division.

In Addition:

Remind prospect of a special interest he or she may have in the university's program.

A campaign of this type can be successful only with leadership gifts from individuals.

Tell prospect of gifts of specific sums needed to make the campaign a success.

Show prospects large gifts received to date.

Remind prospect of any special tax considerations and of opportunities to make gifts of stock or property.

Review special gift sponsorship opportunities for special programs, equipment, endowment, or scholarships.

Ask prospect to consider gift at a particular level, within a given range.

Faculty Division

Repeat general points above.

In Addition:

Point out increasing cost of education to student: tuition, room, board.

Remind faculty of reduction in federal funding.

Future of the institution and their professional careers depends upon the ability of the university to progress and adapt to new circumstances.

Faculty constantly needs new challenges.

Generous gifts from faculty show their belief in the institution and their willingness to make sacrifices on its behalf. A good response from the faculty sets a good example for the other givers.

Figure 9-4. Sample campaign promotion timetable for a corporate division.

Function	Responsibility for Implementation	Deadline					
		Jan.	Feb.	March	April	May	June
Establish campaign goal	Board of directors	5					
Set campaign theme	P.R. comm. staff Camp. chpsn. staff	10					
Set division goal	Camp. cabinet	15					
Campaign case developed	Camp. staff P.R. staff	30					
Campaign slogan	P.R. comm. staff Camp. chpsn. staff		7				
Corporate rating complete	Rating comm.		1				
Corporate solicitors obtained	Corp. div. chpsn.		12				
Corporate cultivation meetings							
Meeting dates and arrangements	P.R. staff		10				
Invitations to CEO	Camp. staff		20				
Visual presentation ready	P.R. comm. and staff		25				
Campaign brochure complete	P.R. staff		20				
Prepare individualized case presentations	Camp. staff		25				
Suggested remarks to be made by chairpersons	Camp. staff P.R. staff		24				
Start corporation cultivation meetings	P.R. staff Camp. staff			7 14 20			
Corporate solicitation begins	Corp. div. chpsn. and workers				1		
Start reporting results	Camp. staff P.R. staff				15	15	15
Special features in newsletter	P.R. staff		30	15	30	15	
Final report							30

Teaser Campaigns

Teaser campaigns are used in the advertising business to arouse attention and pave the way for a fuller promotional effort. Basically they consist of a few words or a phrase that tells an incomplete story but piques the public's curiosity to learn the full message.

Print Materials

Campaign graphics should be designed to carry out the theme and to give all print materials a unified look. This centralizes the promotion and makes it possible to emphasize the campaign story repeatedly. General-distribution pieces for all potential contributors, speakers' bureau manuals, posters, and other specialized brochures should all be designed to carry out this objective. Using differing graphics will weaken the recognition factor and the response of potential contributors.

Radio and TV Spots and Documentaries

Whenever available, the electronic media should, of course, be used. Brief public service spots and taped messages illustrating the institution's needs are especially effective. The degree to which these are personalized is very important. Since most radio and TV stations are limited in the amount of public service time they can provide, professional help in preparing spots should be obtained. Professionals in the advertising business know how to tell the story succinctly and dramatically in 10 to 30 seconds. The organization should also take advantage of opportunities for appearances on interview shows and for comprehensive documentaries on topics that a station may be interested in presenting.

Speakers' Bureaus

Many campaigns will have the need for speakers; they may be few in number or quite numerous. Even a church campaign geared to a limited constituency can use a few well-trained speakers to appear at meetings of the congregation and before men's and women's church groups. For larger campaigns, trained speakers are essential to appear before business, civic, labor, employee, and club groups.

Tours

An effective technique for telling the institution's story is by taking potential contributors on tours of the institution. This is an easy way of showing them what is being accomplished, and also pointing out what is needed in the way of new programs, operating support, and capital expansion.

Films

Much has been made of the need to personalize the campaign and to dramatize it. It is not always possible to do this by using the spoken word or by taking people on tours. A very effective approach is to develop motion picture films or slide sound presentations, depending upon the budget of the institution. When available, professional help should be obtained in developing films. Some organizations have within their constituencies professionals who can be helpful in writing and developing visual productions. Others will need commercial help. National organizations often make films available to local affiliates as part of the national's service. Films are especially helpful in solicitor training, in divisional instruction meetings, and at the campaign kickoff. They also strengthen a speaker's presentation to civic groups and company employees.

Press

General-circulation newspapers, neighborhood newspapers, the labor press, and other specialized media can all be very useful in promoting the campaign. Some organizations may find it quite difficult to get much space in the daily press, but neighborhood newspapers are frequently happy to print articles about the campaign and they do reach specialized audiences that may be closer to the institution.

Displays

Displays placed in strategic locations are helpful in telling the campaign story. Free-standing displays are effective in a church, college, bank lobby, or other public facility that has good pedestrian traffic. Also, 24-sheet billboards are valuable in certain types of campaigns. Often the space will be contributed by the outdoor advertising company as a public service.

Internal Publications

Publications—house organs and employee newsletters—distributed by organizations as a way of keeping employees informed about changing policies and practices can also be used to promote certain kinds of campaigns, primarily those that have a reasonably wide spectrum of contributors. Stories telling how the organization has helped employees of the company are particularly helpful. For example, a college publication might discuss the number of graduates employed by a company and quote them as to how their education enabled them to advance their careers. A human services agency can relate the services that have been provided to employees and their families.

Newsletters

A newsletter published by the nonprofit organization and directed to its campaign organization and potential contributors is helpful in keeping them advised of the approaching campaign, its needs, and the progress made. Such a publication helps keep the campaign alive and maintains the interest of workers and contributors. It makes it possible to tell the human story. Newsletters also can announce the results received from certain contributing groups, individuals, and corporations in order to stimulate giving and competition.

Contests

Another effective way of stimulating interest in the institution is by organizing contests among specific media groups for the best stories or the best promotion of the campaign. Essay contests or prizes given to industrial editors, special recognition of reporters, and awards for best displays are all ways of providing recognition and gaining interest.

Sports Promotions

Planning for the participation of individual athletes and teams in the campaign is the job of a sports promotion committee. Many organizations find it helpful to arrange the appearance of well-known athletes at their campaign meetings. Such appearances help draw a crowd to hear the organization's message.

Americans are very sports-minded and sports personalities and sporting events represent a very natural means of promoting philanthropic programs. A special band formation at half-time of a football game can be used to salute the charity. Marathons and long-distance runs are being used with increasing frequency. They can popularize the cause and raise money. Some athletic teams will dedicate a game—and its winnings—to a particular charity to raise funds.

THE CAMPAIGN KICKOFF

If the campaign plan has been carefully implemented and the soliciting organization is complete, the next major step is to have a formal campaign kickoff announcing the official beginning of the campaign. It is a signal to solicitors that it is now time to begin work in earnest in carrying out the campaign plan. It is like the gun at the start of a track meet signaling that it is time to get off the starting blocks and go full speed. The kickoff is not a time for handling the mechanics of the job, but should be designed to provide motivation and inspiration. It may involve as few as a score of people or many hundreds, depending on the size of the campaign. Generally it is best to use a breakfast, luncheon, or dinner for this purpose.

The kickoff provides an opportunity for the president or campaign chairperson to outline the needs of the institution and to dramatize those needs through a film or through an inspirational message. If an advance solicitation of major givers, corporations, or employee groups has been conducted, the kickoff also provides an opportunity to report on results that have been received to date. This is the time to announce that some of the top givers have responded with generous gifts. It is the time to announce the results of any pilot campaigns in employee groups. The announcement of leadoff gifts sets the pattern for the rest of the campaign and demonstrates that major givers are firmly behind it and that the campaign goal can be achieved.

Of course, holding a kickoff and inspiring workers are of little use unless plans are made to sustain the promotional effort during the formal campaign period. Careful campaign planning will make provision for doing this through feature materials run in the organization's newsletter and in the press and through periodic campaign bulletins that report on results to date.

Each organization will need to select the kind of promotional materials and media that have the greatest impact for it. Not all media are adaptable for every organization. The specific chapters on types of campaigns examine this issue more fully. In any case, once the campaign has begun, the important strategy is to promote, promote, promote.

10

MANAGING THE CAMPAIGN

It has been pointed out previously that success or failure in a campaign has decided psychological components. Givers tend to follow the leader, and prospects are likely to emulate others who have already given. For this reason, if the campaign is started on a negative note, it is very difficult to make it succeed. If it has started on a positive and optimistic basis, the chances of success are greatly improved. Campaign planners must take this psychological atmosphere into account and take every step possible to start the campaign in a positive spirit.

GETTING OFF TO A GOOD START

I recently viewed a campaign of sizable proportions that had received a few disappointing gifts. Staff members permitted word of these disappointments to spread through the community, particularly through the top corporate leadership. By so doing they virtually sealed the fate of the campaign. Other major prospects began to reconsider their pledges and, because they felt there was little chance of the campaign being a success, held back on their own commitments. This magnified the problem so that there was no way the campaign could succeed.

Even when disappointments occur, it is best that campaign staff hold them in confidence and share them only with the campaign chairperson, seizing the opportunity to work out plans for resoliciting the givers concerned. At the very least, they should conduct the balance of the campaign with as great optimism as possible so that some of the disappointments may be overcome by good responses from other major givers.

Bellwether Gifts

One of the best ways of getting the campaign off on the right foot and securing its success is by carefully selecting a small number of major prospects who, in the opinion of the campaign leadership, will support the campaign generously. Typically these are people who have supported the program generously in the past, who are represented on the board of directors, and who are major users of services or leadership companies in the community.

The campaign case should be carefully prepared for these prospects and selective calls made on them well in advance of the general campaign. They are being asked to assume a leadership role and to set the example for others with generous gifts. Once their commitments have been obtained, the gifts can be announced at division kickoffs for major corporations and individuals. Such bellwether gifts demonstrate that the desired level of giving can be obtained and that major givers are solidly behind the campaign effort. Many a corporation has taken a second look at what it had initially planned to give when it found that other major givers were contributing much more than their planned commitments. Such corporations want to follow the lead of others and to be represented in the campaign with gifts that are proportionate to their standing in the community.

Pilot Campaigns

Pilot campaigns are another important way in which the campaign can be started on a positive note. Such advance campaigns, whether among employee groups, faculty, or medical staff, demonstrate to other prospects that substantial support exists for the program and that the desired level of giving can be achieved. Reporting solicitation results from such groups at the general kickoff meeting or at divisional meetings goes a long way toward creating a belief in success. A further discussion of pilot campaigns appears in Chapter 19.

Pacing Results

Another technique that can be used to stimulate giving and create an air of success is to "feed" good results into the campaign on a controlled basis. When a number of individual or corporate gifts of substantial proportions have been received, it is sometimes advisable to hold a few of these back and announce them periodically as the campaign proceeds. This can be accomplished through campaign bulletins, organizational newsletters, and the press. In this way, the solicitor is continually reminded that givers are responding generously to the campaign appeal and gains a feeling that the campaign is going well and will be successful.

The same technique, of course, can be used with employee results as they begin to come in. Highlighting high per capita results among employees in corporate campaigns not only creates a sense of success but develops a certain amount of competition that will stimulate others to do as well or better.

One problem can arise when the total giving of bellwether gifts of major companies represents such an overwhelming proportion of the campaign goal that success appears to be certain. It is important to create an aura of success, but if the solicitation is overwhelmingly large it may create a sense of complacency among other solicitors. Judgment plays a large part in determining how much to report, and when, in order to sustain enthusiasm and competition while generating a sense of achievement.

Don't Let It Drag

One of the greatest enemies of successful campaigning is letting the campaign drag on and lose its momentum. Many solicitors have a habit of putting pledge cards in their desk drawers and delaying solicitation rather than getting the job done promptly. Solicitor training should emphasize the fact that the solicitation is best accomplished and the best results obtained when promotion is at its highest—immediately after the start of the campaign. Solicitors will find that they get their best response if they make their contacts during this period; they will also have a greater sense of satisfaction in a job well done. Delaying solicitation merely puts an additional burden on other volunteers and staff for repeated follow-up with the tardy solicitor and in some cases even makes it necessary to reassign cards if it does not appear that the solicitor is going to complete the agreed-upon task.

One of the ways of stimulating and maintaining momentum is to establish definite dollar objectives for specific points in the campaign. It is possible, for example, to arrive at a reporting schedule such as the following:

End of week 3	40% of goal
End of week 5	60% of goal
End of week 7	90% of goal
End of week 9	100%-plus of goal

Such a timetable, based in part on the kind of campaign being conducted and past experience, not only pushes solicitors to complete their tasks according to a schedule but also enables the campaign leaders to judge how the solicitation is proceeding. When a lag threatens, they can put forth additional efforts in following up on solicitors and in pressing them to complete their assignments.

The ability to show that a campaign is moving according to schedule is a very positive factor in successful campaigning. Everyone wants to be part of a winning team, and good reports stimulate solicitors to match what other campaigners are doing.

ACCOUNT MANAGEMENT

Proper management of accounts begins by having each section leader report in writing on what assignments have been made. (See Figure 10-1.) The next step is to prepare a list of the prospects that are to be handled by each solicitor, showing the amount given the year before and the amount being requested in the current year. Space should be left for filling in the current gift when it is received and for indicating the status of the account. (See Figure 10-2.)

Figure 10-1. Form for reporting campaign assignments.

Name of Section Chair or Captain	Orville Furman
Address	222 Ocean Drive Tel: 555-6702

I have made the following assignments:

Worker James Reiter	Tel. No. 555-2075

Prospect	Address
John Smith	840 Second Street
Sidney Johnson	1020 West 40th Street
Austin Chapman	1st National Bank Building
Julius Owens	67 Prior Drive

Figure 10-2. Account assignment.

Section and Worker, Accounts	Amount last year	Amount requested	Amount this year	Status
Sect. 1-1 George Sweeney 555-0241				
Overseas Corporation	$ 4,000	$ 5,500	$	
ABC Industries	1,000	1,200		
George Seaman	500	600		
Gordon Typesetting	1,500	1,700		
Afton Foundry	5,000	6,500		
Jeffrey Printing	1,600	1,750		
	$13,600	$17,250	$	
Sect. 1-2 Grant Huspie 555-0735				
Mrs. Marjorie Kline	$ 500	$ 550		
Oliver Corporation	2,500	2,800		
James Star Corporation	7,500	10,000		
Gerald Riverside	600	800		
Automotive Corporation	3,000	4,000		
Ajax	2,900	3,500		
	$17,000	$21,650	$	

A very important job of development staff and of volunteers is to track the status of each individual account in each section or group throughout the campaign. This enables the staff to have a good idea of how the campaign is going—whether the calls have actually been made on prospective contributors, whether there are any problems inherent in the solicitation that need to be anticipated and rectified—and to develop strategy accordingly. It also enables the staff to keep volunteer section and division chairpersons alert at all times to the status of important accounts and to when they may be received. Finally, good account management enables the staff and volunteers to know whether the section or group involved is experiencing an increase or decrease in contributions at any stage during the campaign.

Some years ago I observed a division director give all the prospect cards to his section chairpersons for assignment without requiring a listing of the accounts being handled by the solicitors. His idea was to place the responsibility for assignment and success squarely on the shoulders of each section chairperson. The staff director tried to follow through by making occasional calls to the section chairpersons. As the campaign neared completion and his division was falling short, he found it increasingly difficult and unproductive to deal with the section chairpersons. Some were out of town; others weren't returning calls and obviously had not done their jobs. The embarrassed staff director had no way of following the accounts, since he had not insisted on getting the specific assignments to solicitors.

Sometimes, even in the best campaigns, solicitors are unable to make their calls because of illness, job transfer, personal problems, or absence from the community. Unless there is proper account management and follow-up, it is entirely possible that the campaign leadership will not be aware of the difficulties until the campaign is nearly over or is actually complete. At that point, it is very difficult to take corrective action or to initiate the remedies that might have succeeded at an earlier stage.

PROJECTING CAMPAIGN RESULTS

One of the problems confronting development staff is determining how the campaign stands at any particular stage of the drive. Although amounts reported by division and section will show progress toward overall division and section goals, such reports do not give a qualitative analysis of how much "new money" is being raised in the campaign. Nor do they give the staff and lay leadership a picture of what the prospects are for success.

When the solicitation is an annual giving program and there is a past history of contributions, campaign results can be analyzed and final results projected. Every good campaigner should develop a system of doing this. Toward the end of the campaign when the solicitation is nearly complete there may be cards still outstanding (possibly because the donors are out of the city or ill, or because some corporations have not had meetings of their contributions committees or boards of directors). In these circumstances, the campaign committee may want to close out the formal campaign and, by taking into account the possible gifts outstanding, arrive at an estimate as its "final report." This is, of course, the last step of the campaign, when sufficient results are in to judge the current status and likely outcome.

Method

In order to make projections, the organization will need an account-by-account listing in each section or division showing the amount that has been reported for each prospect. This analysis must include the amount given the previous year and the amount received in the current year. Such analyses can be done by computer or, in smaller campaigns, by hand.

Let us assume that a campaign started with a card value (the amount raised the previous year, less any known reductions due to deaths and removals) of $2,175,000. The goal for this year is $2,375,000, or $200,000 more, an increase of 9.2 percent. This means that $200,000 in new money—increased pledges or new gifts—must be received to make goal. Figure 10-3 shows an analysis of the results in Division I, with a goal of $1,100,000 and a card value the previous year of $1,000,000. This division must raise $100,000 in new money, or a 10 percent increase.

From Figure 10-3 it can be seen that the prospects reporting thus far in Division I

Figure 10-3. Analysis of division results.

Total Campaign

Goal this year	$2,375,000
Amount raised prior year (card value)	2,175,000
New money needed	$ 200,000

Division I   Major Gifts

Division I goal	$1,100,000
Division I amount raised last year (card value)	1,000,000
New money needed—10% increase	$ 100,000

Division I   Report to Date

Prospect	Amount last year	Amount this year	New money
ABC Company	$ 50,000	$ 55,000	$ 5,000
Marwill	15,000	17,000	2,000
AC Computer (new)	0	7,000	7,000
Jupiter Corp.	28,000	27,000	−1,000
Joseph Otis	2,000	2,000	0
Good Guy Company	30,000	35,000	5,000
Other prospects (list)	175,000	196,000	21,000
	$300,000	$339,000	$39,000

Projection—Division I

Beginning card value	$1,000,000
Cards reported to date (last year's value)	300,000
Remaining cards outstanding—last year's value	700,000
Amount raised this year—division I to date	339,000
Projected division results based on current increase	$1,039,000
Percent increase to date ($39,000 divided by $300,000)	13.0
New money needed to make division goal ($1,100,000 less $1,039,000)	$61,000
Percent increase needed on remaining cards to make goal ($61,000 divided by $700,000)	8.7%

have made pledges of $339,000 in new money, compared with $300,000 the previous year. This represents $39,000 in new money. Subtracting the value of the reported prospects' gifts last year from the division's beginning card value ($1,000,000 less $300,000), we find $700,000 worth of unreported cards still outstanding in Division I. If we add to this figure the $339,000 that the reporting prospects have given and assume that all the prospects that have not yet reported give the same as last year, we can safely project a division result of $1,039,000 on a goal of $1,100,000 at this point in the campaign.

It can be further determined from this analysis that $61,000 in new money (goal of $1,100,000 less projected result of $1,039,000) needs to be raised from the remaining prospects. We now know that the prospects reported to date have brought in an increase of $39,000, or 13.0 percent, and that the remaining new money needed ($61,000) represents an increase of only 8.7 percent, which has to be raised from the unreported cards.

Quite obviously, Division I is running well in its initial stages and has excellent potential to be oversubscribed. However, we need to bear in mind that the best results almost always come in first and that reductions in gifts and lower percentage increases tend to come in toward the end of the campaign.

If this type of analysis is made for each division, it is possible to show campaign leadership how much of the new money ($200,000) has been raised to date and how much is still needed. It is also possible to project results for each division, as was done for Division I. (See Figure 10-4.)

Figure 10-4. Analysis of campaign status.

	Division I	Division II	Division III	Division IV	Total
1. Goal	$1,100,000	$200,000	$573,000	$502,000	$2,375,000
2. Card value	1,000,000	182,000	537,000	456,000	2,175,000
3. Increase needed	$ 100,000	$ 18,000	$ 36,000	$ 46,000	$ 200,000
4. Percent increase needed	10%	9.9%	6.9%	9.9%	9.2%
5. Amount reported to date	339,000	102,000	400,000	261,000	1,102,000
6. Percentage reported	30.8%	51%	69.8%	52%	46%
7. Last year's card value	$ 300,000	$ 90,000	$377,358	$234,378	$1,001,736
8. Increase to date	$ 39,000	$ 12,000	$ 22,642	$ 26,622	$ 100,264
9. Percent increase obtained	13.0%	13.3%	5.9%	10.9%	10.0%
10. Remaining card value (line 2 minus line 7)	700,000	92,000	159,642	221,622	1,173,264
11. Projected division result (line 5 plus line 10)	1,039,000	194,000	559,642	482,622	2,275,264
12. Increase still needed (line 3 minus line 8)	61,000	6,000	13,358	18,378	98,736
13. Percent increase needed (line 12 divided by line 10)	8.7%	6.5%	9.1%	8.8%	8.5%
14. Number of accounts	122	578	820	1,020	2,540
15. Number reported	47	327	640	550	1,564
16. Number unreported	75	251	180	470	976
17. Percentage of accounts reported	25.9%	56.6%	78.0%	53.9%	61.6%

Conclusions

The preceding analysis allows us to come to some general conclusions about the status of the campaign:

1. The campaign is running well on an overall basis, with 46 percent of goal reported and a confirmed increase of $100,264, or 10 percent, against a needed increase of 9.2 percent.

2. Three of the four divisions are showing the increase necessary to make or exceed goal.

3. The fallacy of depending upon percentage of goal achieved as a measure of campaign performance is demonstrated by Division III. Although this division appears to be in the best shape because it has already reported the highest percentage of goal, 69.8 percent, it actually is in the worst shape. It is registering an increase of only 5.9 percent when an overall increase of 6.9 percent is needed. In addition, the division has already reported a high percentage of its accounts—78 percent. Therefore, its high percentage of goal is related to acceleration or rapid reporting rather than to increased production. The division needs an average increase of at least 9.1 percent on the remaining accounts to make goal.

4. The flag is up on Division III. It is time to pull together section and group chairpersons to determine what the problems are before there is any more erosion of results. Care should be exercised to determine whether there is an overall problem common to most of the accounts or whether some sharp reductions may have occurred in selective accounts that have affected the total division results. In the latter case, leadership must determine a strategy—such as a well-developed callback on these accounts—to see whether pledges can be reconsidered or whether there are special public relations problems. The fact that campaign leadership gave this division only a 6.9 percent goal increase is an indication that it may have had problems in the past or that special problems were anticipated and are now proving to be true.

5. Division I—the largest division—is showing a healthy increase that is essential to success. However, it has reported only 25.9 percent of its accounts, compared with an overall result of 61.6 percent. This may be entirely justified, depending on the types of prospects. An employees division, for example, will generally report more slowly than a special-gifts division because of the large number of employees who have to be solicited and the time required to tabulate results. Nevertheless, campaign leadership should be alert to the possible need to push follow-up calls on workers in this division.

6. Division II is the healthiest division at this time. It is showing a 13.3 percent increase against a 9.9 percent objective. It has already reported 56.6 percent of its accounts. The division shows a good increase and good acceleration.

7. Division IV is in sound position—nothing sensational but just about on target with a slightly better increase than needed and with good coverage of accounts.

8. The campaign has produced $100,264 of the needed increase of $200,000 to date. It is reasonable to project a campaign result of at least $2,274,264 on a goal of $2,375,000 at this time. There is enough card value left—$1,172,264—to register a victory. An increase on the remaining accounts of only 8.5 percent is needed. There is good reason to be optimistic, but not to go overboard. The erosion in Division III needs to be halted, and leadership needs to remember that the best results tend to come in first.

Employee Projections

It is much more difficult to project results for employee campaigns than for individual solicitation divisions. The reason is that employee results in an organization are changing each hour as the solicitation proceeds and it is very difficult, if not impossible, to get the employer to do a card-by-card analysis showing increases by individual from the prior year.

Under these circumstances, it is safe to analyze only when: (1) employee campaigns are completed and the increase or decrease from the previous year can be determined, or (2) the results are incomplete but have already surpassed the prior year's production.

Closing Out the Reporting

In almost every campaign a point will come when the major solicitation is complete, but some prospects are out of town, boards haven't met, or people have been ill. Toward the end of the campaign, when only a small number of cards are outstanding but the chairperson wants to close up the campaign results except for minor follow-up, it is a good idea to take the confirmed amounts reported in each division and to "inventory" the outstanding cards. These accounts should list the amounts given the previous year and, unless there is some question about their being repeated, should be added to the division totals to obtain an estimated campaign result. Some optimistic campaigners will estimate some percentage increase on these remaining cards if the campaign has been a strong one. Conservatism dictates that the best policy is not to count on more than contributors gave the year before. Frequently when gifts are late, it is for a reason. The donor may be pondering a gift or may be indecisive, or a special set of circumstances may dictate that a corporation needs to consider a reduction in gift.

Therefore, the safe policy is to inventory these gifts at no more than the previous level and even to discount them somewhat if there is any question about their validity. A careful card-by-card review with the volunteers who made contacts with the prospects is essential to carry this out. Far too many campaigns have been overreported with embarrassing results to take the chance of being optimistic about unreported cards.

Nonannual Campaigns

When the campaign is not an annual one and there is no history of giving, it is much more difficult to make a final campaign projection. Careful questioning of the solicitor and an indication that a corporate gift at a certain level is going to be recommended by the chief executive officer to the board may be justification to make a projection, but the evidence must be very strong. Sometimes, in their enthusiasm to report goal, solicitors are inclined to latch on to the least bit of evidence of a gift, but the final decision by the prospect may be negative.

If the campaign has run very strong and there is compliance with the "ratings"— that is, the givers have responded to a high degree to the requests—there may be reason for optimism. If only 50 percent of the ratings are needed to make goal and the campaign is realizing 65 percent, the prospects are very positive. In such a case, staff can tell the volunteer chairpersons that of the remaining cards outstanding a certain percentage compliance with the ratings can achieve goal. This will be less than the 50 percent originally needed. However, anything beyond this type of forecast is very risky. Generally, late reported cards are late for a reason, and most are dead—they are not viable accounts. In addition, once the formal campaign is over, the whole impetus for giving seems to stop. Most of the solicitors stop working, the promotional aspects of the campaign are gone, and follow-up is very difficult.

I have seen many red faces and heard many embarrassed rationalizations by staff trying to explain why forecasts based on optimistic projections didn't pan out and why the campaign ended short when the final accounting was made. Conservatism is the better part of valor when making these types of forecasts; furthermore, accuracy in projecting builds confidence in the staff and enhances the reputation of the institution.

11

THE CORPORATE CAMPAIGN

Because corporate gifts represent a major source of income for many types of organizations, it is extremely important that the corporate campaign get off to a good start.

THE CULTIVATION MEETING

An important way of accomplishing this objective is to establish a cultivation program that will set the stage for the formal request to the corporation later. Many organizations have found that a series of luncheons or dinners involving top executives of the major companies is an excellent way to begin the cultivation process. The role of the campaign chairperson or corporate division chairperson is an essential factor in the success or failure of these meetings. The chair's relationship to other top business leaders is most important in getting them to accept the invitation to attend.

Corporate cultivation meetings are best held in groups of 25 to 50. This number is large enough to accomplish the task, yet gives the impression of exclusivity and provides an opportunity for a certain amount of informality in answering questions. The meeting needs to be carefully planned beforehand so that each participant in the program knows what points to make. A typical agenda might include the following:

1. *Chair's introductory remarks*. The chair thanks the participants for coming and stresses their importance to the institution sponsoring the luncheon.
2. *Program summary*. The program of the institution should be described as well as the problem confronting it.
3. *Visual presentation*. Graphic illustrations using a motion picture film, slide sound film, or chart talk can be used to illustrate the problem at hand.
4. *Proposed program and possible solutions*. A summary is made of what has to be done to resolve the problem in terms of program and money and what is needed from the business community if this is to be accomplished.

5. *Questions and answers.* Participants may ask about the proposed program and its cost.

6. *Request for commitment from top leadership.* The chairperson stresses the importance of the program, indicates the amount that must be raised from the corporate community if the campaign is to be a success, and asks for cooperation. A brochure summarizing the program may be given to the participants to read before a personal call is made to get their formal commitment.

It is essential that the meeting be brief, well controlled, and to the point. Belaboring the subject will cause executives to leave and will make a poor impression. Calvin Coolidge is reported to have said that the gift to his church was in reverse proportion to the length of the sermon. It is always helpful if the organization is able to announce that one or more leadership gifts have already been obtained. This demonstrates support by important corporations and begins to set a pattern for others to follow. The corporate executives can then gain an idea of what their companies may be asked to do in comparison to those that have already given. Remember that successful campaigns are built on a follow-the-leader principle.

A merchant who was a newcomer to the community bought a store. Anxious to establish his reputation, as well as that of his company, among people in the neighborhood, he decided to go to a service at the Protestant church located in the immediate neighborhood of his store. It happened to be the Sunday when the annual campaign for the parish was being kicked off.

The minister give a very inspiring message about the needs of the church for increased support and the necessity for each parishioner to do his or her share. He equated the response of parishioners to the principle of charity as enuciated in Christian doctrine.

As soon as the minister had concluded his remarks, the merchant stood up and commented that although he was not a member of the congregation, he had been so inspired by the minister's remarks that he was going to make a pledge of $1,000. Members of the congregation were astounded that someone who was not even part of the parish would give so generously. One after another they began to rise and announce their gifts, all of which were generous and more than they had given the year before.

On the following day, the minister paid a visit to the merchant and expressed his deep appreciation for what the man had done the day before. He said, "I appreciated so much what you did that I wanted to call on you personally and thank you, and I thought as long as I was here perhaps I could also pick up your check." The merchant replied, "Well, Reverend, there really isn't any pledge and there isn't any check. I just wanted to get you off to a good start."

The success of the cultivation meeting in fund raising has popularized the expression, common in corporate circles, "There is no such thing as a free lunch." Corporate executives have learned from long experience that their relationships with others in the business community frequently put them in the position where they will have to respond with contributions to subtle appeals of this type.

THE CORPORATE CALL

Even the best-conducted corporate cultivation meeting will not accomplish the desired result unless it is followed by personal calls on top business executives. When it is impractical to hold cultivation meetings as described above, the personal call on business executives becomes even more important, for here the total selling job has to be done.

Very seldom will corporations respond in substantial and meaningful ways unless an effective and pursuasive volunteer makes a personal call on the executive(s) who can make the decision on contributions in the company. In this regard, there are a few principles that should be followed.

Make an Appointment

A personal telephone call should be made to the top executive by the person who has been assigned the account. Again, it is important to stress that the person making the call be carefully selected and have either business or personal relationships with the executive concerned. It is not always necessary to inform the corporate executive in advance of the purpose of the meeting, although this may come up in the discussion. There is value in avoiding any detailed explanation for the call; otherwise, many of the important questions may be discussed via telephone without the opportunity to make a more meaningful presentation.

Avoid Requests

Whenever possible, do not make requests by mail. Letters are a poor substitute for a personal call unless they are the only way that an organization can get its request considered. Sometimes for one reason or another an appointment cannot be made with the top executive. When requests by mail are necessary, a special case presentation for the corporation should be enclosed if possible. Presentations should always be mailed to the top executive with a cover letter from the campaign volunteer on his or her *own* business stationery. The chief executive officer will give personal attention to those letters sent by someone he or she knows; others will be referred to the person in charge of contributions for the company. In this event, nothing is lost by sending the request to the CEO and there is the chance the request might get his or her attention.

Use Case Presentations

For the larger and more important prospects a carefully prepared case presentation should always be made. The presentation may include some of the material that the organization has prepared in the brochure for general distribution, but it should definitely include information of a more selective nature. Generally, it should highlight the following:

• *Brief summary of the problem*—the problem confronting the institution, the reason for the campaign, and the reasons the corporate community should support it. (See Figure 11-1.)

Figure 11-1. Summary statement to the corporate community.

1. The College of St. Thomas is the largest independent college in Minnesota, with a total enrollment of 4,784 students.
2. Over 1,300 undergraduate students (40 percent) are business administration majors.
3. Approximately 26 percent of all St. Thomas business administration majors are women.
4. St. Thomas has the largest MBA program of its kind in the upper Midwest. In five years it has grown from 79 to over 900 students.
5. Approximately 24 percent of MBA students are women.
6. The Management Center conducted nearly 150 courses, seminars, and conferences on various concerns of business and industry during 1978–1979.
7. The Small Business Institute operates with the SBA to help companies improve their performance and profitability. Over 200 projects have been completed, with 750 students and 16 faculty members participating.
8. The Center for Economic Education provides instruction for present and future elementary, secondary, and college teachers to help reduce economic illiteracy by improving the quality and increasing the extent of economics courses.
9. The Town and Gown Forum encourages mutual understanding and respect between business leaders and members of the academic community by providing a forum for the exchange of ideas.
10. Cooperative education has provided productive work experience for more than 350 students in business, industry, and government as a regular part of their academic program.

(Courtesy of College of St. Thomas, St. Paul, Minnesota.)

• *Programs and services of special interest to the corporation*—services provided to employees of the corporation; the number of graduates employed by the corporation; special research activities that are of interest and help to the corporation; and the improvement that will result in the cultural environment for the corporation. Factual data summarizing the services provided are especially helpful, but keep them brief. Corporate executives are trained to look at facts and respond to them.

• *Program and budget required*—what is needed to accomplish the program and its objectives. These statements should cover what the institution must do, what has to be accomplished on an overall basis by the campaign, and especially what must be raised from the corporate community. Statistical data showing trends in services and projected demands for the future are helpful. The budget needed to accomplish the program objectives and the budgetary implications for the future should be provided. Not only are corporations interested in what they are going to be asked to give to an operating campaign or special building fund campaign; they also want to know the possibilities of increased support in the future. Far too many institutions give this matter little thought. It is often with considerable embarrassment (and sometimes annoyance to the contributors) that they have to request substantial gifts in subsequent years in order to balance a budget that was not explained initially. It is especially helpful if the soliciting institution can show that increased revenue from other sources will help support the project in the future. An organization in the arts, planning an enlarged facility, will make brownie points if it can demonstrate that increased patronage and revenues will help carry the enlarged program in subsequent years.

Budget information should be provided in summary form and should be sufficient to explain the needs, but not in so much detail as to require an intimate examination of financial data. The corporate prospect is a busy person, immersed in problems of his or her own, and does not have the time to extract detailed financial information that can be provided in summary form.

• *Corporate support required*—the amount required from major corporations and, when possible, examples of gifts already received from other corporations. This is the institution's opportunity to put its best foot forward by showing that it has already received commitments from major corporations in support of the project. Most corporations will want to follow that lead, but many are reluctant to give if there is not a good chance that the campaign will succeed.

This section should also include the campaign dates and the projected date by which it is hoped the corporation will make a commitment. It should also cover the payment dates for the pledge—whether one, two, three, four, or five years. If it is an annual campaign, the gift will, of course, be paid during the succeeding 12-month period. However, building and endowment campaign pledges often will be payable over a three- to five-year period. Annual pledges may be payable quarterly. When the request of a corporation is large, the corporation will find it easier to give generously if the payment period is longer. It is easier for a company to give a major gift over five years than in a single year.

• *Basis of the request to the corporation*—how much the organization would like the corporation to consider giving and, possibly, how that figure has been determined. This can be done by comparing the corporation's size or profitability with that of other corporations. If it is an annual campaign, the corporation might be asked to give a percentage increase, reflecting the higher goal and inflationary costs. It might also be asked to make a more substantial increase if its gift is on the low side when compared with those of other companies.

Appeal to Interests

Knowledge of the corporate manager's interests are of special help in making the request. In many cases, the programs of the soliciting organization may be multifaceted. In this case, select that program in which the executive may have the most interest and emphasize it in making the presentation. If his or her interest is research, stress any parts of the program that are research-oriented; if the interest is youth, stress youth services. The prospect and the soliciting organization can then establish an immediate area of common interest and the job becomes much easier.

Ask for the Money

We have all heard about the salesman who made a wonderful sales presentation but forgot to ask for the order. After the presentation has been carefully made, it is important that the person making the solicitation not forget to ask the corporation for the gift proposed. Remember, that's what the solicitor came for. In this connection, the importance of the company's gift to the campaign should be stressed; it should also be pointed out that the effort can be successful only if the response in general from the business community is in line with the gift requests being made.

Give Recognition

If the institution has designed a recognition program for corporations and individuals, this should be mentioned. A plaque in a new building recognizing major gifts may be of special interest. A special listing of leadership corporations in the annual report or in other publications may also provide an incentive. Although most corporations would not give for these reasons alone, they are always interested in knowing what possible recognition they may receive for their gifts.

PRESENTATION TECHNIQUES

Some institutions make their presentations by summarizing the case through visuals presented through a small projector placed on the executive's table or desk.

When a written presentation is used, it should be borne in mind that the more white space on a page and the less copy, the more effective it will be. If the major points can be reduced to a few lines or figures on each page which the executive can thumb through and grasp quickly, this is much more effective than presenting many pages of detailed copy that the executive does not have time to read.

Even when the corporation being solicited is not large enough to justify an especially prepared written case presentation, the same general outline of the organization's case can be followed by the campaign volunteers by using the general brochure plus interpretation. See Appendix A for a sample case presentation from the Children's Heart Fund.

THE CORPORATE CONTRIBUTIONS COMMITTEE

Although we have emphasized the need to approach the top executive in the solicitation of company gifts, philanthropic organizations should not overlook another very important group within many corporations today. This is the contributions committee which, in some corporations, will have the final responsibility for recommending which organizations will be funded and the amount that will be given.

Dennis Murphy's *Asking Corporations for Money*, a study of the largest companies in the country, discovered that in 64 percent of all corporations it studied, the contributions committee—without the involvement of the CEO—made the final recommendations on gifts to charitable organizations. In 46 percent of those companies, the decision was made in conjunction with a high-level staff person in the company responsible for reviewing, analyzing, and presenting to the contributions committee information concerning the organizations that were seeking support. This staff person may have been a vice president or the civic affairs manager, community relations manager, or contributions manager. In the remaining 54 percent of those companies, the contributions committee made the final decision without assistance from another individual or group. This underscores the importance of the committee in nearly all firms and the desirability of cultivating its members by placing them on the philanthropic organization's mailing lists for regular bulletins about the organization's program.

Although the contributions committee is very important, and increasingly so in many corporations, the study also discovered that in 52 percent of the corporations the final decision as to which charitable organizations should receive support was made— at least some of the time—solely by the contributions *manager*. Some companies allow the contributions manager the discretion to approve smaller gifts that fall within a prescribed amount. In 49 percent of all companies, the chief executive officer was also involved at least some of the time in the final decision. It is likely that the CEO will be involved in the giving of large gifts to organizations in which he or she has a personal interest. Even when corporate contributions committees have, at least in theory, the responsibility to recommend gifts to philanthopic organizations, seldom will they act so independently that they do not take into account the interests of the top executive and his or her business relationships.

As to the amount given, the chief executive officer may play a less influential role. This same study indicated that in 46 percent of the corporations the CEO was involved at least sometimes in this decision. But the decision was made in conjunction with the contributions committee or contributions manager at least 81 percent of the time.

Frequently when the chief executive of a corporation is approached for a contribution, he or she will involve the contributions manager, who has the responsibility of processing the request through the contributions committee. In this case the organization will have the advantage of presenting its sales case both to the chief executive officer and to the person who is charged with the day-to-day responsibility of conducting the corporate contributions program. Nevertheless, it should be emphasized again that it is important to start at the top with the chief executive officer. If the CEO does not want to get involved, he or she can always refer the matter to the appropriate person in the company. If your organization just doesn't have access to the chief executive officer, then the next best place to start is with the contributions manager.

The same study mentioned above showed that corporations tend to support those organizations with which they are familiar, and more than half the charities supported received gifts at least once during the preceding three years. It is uncommon for dramatic changes to occur in the organizations receiving corporate support, although there is some evidence that this may be changing. As corporate contributions budgets become larger and more specialized staff is available to look at unmet needs and to consider funding organizations attacking major community problems, corporations may tend to fund new organizations.

What organizational characteristics do corporations feel are most important in deciding on a gift? The study revealed that cost efficiency is the most important (96 percent). The second most important factor is the service provided by the organization in the local community (92 percent). Other important considerations are whether a charitable organization helps people who wouldn't otherwise get help or has a program that would reduce client dependence on public welfare (76 percent); the extent to which the organization uses volunteers (67 percent); and whether the organization is involved in health research or helps the average middle class person (57 percent). Services to company employees also carry a major attraction for corporations (57 percent).

The size of the organization's goals and the gifts of other corporations are two other important factors that help a corporation decide how much it should give.

Contributions committees will be guided in their decisions by a corporate contributions policy which describes the areas of philanthropic interest of the company and the conditions which must be met by an organization seeking a gift. Within these guidelines the committee has wide latitude to establish priorities and make decisions on individual requests. A sample contributions policy—that of AT&T—is shown in the Appendix. Note that AT&T utilizes a corporate foundation to make its gifts.

WHY CORPORATIONS GIVE

There is a growing recognition that the free enterprise system will succeed best if the social, educational, health, and cultural environments of the community provide essential services for employees. There is also a growing concern that if all services are administered by government, this will result in a monolithic set of services that do not provide the varied or innovative approaches necessary to solve problems and keep the American system viable. If all social and health services, all educational programs, and all cultural programs are entirely supported by government, then all policies and decisions affecting those services will eventually be dictated by government.

From a purely practical point of view, it is essential that important problems in the community be solved; otherwise, the environment for conducting business may become very difficult indeed. Putting money into preventive services eventually means a reduction in certain types of taxes that fall heavy upon the business community.

Giving by corporations is one of the fastest-growing sources of funds for many segments of philanthropy. Total contributions by corporations have now surpassed the total giving of foundations in the United States and show promise of continuing upward. While this record is admirable, it still falls far short of what corporate giving might be in this country.

The concept of giving by corporations developed in the 1920s as more and more business enterprises were transformed from individually owned companies to corporations. As corporations grew in number and size, they recognized the increasing problems of local communities in which their plants and offices operated. Problems of housing, health, dependency, and child welfare all accompanied the growth of major industrial corporations.

Business has learned that a productive labor force exists only where necessary and essential community services are available. Good hospitals, schools, day care centers, clinics, family counseling programs, assistance for retarded children—all are examples of the kinds of services that productive members of the labor force and their families require. Organizations in the arts enrich a community and make it more attractive for an executive considering a transfer.

It is easier and more efficient for a corporation to make such services possible by cooperating with the rest of the community through contributions than by attempting to provide all these services itself. The corporation's precise policies for giving are affected by several factors.

Tax Deductibility

The major impetus for corporate giving came with the recognition of its importance by the federal government in the 1920s. Corporate contributions were stimulated by federal legislation that permitted them to be deducted when determining income tax liability. This meant that government not only acknowledged the importance of corporate giving and of the private philanthropic sector but actually encouraged corporations to give. In effect, government became an indirect partner of the corporation because for every gift made by the company, the government shared in the cost. As tax rates changed, the cost of a gift in aftertax dollars to the corporation diminished or increased, depending on federal tax policy, but the deductibility factor made it possible for corporations to experience some tax savings through their giving programs regardless of the tax rate.

Recent federal legislation has raised the ceiling on corporate giving from 5 to 10 percent of pretax profits, but the actual experience at present for all companies in the country is still only about 1 percent. Therefore, while corporate giving has been growing, there is still a substantial distance to go before corporations use the full deductible privilege permitted by law.

Growth of 2 Percent and 5 Percent Clubs

Within recent years corporations have been encouraged to give from 2 percent to 5 percent of their pretax profits, the former limit permitted by government. This action springs from the growing sense of corporate social responsibility and the recognition by top management that corporations must help to solve important social, health, educational, and cultural problems. Thus 2 percent and 5 percent clubs have sprung up in a number of cities, led by Minneapolis, as a way of recognizing corporations that are generous and encouraging others to do likewise. Generally, such recognition is given through an annual dinner and an award, and the corporation's name is included in a brochure circulated in the business community.

One word of caution: Although it is commendable to encourage corporations to give a certain percentage of their income, it should be recognized that there are some hazards. Profits can go down as well as up, and when contributions are tied to falling profits, giving goes down as well. Profit patterns are highly cyclical; therefore, any corporate contributions program should emphasize the establishment of corporate foundations, so giving can be stable in bad economic years as well as good. Otherwise, the future of nonprofit organizations could be bleak indeed.

Response to Criticism

Corporations have become increasingly sensitive to the charges by some activist groups that they are interested only in profits, or the bottom line. Accordingly, enlightened corporations now recognize that it is necessary to support philanthropic services if for no other reason than to demonstrate that they want to be good corporate citizens.

Government Policies

While some government policies have been conducive to corporate giving, other policies, strangely enough, have worked in an opposite direction.

Government policy generally does not permit contributions to be included as an element of cost in defense contracts. In other words, if a corporation with large defense contracts wishes to make contributions it cannot include them in the bid it submits to the government. Such costs must be borne directly out of profits. Many argue that this situation is justified because government should not indirectly be paying contributions through its contracts. However, the contradiction in this practice is that if the social, educational, or cultural services are paid for by local taxes, the defense contractor can then include them as an element of cost in submitting its budget to the government. In other words, a double standard exists between services supported by private contributions and those supported through taxes. Over a long period the result of this practice could be that more and more services are supported by government and fewer by private contributions.

A similar situation has recently confronted the utilities industry. For years the public service commissions in most of our states permitted the utilities to include contributions as an element of cost when determining the rate to be charged customers for gas, electric, and telephone services. More recently, some utilities commissions have ruled against the inclusion of contributions in the rate structure, and this has resulted in serious cutbacks in the contributions of utilities to some nonprofit organizations. Although the contributions made by utilities were substantial, their actual cost to each customer was minimal, amounting to only a few cents a year. In the long run this new ruling may turn out to be quite shortsighted and to harm essential nonprofit services.

It is rather difficult to understand why government policy has been so inconsistent, particularly when government itself has often made direct grants to nonprofit organizations or entered into purchase of service contracts through which it has paid for services provided to patients in hospitals, clients of social agencies, and students in colleges and universities. Current policy is also difficult to understand in a period when government is attempting to reduce its own expenditures and is encouraging the private sector to do more. Certainly it is making this objective more difficult to attain.

Stockholder Attitudes

Occasionally a corporation will be challenged by a stockholder who questions the validity of corporate contributions. In effect, the stockholder is saying, "Why should management be spending the stockholders' money for contributions to nonprofit organizations? These eventually come out of the pocket of the stockholder." Such stockholder challenges have become less frequent in recent years as the concept of corporate responsibility has been more widely accepted. Nevertheless, stockholder challenges are a factor that top management and boards of corporations must consider when determining what the company will give through private contributions.

Mergers and Acquisitions

Another factor that affects corporate giving is the rise in the number of mergers and acquisitions. Competition is becoming more intense as market conditions change and as capital becomes more difficult to obtain. In addition, our economy has entered a phase in which companies are competing internationally rather than competing only with other U.S. companies. Markets today are worldwide and corporations span continents. Because of this, more and more corporations are merging with or acquiring other companies. The multinational corporation is increasingly confronted with widely different circumstances and cultures with which it must relate.

The larger the company, presumably the stronger its financial base and the better able it is to compete and have the necessary capital to meet needs for new products, plants, and machinery. A rather unfortunate result, however, is that larger corporations tend to give a smaller percentage of pretax income in private contributions. The very smallest corporations give the least or not at all as they struggle to survive and accumulate capital for expansion. But once they are established and become profitable, they are more generous than the very large companies.

A study by The Conference Board of corporate contributions made in 1982 shows that companies with U.S. assets under $100 million gave a median 1.92 percent of pretax income compared with 1.14 percent for companies with assets over $10 billion. The upper quartile of these companies showed again that the smaller companies were more generous, giving 2.46 percent of pretax income, compared with 1.82 percent for the most generous larger companies.

When the comparison is made relative to the number of employees rather than assets, the same holds true. Manufacturing corporations with fewer than 1,000 employees had median contributions of 2.20 percent of U.S. net pretax income compared with 0.98 percent for companies having 5,000 to 10,000 employees and 1.50 percent for companies having over 50,000 employees.

The growth of mergers and acquisitions often means that the total amount of money available for contributions in local communities becomes less. This results from the fact that a company that was previously headquartered in a community now becomes only a branch operation there. Its officers and top management no longer live there and do not have the same in-depth interest in the community. Policies on contributions tend to be established by the corporation at a national level and many of the decisions on contributions are made at headquarters. There is also a tendency to standardize or reduce to formulas the giving by such corporations, which often means a reduction in support to charities in local communities where the companies have branches.

What may happen is that as a corporation becomes larger, the amount appearing in its budget for contributions appears as a large item compared with the amounts previously budgeted by the individual companies before the merger. It is important for campaign chairpersons and development directors to recognize that this trend does exist because it will have a substantial effect upon their ability to raise money.

SPECIAL CONSIDERATIONS

Although corporate support of United Ways is virtually universal, corporations differ to a considerable degree in the other areas of philanthropy that they support. Some may give more generously to higher education while others stress human services. Part of the job of a good campaign chairperson or development director is to learn what these special areas of interest may be and what the corporate giving guidelines are. Some corporations handle their contributions program in a rather confidential manner, but an increasing number are quite open about their areas of philanthropic interest and make guidelines available to organizations for determining whether they qualify for support.

When corporations have established foundations, information of this kind is often published at the community or state level by groups such as the Council on Foundations.

In the absence of published material, the best action is for development staff to make a personal call on the corporation and ask whether it has a corporate contributions program and whether it publishes guidelines for gift applications. This also presents an opportunity to outline the program of the institution briefly and to determine whether it will qualify for support. If time does not permit a personal visit, a telephone call to the company may elicit the same information.

It is important to recognize that corporate giving programs tend to reflect the personality and interests of the chief executive officer. If the CEO has considerable interest in the arts, for example, organizations in the arts will obviously have a good opportunity for support and educational or other organizations may have only a remote chance of obtaining a gift. Also, there is an increasing tendency among major corporations to act more like private foundations by sponsoring special projects with which the company may be identified rather than giving general, unrestricted support.

Branch Operations

In many communities a substantial number of the companies solicited are branch operations of major national corporations. It is important that nonprofit organizations conduct research to determine whether the decision on giving is made at the local branch level or has to be referred to the national headquarters for approval. Some national corporations provide their branches with a contributions budget and allow wide latitude within certain guidelines for branch management to make decisions. In other cases, all requests received by the local branch are funneled to the national headquarters, which gives high-priority consideration to the recommendation of local management in approving or disapproving the gift request. Once again, the relationship established with the management of the local branch is extremely important. In a few situations branch managers prefer that the request be made directly to national headquarters.

One of the most important considerations here is timing. Many organizations approach a corporation for a gift only to find that the branch has not provided for that organization in its current year's budget. A good solution is for the nonprofit organization to submit its request in writing in October or November, since most corporations formalize their contributions budgets in the latter part of the year, with formal action being taken in December for the succeeding year. This will not ensure an organization that its request will be approved, but the organization will certainly stand a better chance of obtaining support if it submits an early request. The corporation will then have a better chance to review all the requests it has received together and give appropriate consideration to each.

Intercampaign Cultivation

Making calls on corporations during a period of the year when the active campaign is not being conducted is also a helpful way of establishing relationships and getting the organization known. There is always an opportunity to discuss the needs of the organization, the program requirements, and the overall amounts that will likely be needed when the formal campaign commences.

Matching Gifts and Challenge Gifts

An increasing number of corporations are making matching or challenge gifts to organizations. The corporation may match employee gifts on an equal basis or even a better basis. Or the corporation may promise that it will give a sum of money provided the charitable organization is able to raise a specific amount from other prospects. Many organizations now find the challenge gift a very helpful tool in approaching new prospects.

A recent study of matching gifts by the Council for Financial Aid to Education showed that 777 major companies matched gifts of employees to institutions of higher learning. The number of gifts received by these institutions was 233,153 and the average gift was $193.55. Some companies matched contributions up to $1,000, but 90 percent of the participating companies matched employee contributions up to $500.

Primary and Secondary Schools

Public secondary schools are rarely included in corporate contributions program, but some private independent secondary schools do receive support. The National Association of Independent Schools reported that in 1981 9,576 gifts amounting to $3,113,682 were made to private independent secondary schools, for an average of $8,237 per school and an average corporate match of $325.

Approximately 97 percent of America's private secondary schools are affiliated either directly or indirectly with churches. In some corporate programs, schools operated and supported by a church, parish, or diocese do not fall within the definition of an independent school. But a number of corporations do include them as well as other independent schools.

Cultural Organizations and Hospitals

A number of corporations offer matching programs to cultural organizations and to hospitals. The Council for Financial Aid to Education study showed that in 1980 hospitals received $749,000 from 26 companies.

In the study cited, 0.6–1 percent of the corporation-matched employee gifts were given to the arts while a 48 percent share of the matched gifts went to education. The cost of a matching gifts program in the arts was less than 10 percent of the amount given to education in 18 of the 41 companies, between 10 and 25 percent for 17 companies, and between 25 and 48 percent for 6 companies. Further, the arts received only two gifts for every 54 going to education. Half of the companies reported 25 or fewer gifts to the arts for every 100 to education.

The cost of corporate matching gifts to hospitals was less than 10 percent of the cost of matching gifts to education in 18 out of 35 companies, between 10 and 25 percent for 11 companies, and over 25 percent for only 1 company. Education received 2.68 gifts per 100 eligibles, with an average gift of $165.42. Culture and the arts received 1.27 gifts per 100 eligibles, for an average gift of $95.12. Hospitals received 0.42 gifts per 100 eligibles, for an average gift of $143.26. It is obvious that a matching gifts program in the arts and hospitals could be accomplished for considerably less corporate money than is required for a similar program in education—probably about 25 percent.

United Ways

Some companies have attempted to stimulate employee giving to United Ways by matching the gifts of their employees. In some cases, this has had the desired effect and employee gifts have increased substantially. However, a word of caution is in order here. Unless the corporation agrees to a base figure for its gift, a poor result among employees because of unfavorable economic circumstances, work stoppages, layoffs, or other unsettled conditions within the company can result in the corporation reducing its gift. It has always been my belief that a corporation has a responsibility to the community regardless of what its employees give. Accordingly, when a matching gifts program is being considered, it is best to suggest to the company that it agree not to reduce its gift if the employee campaign is unfavorable. Otherwise, the results can be rather disastrous for the community and the agencies that depend upon United Way support.

DETERMINING THE SIZE OF THE REQUEST

Over the years a number of methods have been used to determine how much an organization should ask of each corporation approached in the campaign. Regardless of the method used, the total amount of corporate requests or goals (in a campaign for operating purposes) should exceed the amount needed from corporations in the campaign by at least 15 to 20 percent. Realistically all corporations are not going to give, and others are not going to respond at the level of the request. Therefore, a margin has to be built into the requests in order to ensure that the overall campaign goal is achieved.

Corporations will always want an indication of what is expected of them in the campaign. Without such a guideline they have no way of determining what the level of their gift should be. Accordingly, the soliciting institution should not hesitate to give a company a suggested gift for its consideration. Frequently corporations will ask what other companies are doing, since this may have a bearing on their gift. It is important to recognize that there is no such thing as a perfect corporate giving formula. All formulas have strengths; all have weaknesses. The important thing is to have some system that tries to bring equity in giving.

Three Basics

Three basic factors need to be taken into consideration in determining an equitable request for each corporation.

1. *Corporate responsibility.* Companies use the services in a community and, in return, have a responsibility to support them. One basis for evaluating the amount a corporation should give is by establishing its relative responsibility to the community. This can be accomplished by determining the number of employees in the company,

related either to total employment or to employment in other companies. In effect, this factor in a corporate giving formula implies that a gift at a particular level will be necessary if the campaign is to succeed and if the services needed by its employees are to be available.

2. *Ability to give.* A further consideration in determining corporate gift requests is the relative difference in ability to give because of widely differing profits. Some companies have a high profit margin and a relatively small number of employees; others have a relatively low profit margin and a high number of employees. Petrochemicals companies are a good example of an industry group with relatively few employees and high profit margins. The garment industry, on the other hand, has low profit margins and a high number of employees. If the number of employees only is used as the basis for making a request, some companies will be asked to give quite disproportionately in relation to their ability. Corporate goal setting based on profits, on the other hand, asks companies with the highest earnings to give the largest amounts.

3. *Propensity to give.* Over the years many companies have developed a pattern of generous giving to nonprofit organizations. This policy stems from a highly developed sense of social responsibility on the part of the management and the company's board of directors. Although most companies in the United States are giving at a level of approximately 1 percent of pretax earnings, a number of companies are giving 5 percent of pretax profits. This propensity to be generous is another major factor in the amounts that may be asked of corporations. Fund raisers will quickly recognize that no matter what formulas are put together on paper—based on number of employees or on profits—the actual response will be greatly influenced by the previous giving habits of the corporation.

Corporate giving formulas help organizations establish requests that are equitable, but experienced fund raisers know that corporate philanthropy is not perfect and that some corporations are just going to be more generous than others.

There are ways to glean information about the giving habits of corporations. Many large companies publish annual reports that review their activities in the area of social responsibility and include a report on their contributions. To obtain a copy, a letter or telephone call to the company is generally all that is necessary. Annual reports of charitable organizations frequently list their major donors.

Rating Method

One of the simplest and most widely used approaches to determining the amount to be requested of corporations is through the establishment of a rating or prospect evaluation committee.

Basically this involves gathering together a small group of well-informed volunteers—bankers, brokers, insurance agents, and other knowledgeable businesspeople—to review each corporate account that is to be solicited and establish a request or objective for that corporation. Using their knowledge about the profit structures of the companies, these people rate the companies according to their size and ability to give. Typically, this is accomplished by establishing an objective for the 10 potentially largest gifts first and then relating the others to them. The rating will take into account the profitability of the company as well as the number of employees it has in the community.

This is not a precise method, but over the years it has proved to be highly effective in setting goals for corporations. Its weakness, if any, is the fact that if an executive asks how the amount requested was determined, there is no objective, persuasive answer. The organization can simply explain that it was the judgment of a knowledgeable group of the corporate executive's peers that the amount was fair in relation to the amount requested of other corporations.

Requests Based on Employee Formula

Another method for determining the amount of giving by corporations is to base requests on the relative number of employees in the various companies. This method, in effect, bases its request upon the relative responsibility the company has to the community as measured by employee size.

Under this method, the soliciting organization determines by telephone call or census letter the number of employees in each of the major companies to be solicited. After this information has been determined, the total number of employees in the major companies is tallied. Once the goal has been broken down by divisions in the campaign, it is a relatively simple matter to determine what the amount of gift per employee should be in order to achieve the division goal.

> The Department of Labor sent a questionnaire to business firms asking them to report the number of employees broken down by age and sex.
>
> One company responded: "Very few; alcoholism is a much more serious problem."

Let us assume, as shown in Table 11-1, that the census has determined that there are 2,065 employees in all the major firms. A division goal of $41,300 has been established. In order to ensure that the division goal will be achieved, the organization must have a 20 percent markup or override. A simple arithmetic computation determines that if the corporate requests are based upon $25 per employee, the total amount of the individual firm goals would be $51,625, which covers the organization's need for a minimum of $41,300 from the division plus the 20 percent markup.

Table 11-1. Employee formula for determining requests.

Name of Company	Number of Employees	Amount of Corporate Gift Needed per Employee	Corporate Request
Allied Finance	25	$25	$ 625
Brand Dry Goods	55	25	1,375
Crawford Wholesale	75	25	1,875
First National Bank	125	25	3,125
Cart Insurance	525	25	13,125
Hobart Manufacturing	1,260	25	31,500
Total	2,065		$51,625

The advantages of this system of goal determination are that it is relatively simple and easy to administer and it is easily understood by volunteers and corporate executives. On the surface it appears to be equitable because all companies are being asked to give on the same basis.

The disadvantages of this method of goal setting are that not all corporations are the same. As pointed out, they differ widely in their ability to give on the basis of profits, and there is wide variation in the profitability per employee among companies. From this point of view the formula is less desirable. It is also true that not all companies are willing to disclose the number of employees.

Employees by Trade Classification

In order to overcome the obvious weakness in the preceding method, a somewhat different system may be used. If all companies are placed in broad trade classifications, the wide variations between companies according to profitability can be eliminated, at least in a general way. It is then possible to vary the amounts asked of the various companies according to the employee count and company trade classification. In other words, banks may be asked for $50 per employee and manufacturing industry for $15 per employee.

This method of goal setting, illustrated in Table 11-2, has the advantage of basing requests on like kinds of companies with like kinds of problems and, in general, with proportionate employee forces. In other words, the assumption is that banks, for example, will require a proportionate number of employees to generate proportionate profits.

The weakness of the program is that banks, too, differ in the number and kinds of services they offer to the customer, and their profit structure is often quite different depending on their size. However, this method is more acceptable to most companies than the employee formula regardless of type of industry. It also eliminates to some degree the wide difference that exists in profitability between types of industry.

Table 11-2. **Assessing requests by trade classification.**

Industry Group and Company	Amount of Corporate Gift per Employee	Number of Employees	Amount of Corporate Request
Banks			
Commercial Bank	$50	250	$12,500
First Bank	50	600	30,000
Old Second Bank	50	75	3,750
Retail			
Apex Dept. Store	25	175	4,375
Emporium	25	450	11,250
Quality Dept. Store	25	90	2,250
Manufacturing			
Reed Manufacturing	15	200	3,000
Major Controls	15	1,000	15,000
Widget Manufacturing	15	60	900

Table 11-3. Assessing requests by trade group averages.

Trade Group—Banks	Number of Employees	Amount of Gift	Corporate Gift per Employee
First National	500	$100,000	$200
Commercial	75	7,500	100
Security	50	3,750	75
Continental	200	30,000	150
American	275	48,125	175
Western	125	7,500	60
First State	90	8,100	90
Total	1,315	$204,975	$155 average

Another difficulty with this system is that if an organization's campaign is annual it may build in inequities between companies and trade groups over the years rather than eliminating them. Still another problem is that there is no exact method to determine the ratio of requests among the various trade groups. For example, who is to determine that a bank should give $50 per employee and a manufacturing company $15 per employee?

Trade Group Average

A variation of the trade group method is the trade group average. Here companies are grouped by trade and the amount given the previous year is listed, along with the number of employees. The amounts of the gifts are totaled and the results divided by the total number of employees. This gives an "average" corporate gift per employee for the trade group.

In the formula shown in Table 11-3, the trade group average for all banks is $155 per employee. In this situation, companies below the trade group average are asked to move toward the average by taking a major step. First State Bank, for example, would be asked to move up from $90 per employee toward the $155 average for the group. Companies that are at or above the trade group average would be asked to give the percentage increase in the campaign goal. If the goal were increased 10 percent, for example, American Bank would be asked for a 10 percent increase, or a total of $52,937.

This type of formula assumes that like kinds of companies have like kinds of responsibilities and that the number of employees is a relatively good measure of ability to give and of community responsibility. It has the advantage of being a relatively simple formula that is easily understood, and it can be devised without having to get corporate profit figures.

Trade Groups and Profitability

A further refinement and a fairly sophisticated one that attempts to answer these objectives relies on both the number of employees and the profitability factor. Here again, all companies are first put in trade groups. A convenient way of doing this is to use the Standard Industrialization Classification, available from the U.S. Department of Commerce. Every company is classified by the Department of Commerce according to its major type of business activity. The listing may have far more groups than the average campaign wants to utilize, but it can be combined into broader categories.

Next, a determination of the profitability per employee will help establish the relative relationship that each industry group should have to the other. If, for example, one industry group makes an annual profit of $1,000 per employee (its profit divided by the number of employees) and another industry group makes $5,000 profit per employee, it can be assumed that the corporate gift formula should ask the companies in the more profitable trade group to give five times as much as the less profitable group.

As can be seen from Table 11-4, there is wide variation in the profitability of companies with respect to the number of people they employ. Accordingly, a corporate gift formula taking this into account will more fairly base the request both on number of employees (community responsibility) and on profits (ability to give). The formula can set the corporate gift guidelines so that they reflect the differences in profitability. Using one of the above classifications as a base, the relationship of one trade group to another can be easily determined by dividing the profitability per employee for the base trade group into all others.

Let us assume that the services and retail firms make a profit of approximately $1,400 per employee and the financial institutions, $6,500 per employee. Under these circumstances, it would be appropriate to ask financial organizations (banks, savings and loans, and so on) to give 337 percent more than retail stores or $43 compared with $10 for retailers, based on profitability per employee. Since a high percentage of retail employees are part time, which reduces the profitability per employee, the gross number of employees—full and part time—should be used in computing the formula.

Thus if "retail" is established as the base trade group at a gift request of $10 per employee, companies in other trade groups would be rated as shown in Table 11-5. These broad trade groupings now reflect the differences in the ability of various types of industry to give, and the system overcomes part of the objection of using employee figures as a base. The formula will be accepted by most corporations because it, in

Table 11-4. Profit per employee by major industry group.

Industry Group	Corporate Net Income (billions)	Number of Employees	Profit per Employee
Construction	12.6	5,504,000	2,288
Manufacturing	101.4	20,637,000	4,913
Transportation	20.5	5,833,000	3,514
Wholesale	20.1	3,597,000	5,587
Retail (including part time)	22.6	15,109,000	1,495
Finance	32.6	5,038,000	6,470
Services	38.0	25,658,000	1,481

Source: U.S. Department of Commerce, 1977 data.

Table 11-5. Corporate request per employee by major trade group.

Trade Group	Profitability per Employee	Percent of Base Trade Group	Corporate Request per Employee (rounded)
Retail (base trade group)	$1,495	—	$10
Services	1,481	—	10
Construction	2,288	153	15
Transportation	3,514	235	23
Manufacturing	4,913	328	32
Wholesale	5,587	374	37
Finance	6,470	433	43

effect, reflects the average profitability of companies in a given trade. The only disadvantage is that even within a trade group companies do vary appreciably in their profitability.

Profits Only as a Basis

Another method of establishing corporate requests is to rely entirely upon the profitability of the companies as a reflection of their ability to give. In using this formula, the campaign organization must have gathered data about the pretax profits of a corporation. These figures are usually available through corporate annual reports and through brokerage houses. By totaling the pretax profits of the corporations in the group and dividing those into the amount that needs to be raised by the division, staff members can determine what percentage of profits needs to be asked of each of the corporations involved. If, for example, the total pretax profits of all the corporations in the group are $100,000,000 and the amount to be raised by the division is $100,000, then the amount required of each corporation is one-tenth of one percent of pretax profits. If the division goal is $1,000,000, the amount requested would be 1 percent of pretax profits, presumably payable over a period of years. This figure can be raised slightly to gain a built-in safety factor.

The method is illustrated in Table 11-6. Its advantages are that the formula can be easily demonstrated, the factors of profitability are commonly known, and the basis can be easily explained to top executives. Further, the requests are based entirely upon profitability. The formula automatically brings companies into perspective on the basis of their ability to give.

The problem with this method is that earnings of privately held companies are unknown and, therefore, cannot be included in the formula. In these cases, estimates must be made. Profits are cyclical—up some years and down in others—which can create a problem. Use of average profits over a three-year period can help eliminate this problem.

It is often difficult, too, to determine the profitability of banks since their public balance sheets do not disclose profits. Generally estimates for bank profits can be made within a range. Normally very large banks will realize profits of 0.6 percent of assets; medium and smaller banks, 1 percent. It is probably safe to estimate 0.8 percent.

Table 11-6. Requests based on corporate profitability.

Company	Pretax Profits	Times Formula for $100,000 Goal	Amount for $100,000 Goal	Times Formula for $1,000,000 Goal	Amount for $1,000,000 Goal
Com-N-Get-It Corporation	$ 1,000,000	.001	$ 1,000	.01	$ 10,000
ABC Corporation	4,000,000	.001	4,000	.01	40,000
Overall Corporation	12,000,000	.001	12,000	.01	120,000
Top-It Corporation	13,000,000	.001	13,000	.01	130,000
Excel Corporation	20,000,000	.001	20,000	.01	200,000
U-Got-It Corporation	50,000,000	.001	50,000	.01	500,000
Total	$100,000,000		$100,000		$1,000,000

Finally, many potential corporate contributors are only branch operations of the parent company, and the profits of a branch cannot be determined. This problem can be overcome in part by determining the total employment of the corporation and ascertaining what percentage branch employment is of the total. The resulting percentage is applied against the corporation's profits to determine the "branch profit," as shown below:

Corporate pretax profits		$50,000,000
Total corporate employment	10,000	
Local employment	1,000	
Local employment as a percentage of total employment	10%	
Estimated "profits" of local branch based on employment (10% of $50,000,000)		$5,000,000
Suggested gift of local branch—0.1% of (request formula) × $5,000,000 (estimated branch profits)		$5,000

This is not a scientific method, but it is usually accepted relatively well by top management. The assumption here, of course, is that the local branch of the company is earning, on average, the same as other branches in relation to the number of employees. This may or may not be true; the branch may be more profitable or it may be less so.

Return on Equity

Another potential way of measuring corporate goals is to use return on equity. This represents the return or profit a company makes as measured by the amount invested in the firm from capital surplus, reinvested earnings, and common stock issued.

Business Week annually produces data on the largest corporations giving a variety

Table 11-7. Relative profitability by trade group, based on 1982 return on equity.

Trade Group	Percent Return on Equity
Building materials	2.8
Real estate	6.3
Railroads	8.7
Retailing (nonfood)	10.4
Retailing (food)	12.9
Utilities	12.7
Banks	12.7
Electrical, electronics	15.1
Publishing, radio, TV	16.6
Personal care products	16.7
Beverages	17.2
Drugs	19.2
Tobacco	20.2

of information including return on equity both for individual companies and for trade groups. Return on equity figures are also easily obtained from the corporate listings produced by most large brokerage houses. Return on equity can be used in the rating system as part of the information the committee takes into account when setting requests for individual companies, or the campaign organization can set up a corporate formula using equity return by trade group.

Return on equity data can be used to show relative profitability by trade group, as shown in Table 11-7. The data are illustrative only. *Business Week* actually reports on 39 trade groups and these can be used in the rating process to develop a relative measure of profitability. Or, using the number of employees, the campaign staff can develop a formula similar to that shown using profits as a base.

An advantage of return on equity is that the figure is available for all publicly held companies and is considered by executives to be a good measure of profitability and, therefore, of ability to give.

Other

Some national organizations such as the United Way collect data from local affiliates on the average corporate gift per employee of major corporations. (For example, if a company with 2,000 employees gives a $20,000 gift, the corporate gift per employee is $20.) In these cases, the corporate gift request of a company branch may be based on the average corporate gift per employee in the company as a whole.

Which Formula Is Best?

Which corporate formula is best? Obviously that which works. Which is most likely to work? That depends greatly on the acceptability of the formula to the corporations themselves and on their conviction that the approach is fair. A most important consideration in this regard is the process used in adopting a corporate formula.

A man heard that his wife was having an affair with another man, wrote to the lover, and said:

"I understand you have been having an affair with my wife. Please meet me at my office Monday morning at 9:00 A.M. and we will discuss the arrangements that need to be made."

The alleged lover received the letter and responded:

"Thank you for your mimeographed letter, which I received today. Unfortunately I cannot come to your office on Monday as I will be out of town. However, I do want you to know that I will go along with whatever the group decides."

It is essential that top leadership of the campaign be given the opportunity to review one or more goal-setting methods and decide which is most equitable or salable in that community for that institution. Even so, organizations should be careful not to get leadership so lost in a maze of detail that it cannot come to a conclusion. It is best that the staff make a brief and general description of one or more suggested approaches and let leadership decide.

In approaching corporations, I frequently used the device of presenting several ways in which a company could determine its fair share, particularly with companies whose giving was on the low side. For example, I might portray what the company's gift would be if it were based on profitability, on the number of employees compared with similar companies, or on the giving of other major corporations. A company is not likely to reject all the formulas suggested, and it will see that a fair attempt has been made to establish an objective request.

12

SOLICITING THE WEALTHY

An essential element in the success of any campaign is a plan to solicit major individual gifts from people of substance or wealth. Some of the most substantial gifts received by institutions come from people who have had a pleasant experience with the organization and who will respond generously. Large gifts from individuals can range from $1,000 to $1,000,000 or more if a proper approach is made.

IDENTIFYING PROSPECTS

An initial problem is to identify these prospects. Most institutions can readily recognize wealthy people whose prominent activities or reputations make them highly visible. However, there are many people of considerable wealth who may not be well known.

During World War II, I was heavily involved in raising funds for war-related causes—war relief, USO, and prisoners of war. A section leader who was working in the small business division came to our staff and reported that one of her small business prospects appeared to be living in dire poverty. Instead of asking the man for money, she suggested we see what we could do to help him. We called family services and asked the agency to look into the situation.

The next day the same volunteer was on the platform for an appearance by Dorothy Lamour in selling war bonds. The volunteer looked into the crowd and spotted her poor little businessman in the front row. Can you imagine her shock when the "poverty-stricken" gentleman stepped up on the platform and bought $150,000 worth of war bonds?

The moral of the story is that wealth is conspicuous in some and concealed in others. Many small businesses are very successful, but because they are privately held and not particularly large, they are never thought of as potential big gifts prospects.

Recently I talked to two business partners who had given the entire firm to their employees through a special trust. They reasoned that they didn't need the money and that the company had been successful as much because of the efforts of loyal employees as of their own. The company was worth $40 million—and not a word had ever been printed about it in the press.

The identification of potential large givers demands special alertness on the part of campaign or development staff, who must utilize all the contacts they can through their volunteer structures. Certainly a review of country club lists, memberships in civic organizations, managements and boards of major corporations, and lists of contributors to other organizations will assist in putting a prospect list of this kind together. But there is no substitute for spending time reviewing the names of possible prospects with knowledgeable volunteers who are in a position to know about people of substantial wealth. Usually the review of a prospect list will trigger other names from knowledgeable campaign volunteers.

Some years ago, while conducting a campaign for a religious organization, I found that the prospect list had very few names that might be expected to give substantial amounts of money. After giving this matter some thought, I asked all the members of our large gifts solicitation committee to complete a form listing the people they thought were capable of giving gifts of $2,500 or more. It took a good deal of pushing to get the completed forms returned, and there was considerable duplication, but the resulting prospect list yielded gifts ranging from $2,500 to $250,000. Many of the givers had been unknown to the institution. As we reviewed the list with our special gifts rating and evaluation committee, new names kept surfacing as one name triggered another.

Time can be spent productively during the year and between campaigns by reviewing organizational lists of potential prospects with knowledgeable volunteers—bankers, insurance executives, brokers, and corporate executives. Although many volunteers are constrained for professional reasons from giving information about a person's wealth, they frequently can indicate whether a person is a big gifts prospect, and the organization can take it from there.

ASSIGNMENT

The solicitation of wealthy individuals involves the same basic procedures that work well in making calls on corporations. Here again, personal and business relationships are extremely important. All of us have someone who has our ear, who acts as our confidant, or to whom we listen and turn for advice. Good campaigning dictates that a development director, through his or her volunteers, learn who these contacts are and then make assignments accordingly. This is, as a matter of fact, the most important part of the campaign preparation, since it will make the solicitation much easier. I have seen many organizations flounder and then have to reassign cards for resolicitation because they failed to make the correct prospect assignment initially. Resolicitation is never as productive as making the approach correctly in the first place. Special cultivation meetings similar to those used in a corporate setting are also helpful in presenting the organization's needs.

PRESENTING THE CAMPAIGN CASE

Presenting the case for support to a wealthy individual is similar in many respects to presenting the case to corporations. Many wealthy prospects will have the same interests as corporate executives. As a matter of fact, many will be top corporate executives; others will be wealthy individuals who are retired or who live on investment income entirely.

However, it is wise to individualize the case presentation and, if the prospect's particular philanthropic interests are known, to pitch the case accordingly. A college or university, for example, might stress a program in business, science, or medicine if it knows one of these is of interest to a prospect.

Always solicit the most generous and dependable contributors first. Leadership gifts set the pattern for others and serve as an example for others to follow in making the campaign a success. Most contributors want to know what their share of a program is. On a confidential basis potential contributors can be told what some of the other large gifts have been, whether by name of contributor or only by amount. This gives the prospect an idea of where he or she fits into the campaign and what type of gift might be expected.

It is helpful to point out any tax implications of recent legislation that might benefit the contributor, so that the prospect can judge the tax advantages that might accompany a gift. However, very few people give generously for tax purposes only. The key is motivation, and therefore the case presentation, the personal call, and the direct involvement of the prospect will be the prime factors in motivating him or her to give. People who want only tax savings have other ways of accomplishing this objective through various tax shelters—and in my experience very few of them are generous to philanthropy. If the motivation is not there, people will not give—tax savings or no tax savings.

A conscience-stricken taxpayer wrote a letter to the Internal Revenue Service as follows:

"Gentlemen:

The income tax report I filed with you was wrong. It has been bothering me very much, so much that I can't sleep at night. So, enclosed find a check for $100.

Sincerely,
John Taxpayer

P.S. And if I still can't sleep, I'll send you a check for the other half."

The formal case presentation may ask the giver to consider funding a specific project for a definite amount or may present the giver with a list of projects, all of which are needed by the institution and which he or she could afford. The case presentation is similar to the one used for universities (see Figure 9-3 in Chapter 9) with variations to accommodate an appeal to individuals. The case presentation should also point out the period over which the pledge can be paid; this is important in helping contributors make a decision because they can fit the payment plans into a schedule, making allowance for other pledges they have made. The longer the payment period, the more feasible and more potentially generous a pledge will be, since conflicts with previous pledge commitments will be minimized.

Many organizations can present specific projects that the individual may be interested in supporting and that he or she can be identified with. Building programs present natural opportunities for this kind of giving. A person might be interested in funding a new gymnasium, physical sciences building, chapel, or any other of a variety of facilities that can be specified concretely and costed out.

It is also possible to present proposals to help the institution fund ongoing programs. For example, a donor may choose to endow a specially designated professorship, fund a chair in a symphony orchestra, or sponsor a scholarship in his or her name. Only the imagination of the soliciting organization restricts the possibilties for giving.

GUIDES TO GIVING

It has been pointed out that motivation is the principal factor in giving. However, recognition is also an important incentive. Specially designated gifts are one way of giving this recognition. However, not all people are able to make gifts of such proportions as to finance an entire program or facility. In these cases, a donor classification system should be used with prospective givers that divides them into categories for special recognition in the organization's annual report or on special plaques installed in the institution. Some of the names commonly associated with this kind of recognition are the following:

Founders	Dean's Club	Chairpersons
Major benefactors	Builders	Century Club
Benefactors	Patrons	$500 Club
Donors	Members	$1,000 Club
Sponsors	Fellows	$10,000 Club
Guarantors	Sustaining fellows	
President's Circle	Sustaining members	

The presentation to the prospective donor should also stress special kinds of gifts that could be made. Cash payments, of course, are obvious, but there are many cases where an individual may find it profitable to give appreciated securities and thereby obtain a tax deduction and also escape the capital gains tax. Gifts of appreciated real property are also potential sources of income.

Unless potential contributors receive some suggestions, it is difficult for them to know what they should give. This can be accomplished by suggesting a specific amount in the written request, as determined in the rating process, or by preparing a guide based on income. Guides for giving have been used extensively by United Ways for many years for executive and employee solicitation. A further discussion of giving guides is included in Chapter 19.

THE COST OF A GIFT

Recent legislation has reduced the income tax rates for wealthy individuals and thereby "increased the cost" of making a gift. The higher the tax rate, the more the government assumes through the charitable deduction, and the less the cost to the contributor. A wealthy individual in the 70 percent tax bracket may make a gift at a net cost of only 30 percent. With a tax rate of 50 percent, the cost to the individual is 50 percent. State income tax rates are also a factor. As mentioned earlier, the gift of securities or real property is often an excellent vehicle for a major gift because the income escapes the capital gains tax and the giver still obtains a maximum charitable deduction.

There has been much debate as to whether or not the reduction in income tax rates will result in decreases in giving by major givers. Lower tax rates do increase the net cost of a gift, but they also mean that contributors have more discretionary money to spend. In my opinion, the decrease in tax rates will undoubtedly cause some to reduce their gifts, but if the motivation is there, the desire of the individual to be generous to an institution may overcome some of the differential in the rates. Charitable donors know that "the gift without the giver is bare."

13

SOLICITING FOUNDATIONS

The importance of foundations to a successful campaign will differ widely from community to community and from organization to organization. Some communities have a number of foundations with substantial assets that represent tremendous sources of potential income for nonprofit organizations. Other communities have virtually none. Even when local foundations do not exist, there are a number of national foundations that offer possible sources of funding depending on the nature of the requesting organization and its program.

It is important to recognize that no rule applies universally to soliciting foundations. Because they represent vehicles for giving by individuals or families, of whom some are living and others deceased, the purposes and interests of the foundations will differ as widely as the interests of those who founded them. For this reason, research is an essential factor in the successful solicitation of foundations and trusts. There is no point in making a proposal to a foundation for a program in which it has no interest. Not only is it wasted time for the soliciting organization, but it will get little or no attention at the foundation level.

WHERE TO START

The first step in the successful solicitation of foundations and trusts is, of course, to identify those that exist in your particular area or that, even though out of your geographic area, might consider a request from your organization. This can be done in a variety of ways. Since all foundations must complete a financial statement for the Internal Revenue Service, the federal government has an up-to-date report on every foundation in the United States. Many states have taken these reports and compiled them into a foundation directory that can be used by nonprofit organizations. The National

Council of Foundations can inform you whether directories of this kind exist in your state. Another organization, The Foundation Center, 888 Seventh Avenue, New York, NY 10016, publishes a directory giving pertinent information on all foundations, including a list of foundations in each state and city. Trust departments and banks are also helpful in identifying foundations and trusts that might be potential donors.

Once a list of prospects has been obtained, you will need to determine whether they are potential donors for the kind of program your institution represents. All the larger foundations and most of the smaller ones have established written policies or guidelines that define their areas of interest and outline the information they require before considering a grant. This information can be obtained by a call to the foundation office.

PREPARING THE PRESENTATION

As pointed out, most of the major foundations will provide applying organizations with a list of items they would like to have. This may include:

1. A statement of the purpose of the grant: What is the problem to be addressed and how does the program intend to resolve it?
2. Specifics of the program.
3. Budget information—cost of the program, amount sought from foundations and why, amount sought from other sources.
4. How the program will be financed later.
5. How the effectiveness of the program will be evaluated.
6. A brief history of the organization.
7. Necessary IRS exemption letter.
8. Names and experience of major staff members.
9. A list of directors of the applying organization.

It is important to recognize that even though all this information may be required, it need not be prepared in exactly the sequence listed by the foundation. As a matter of fact, it is important to remember that the initial impression made by your written presentation will go a long way toward determining whether you will receive a grant. Starting the presentation by a long and laborious history may be the worst thing to do.

Getting the Right Person's Attention

In preparing presentations through the years, I have always worked on the principle that it is best to get the immediate attention of the staff person or trustee who is going to be reading the presentation. This can be accomplished with a succinct opening paragraph stating the problem facing the community or organization in question, followed by a description of the program that the institution plans, how it will address the problem, and how the program will be carried out in terms of structure and staff. Other information such as history, IRS exemption letter, and so on, can be included later or attached as appendixes.

Consider, for example, these two entirely different approaches in the first paragraph of a proposal requesting a foundation grant:

Proposal 1

Four years ago a number of organizations came together at the invitation of Wilbur Hines to discuss what might be done about the growing problem of drug abuse in our community. After an initial meeting, a number of subcommittees were appointed representing parents, teachers, police, and social agencies to discuss the problem further and come up with a concrete program. After a full year's work, an organization representing the various groups has been recommended and is ready to adopt a constructive program. Foundation funds are greatly needed to make possible the formation of the organization and the implementation of its program.

Proposal 2

Drug abuse is the most important single health problem in our community today. Not only is the use of drugs harmful to the individual, but drug use is the single most important cause of the battering of women and the physical abuse of children. Chemical substances—both alcohol and hard drugs—cause more automobile accidents than any other factor. According to police records, there is a direct relationship between the use of chemical substances and crimes of all types, including violent crimes. Drug users must steal and often abuse to get funds to maintain their habit. Alcohol and other drugs are principal reasons for the poor performance and decreasing grades of students. Drug abuse is no longer a minor problem; it is a problem of major proportion in our society and it is expensive. Bold and positive programs are needed to deal with its cause and prevention.

Although there is technically nothing wrong with the first proposal, it is not constructed to get the immediate attention of the foundation staff person or trustee. The reader cannot help but be alert to the problem and the subsequent request after reading the introductory paragraph to the second proposal.

Past Trends

A factor that should not be overlooked by an applying institution is that past grant-making trends are a helpful guide in determining how a foundation request might be presented. Reading the annual report or conversing with other institutions will give you an idea of what the foundation might fund. Since most programs have more than one facet, it is possible to emphasize those portions that may be of particular interest to the foundation in light of its past grant-making experience. If the program is multifaceted and the foundation's interests are, say, in the field of health, the organization can emphasize the health-related portions of the proposals. Similarly, it may be advantageous for the applying organization to emphasize the educational, research, or demonstration aspects of a program.

Many foundations prefer that the detailed proposal be preceded by a synopsis or summary that briefly outlines the problems and the project being presented.

Monsignor Murphy was getting old and a little forgetful. After 40 years of weekly sermons he noticed that his congregation was not very attentive. He approached a young pastor who was having great success in attracting new parishioners because his sermons were so interesting.

"Father," the Monsignor asked, "how is it that you give sermons that are so interesting to the congregation?"

"Well, Monsignor," the young pastor responded, "I always try to say something at the very beginning to get the congregation's attention."

"Can you give me an example?"

"Well," said the priest, "last Sunday I started as follows: 'I'm in love. (*pause*) I'm in love with a beautiful woman. (*pause*) I'm in love with the Blessed Mary.'"

The Monsignor thought this was an excellent idea and the following Sunday mounted the pulpit and said:

"I'm in love." There was an immediate reaction from the congregation and all ears were attentive.

"I'm in love with a beautiful woman." The congregation was now really awake. What could the elderly Monsignor be up to? All eagerly waited for him to disclose this mysterious announcement.

The Monsignor looked at the congregation and a confused look spread over his face. Puzzled, he paused and passed his hand slowly over his brow.

"Now what was that woman's name anyhow?"

THE OVERALL APPROACH

Foundations differ in the way they like to be approached with respect to a grant request. Some of the very large foundations have multiple staff and are in a position to acknowledge a fairly high percentage of the requests for contributions. However, this is an unusual situation and most foundations do not have sufficient resources to acknowledge more than a small percentage of requests.

For this reason it is important that proper steps be taken in approaching the foundation. Timing is often critical. Foundations meet at various times of the year, and only the largest hold monthly meetings. Therefore, it is important to determine when the application should be sent and when it is likely to be reviewed. A call to the foundation office or use of a foundation directory should provide this information.

The next important step is research. Call the foundation office and ask for a copy of its most recent annual report as well as its guidelines for making an application. (See Appendix B.) After reviewing the annual report and some of the larger grants that were made, make contact with the people responsible for foundation cultivation in several of those institutions that received grants. Ask them how they approached the foundation and what steps they took that they felt were helpful. Most institutions are willing to be helpful in this regard.

A follow-up call to the executive of the foundation or a designated staff person indicating, in summary form, the problem your organization is addressing and the kind of program it seeks to have funded will give you a preliminary idea of whether the project will be given reasonable consideration. If the program is not in the foundation's area of interest, or not consistent with its policies, the foundation staff will generally inform you so you need not go through a lot of wasted motion. On the other hand, if you have done your homework well, your request should qualify for consideration, and the foundation staff will tell you to send in a written proposal for review.

Because of the number of requests received, it is not possible for foundations to interview representatives of every applying institution; therefore, the written proposal is especially important. However, when the foundation staff or individual trustees have displayed initial interest, representatives of the applying organization may be invited for an interview to explain the proposed project further. In these situations, very few grants are made solely because of personal relationships; but certainly these relationships, if they are good, will never hurt and can go a long way in obtaining a grant, especially with the smaller foundations. Therefore, provided the program is a worthy one, the relationship between the staff of the applying institution and the foundation staff and the relationship of the organization's board members to the trustees of the foundation can be important factors.

THE DECISION-MAKING PROCESS

Decision-making procedures on grants differ widely among foundations. Major foundations have trained staff, some of whom may be specialists in certain areas such as education, health, human services, and the arts. Normally, the staff will make a quick review of the application to determine whether it complies with the policies of the foundation and its areas of interest. If it does not, the application will be quickly rejected. If the application appears to meet policy requirements, it will be assigned to a staff person who will then make a detailed review of the application itself. If the proposal is a particularly complicated one, the staff member may ask for a personal presentation and explanation.

Taking into account the foundation's policies and guidelines, the amount of money available, and the amount of the grant request, the staff person will then make a recommendation to the board of trustees for consideration. The board will review the recommendation and again, guided by the foundation's policies and financial resources, make a decision on whether to approve the grant.

Smaller foundations do not have such staff services. Generally it is up to the president and individual trustees to review the proposals and make a decision on the grant. Smaller foundations are generally more narrow in interest and more parochial in their grant-making policies, and many of them will be guided by family interests in philanthropy.

Many of the better-organized foundations do recognize that some institutions lack the skills necessary to make an adequate presentation of their program. As a result, they may reach out to institutions of this kind and give them help. Occasionally foundation staff, if they are particularly impressed with a need and a potential program, may meet with the applying institution and make helpful suggestions for polishing a presentation. This is not an excuse for shoddy work—nor should it permit applying organizations to be complacent about doing their own work—but it does illustrate that many foundations want to be helpful to the "little guy."

Although individual board members generally will not become involved in specific projects, the interests of these members, as they are reflected in foundation policies, are important. Foundations differ widely, however, in their reaction to approaches made to individual board members for grant requests. In the larger and more sophisticated foundations, the inquiring institution will generally be turned away with the suggestion that the proposal be made to staff. In foundations that do not have highly specialized staff, approaches to individual foundation trustees may be helpful. Just as in real estate the important thing is location, location, location, so in foundation cultivation the important thing is research, research, research. Only research will determine what the proper approach should be.

FAVORABLE AND UNFAVORABLE FACTORS IN GETTING GRANTS

In visiting with executives of some of the larger foundations, I have learned that a variety of factors influence positive or negative grant decisions.

Positive Factors

- The program presented must be truly designed to meet an urgent community need.
- The organization must have done its homework and developed a well-conceived program that seems to have a reasonable chance of success.
- The program must be truly innovative and creative, not just a rehash or warming-over of old programs. Sometimes organizations will try to disguise old programs by giving them a facelift, but most foundation people are smart enough to recognize new wine in old bottles.
- Foundations are impressed by low management costs and high value for the services rendered. Most foundations feel they cannot afford to support high-cost programs.
- Foundations like proposals that have focused interests and that clearly delineate a problem as well as the program being proposed as a possible solution.
- Foundations tend to react positively to proposals that are proactive rather than reactive. They like proposals that anticipate a problem and come up with innovative solutions rather than merely reacting to critical situations.
- An institution is best served if it gives a history of the problem rather than a history of the organization requesting the grant.

Negative Factors

- Foundation executives are turned off by a lack of candor—organizations that pretend they need money and really don't, or organizations that pretend they know what they are doing and really don't.
- Some foundations are turned off by expensive packaging of proposals and unnecessary paperwork.
- Some foundations are not particularly impressed by awards given them for grants, whereas others do appreciate it.
- Foundations react unfavorably to what appear to be unrealistic expectations. An institution makes a mistake if it tries to present itself as having all the answers to a serious problem. This does not mean, however, that the applying organization should not put its best foot forward and present itself in a positive way.
- More detailed and sophisticated presentations do not necessarily have a greater chance of being accepted. Many foundations dislike having to wade through a lot of jargon to find out what it is the institution wants to do. Good foundation staff will be more impressed with conciseness and directness and clearness of program thinking than a great deal of rhetoric.

Martin was an expert in space aviation. He served as a consultant to a number of industries and was frequently invited to speak to the engineering classes of various colleges and universities. He had a driver by the name of Smith who would take him to the various colleges for his lectures.

One day after his lecture had been completed Smith was driving Martin back home and remarked, "You know, I've heard that lecture of yours so often that I think I could give it myself."

"Well, I know you've heard it a lot," Martin said, "but I really doubt that you could give it. What do you know about space aviation?"

As they proceeded, they talked about the probability of Smith delivering Martin's lecture and a $25 bet was arranged: At the next college Smith would represent himself as Martin, the expert on space aviation, and give his speech for him. Martin would take the driver's place in the audience to see how well he did.

On the day of the lecture, Smith approached the podium and gave Martin's presentation in a most persuasive and authoritative way. When he completed his talk, he was greeted with an enthusiastic round of applause by the engineering students in the audience. He was so overwhelmed with his success that he made a gross mistake. Smith said, "Are they any questions?"

A student in the front row raised his hand and asked a very difficult question about a factor of lift.

Smith was totally overcome at this point, but suddenly gathered his resources and said, "What class are you in?"

"I'm a senior," the student responded.

"You mean to tell me you're a senior in engineering and you don't even know the answer to that question?" Smith said. "Why just to show you how simple that is I'm going to ask my driver out there in the audience to answer it."

IMPORTANT CONSIDERATIONS IN OBTAINING FOUNDATION GRANTS

Although foundation grants are extremely helpful in getting new plans started and in funding innovative programs, there are some important factors in foundation funding that applying institutions need to recognize.

- Foundation grants are frequently short term—one to three years—after which they terminate. This means that the institution must have made plans to assume the financial obligation of the program at the end of the period. Occasionally foundations will consider funding a second phase of a program, but this is fairly unusual.
- Foundations do not like to be asked to fund debts of institutions and generally will not consider doing so. Nor do foundations like to fund financial situations that are critical because of ill-considered action taken by an organization's board. Many an organization has embarked on new programs or capital expansion without giving careful thought to future costs and realistic sources of funding. Such programs show lack of good management and board control and do not make a favorable impression with foundation personnel.
- Foundations generally do not like to be asked to assume financial responsibility for programs that have been defunded by some other financing group, such as the government. Also, many foundations will not make grants for general annual operating expenses except to federated drives. Some foundations will not consider making gifts for capital purpose or will restrict the amount they do give.

Despite these problems, many foundations work on the principle that their purpose is primarily innovative. They do not expect all projects to succeed and are aware that many involve ideas and techniques that have not been tried before.

TYPES OF GRANTS

Foundation grants vary in amount and purpose. They can be given in several different forms.

Matching Grants

A growing practice among foundations, as well as some corporations, is to make grants on a matching basis. In this situation, the foundation or corporation agrees to match dollar for dollar, or on some other type of basis, the gifts that are raised by the institution in its campaign. Such a program gives the organization an incentive to do a thorough job of organization and campaigning, since every gift received will be doubled in amount. The matching gift program also provides a powerful incentive for alumni and other contributors to make gifts because they know they will be maximizing their contribution when they do so.

Challenge Gifts

Challenge gifts are similar to matching gifts except that there are certain conditions attached. Frequently the foundation will specify that it will make a contribution on the condition that the institution raises a certain amount of money from other sources. If, for example, an organization wants to raise $5,000,000, the foundation may decide to give it $200,000 conditional upon the organization raising at least $4,800,000 from other sources. This gives the organization an incentive to mount a strenuous campaign and also serves as a powerful stimulus for givers to make their gifts generous ones.

A matching gift or challenge gift program may also be made on the basis of the foundation matching all the "new money" raised in the campaign. In this case the organization has a powerful sales tool for appealing to new givers and inducing former givers to increase their gifts.

Program-Related Investments (PRIs)

Although private foundations are generally known for their direct financial grants to nonprofit organizations, a new method of assisting such organizations and of meeting pressing community needs has developed in recent years. The 1969 Tax Reform Act permits foundations to make program-related investments in areas of social need provided that the program meets certain requirements.

Under present Internal Revenue Service regulations, foundations can make investments comparable to those made by institutional investors to tax-exempt or profit-making organizations or to individuals provided that the investment objective relates to religion, science, literature, education, amateur sports, the prevention of cruelty to animals or children, the promotion of health, or any other legitimate charitable activity. The requirement is satisfied if the investment significantly furthers the accomplishment of the foundation's tax-exempt activities. The investment cannot be made for the production of income or appreciation of property or for the development of profits, and it cannot be made for the purpose of influencing legislation or participating in political campaigns. The foundation can make loans to profit-making or nonprofit-making organizations only if the purposes of the investments are compatible with its philanthropic objectives.

Under these circumstances, it is possible, for example, for a private foundation to make a loan to a profit-making company to assist the corporation in financing low-income housing in a blighted area or in attracting new industry to help reduce unemployment—provided these purposes are compatible with the foundation's objectives. It is also possible to make a program-related investment to a nonprofit organization at below-market interest rates if it will assist the nonprofit organization in instituting a new program, completing a building, or otherwise carrying out a useful social purpose. However, the nonprofit organization is expected to repay the loan. If it fails to do so, the loan will have to be considered a regular grant.

A foundation gains some benefit by making loans of this kind since their repayment replenishes the amount of funds available for future loans or grants. The foundation also gains some benefit with respect to the excise tax on its assets. An organization in the nonprofit field will want to explore this possibility when direct grants are not available and when the organization is in a position to repay the low-interest loan.

MONITORING AND EVALUATION

Most foundations require that an institution give a report at the end of the project describing what has been accomplished in relationship to the goals that were originally established. The institution may be asked to outline the criteria by which the program will be deemed successful. When large grants are made, some foundations will ask for interim financial and program reports describing what has been accomplished. If a program does not show that steady progress has been made in meeting objectives, the grant may be interrupted, reduced, or terminated.

14

SPECIAL CAMPAIGN MARKETS: SMALL BUSINESS, RESIDENTIAL, AND THE PROFESSIONS

A campaign chairman was once asked to describe the proper way of soliciting small businesses. "Soliciting small businesses is like feeding pablum to a baby," he replied. "Any way you do it, it's a mess."

Perhaps no group of prospects is as frustrating to the volunteer and professional campaigner as small businesses, which represent, in theory, a considerable potential but pose a difficult organizational problem for most campaigns.

SMALL BUSINESS SOLICITATION

Generally speaking, small businesses are those that employ fewer than 10 or, in larger communities, fewer than 25 employees. They may be proprietorships, partnerships, or small corporations. In most communities their numbers range from the hundreds well into the thousands so that the problem of contacting them is an enormous one. Nevertheless, U.S. Department of Labor data show that these small businesses, in total, often employ as many people as the largest corporations in a community, but they are dispersed over broad geographic areas.

Dun & Bradstreet reports that 68 percent of small businesses are corporations; 32 percent are proprietorships or partnerships. Some 41 percent have a sales volume of $500,000 or more, and 25 percent have sales of $100,000 or more. When first started, they average only 3.3 employees; after they are established, they average 7.2 employees.

Despite this fact, small business solicitation is still important to campaigns that must conduct a saturation solicitation in order to be successful. This includes United Ways and some major building programs. Even though small businesses may account for only a small percentage of campaign results, those results can spell the difference between success and failure. Thus it is not possible to ignore their potential totally.

Campaigns other than United Ways, however, are probably well advised to put most of their efforts elsewhere. Their campaigns will be more productive if they spend their time soliciting major corporations, foundations, executives, and the individually wealthy who are not connected with a firm. The effort required to take a census of small businesses, the enormous complement of personnel required to solicit them, and the amount of staff time involved will just not pay off for most institutions.

This is not to say that small businesses should be ignored entirely. Three smaller-scale approaches are suggested:

1. Conduct a mail campaign directed to small businesses.
2. Utilize a phone campaign (telemarketing) in order to reach these groups.
3. Isolate those small businesses that are the most profitable and that have a greater potential for gifts than the ma-and-pa grocery store, and solicit them personally or by individualized letter or phone solicitation. Such businesses may also be included in another division (for example, special gifts).

Geographic Organization

Organizations like the United Ways, which must solicit small businesses, can best do so by dividing the community into geographic areas by ward, census tract, or natural neighborhood. A complete census of all the firms in those areas is made and they are listed by geographic region down to the block level. The number of personnel required for the solicitation is estimated on the 7/7 principle previously described, and the appropriate number of solicitors and group and section chairpersons are recruited.

Because of the nature of small business, a "unit" approach is best conducted here by soliciting a gift from the owner of the company and asking the owner to make a solicitation of his or her employees. In companies with fewer than five employees, the campaign volunteer may ask the employer if he may solicit the employees himself.

Office Buildings and Shopping Centers

Many small businesses are located in office buildings. In these cases a chairperson is obtained for the building, and for each floor of the building he or she in turn recruits a chairperson responsible for soliciting all small businesses on that floor. When major companies are located on a floor, "stop" cards are prepared, informing the small business solicitor not to approach those companies because they are being covered by another division. When companies have 10 or more employees, a firm captain for the solicitation is named by the head of the company. Once the organization of the building is complete, a kickoff for all floor chairpersons and firm captains is held. A film is shown and solicitation instructions given. Figure 14-1 shows the organization of a typical small business division.

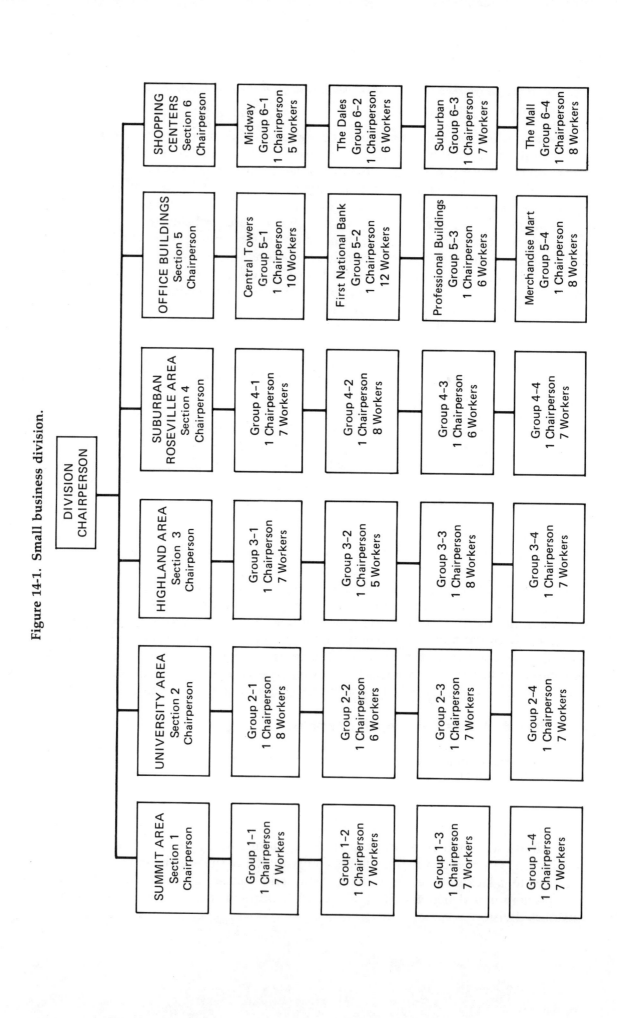

Figure 14-1. Small business division.

Shopping centers represent concentrated areas of small businesses—dress shops, restaurants, boutiques, and so on. Here the best approach is to get a chairperson for the shopping center, preferably someone from one of the major stores located there, who recruits other solicitors who in turn make contact with the individual businesses. Company chairpersons are obtained for those businesses with 10 or more employees. When all solicitors have been obtained, a training session is held to explain the campaign and its procedures.

Year-Round Cultivation

As pointed out previously, some small businesses, although rather obscure, are very profitable and the owners capable of making substantial gifts. The identification of such prospects, and their cultivation, is the year-round job of the staff. These companies should be cultivated in person, leaving the less responsive companies to a mass coverage by mail. It is also helpful to review small business lists with volunteers between campaign periods to identify those that have proved profitable and that deserve special attention through one of the other divisions. Again, keep in mind that, except for United Ways, most organizations will not be well served by an extensive investment of time and money in the solicitation of small businesses.

Future Trends

Wise development and campaign staff will not ignore small businesses entirely, because the number of large manufacturing corporations with masses of employees has been steadily decreasing. The increased use of robotics and automation will, in the future, seriously erode the contributions from large employee groups. More of our economic organization will rely on the service industries—most of which will be small businesses. Thus it is wise to keep small businesses in your campaign planning and to experiment with new techniques for reaching them.

Quotas

Since employee data are generally not available for small companies, a simple quota system is often helpful. Here the solicitor inquires concerning the number of employees and suggests a company gift based on a certain amount per employee, with some kind of minimum. A quota plan might suggest $10 per employee, for example, with a minimum company gift of $25. When gifts are available by trade classification—retail, wholesale, food service, and so on—the solicitor may use the trade group averages per employee and relate them to the particular firm's employee count. In cases where the company has given in prior years, a percent increase may be suggested.

With companies that have been identified as having substantial potential, an individual "rating" should be made by knowledgeable volunteers, and that company should be asked for a generous gift. Some arts organizations solicit such companies by offering a "package deal." In return for a minimum gift, the company receives a certain number of tickets to a concert, musical, or theater production.

Employee amounts can be suggested ranging from $.25 to $.50 per week, payable in one payment semiannually or quarterly on a direct-billing basis. If the employer is willing to provide payroll deduction, employee gifts become much easier. The number of deductions depends on the degree to which the proprietor is willing to cooperate. The longer the period of the payroll deduction, the better. One year is best.

RESIDENTIAL CAMPAIGNS

At one time many philanthropic organizations, particularly health organizations, considered the residential campaign a primary vehicle for developing support for the institution. A large cadre of volunteer women was available to serve as campaign solicitors and was willing to work on behalf of the agency. Organizations also saw the residential campaign as a prime way of conducting their educational programs. It provided a means of distributing material and offering word-of-mouth interpretation. This objective was a primary reason that the American Cancer Society and the American Heart Association refused for many years to participate in federated campaigns. They saw the residential program as a great opportunity to familiarize people with the "seven danger signals of cancer" or of appropriate health measures that should be taken to prevent heart diseases.

The climate for residential campaigning, however, has changed drastically in the last 10 to 15 years. Fully 50 percent of the women in the United States are now employed on a full-time or part-time basis outside the home and thus are not available to serve as campaign volunteers. In addition, the growing concern about crime in the streets has led many prospective contributors to refuse admission to volunteer solicitors for their favorite charity. Many apartment buildings and condominiums will not permit volunteer solicitors to conduct a campaign within their facilities; in fact, many make this a sales point to prospects considering a move into the facility.

These circumstances, together with the fact that residential gifts tend to be casual in amount, have resulted in disproportionately high fund-raising costs and disproportionately low campaign results. Philanthropic organizations have, therefore, recognized that their needs are better served by developing more specialized approaches to fund raising through the solicitation of large individual, corporate, and foundation gifts. For those institutions that are eligible to participate in federated United Way campaigns, membership has distinct advantages. Many have found that their educational purposes are better served through the combined campaign because they receive the cooperation of corporate management in informing employees about their programs.

Selective Approaches

Today it is generally better to resort to a selective type of residential campaign directed to higher-income sections of the city, to retired people who are able to make a reasonable contribution, and to those who work out of their own homes. The day of the door-to-door campaign is effectively over for the reasons previously mentioned.

Organizations planning to conduct residential campaigns can more appropriately do so by getting census tract data and focusing their attention on those areas of the

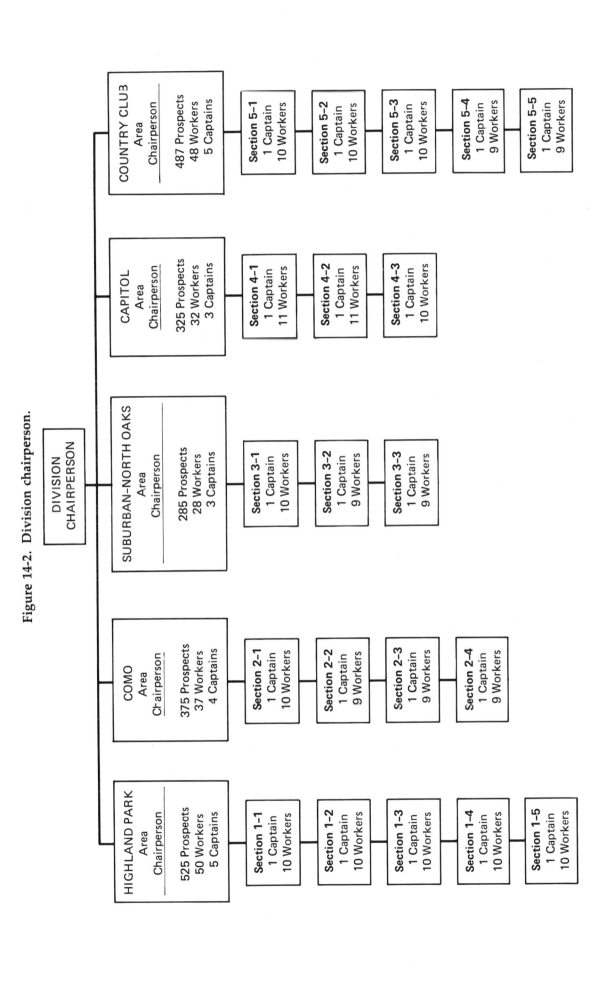

Figure 14-2. Division chairperson.

city with the highest income levels. In this way, available volunteers will be used more productively among prospects who are able to make reasonable contributions. However, smaller givers who have contributed in the past should not be ignored; the organization can give them an opportunity to contribute through mail solicitation, capitalizing on the low postal rates available to nonprofit organizations, or through telephone solicitation.

In residential campaigns, the community is generally divided into geographic areas by neighborhood, census tract, or ward, utilizing only the higher-potential income areas. Prospects are determined through past giving records, review of the city directory, or personal knowledge of campaign workers. The number of volunteers required is estimated according to the number of prospects in each area of the city. Generally speaking, a campaign volunteer will serve best if he or she is assigned no more than 10 to 15 persons to solicit on a residential basis. After the number of solicitors required is determined, a chairperson can be assigned to each area or zone and a captain chosen for each ten workers in that area. When the organization plan is complete, it might look like Figure 14-2.

Solicitor Training

It is essential in conducting a residential campaign that appropriate measures be taken to train solicitors. A centralized training session can be held if the campaign organization is not too large, or the training may be conducted in each neighborhood. Sessions may be held in the home of one of the captains or division chairpersons, again depending upon the size of the group involved. Staff from the soliciting organization and the residential chairperson should be in attendance. A visual presentation outlining the needs of the organization should be made and solicitors should be briefed in the appropriate way to approach their prospective donors and to deliver the sales presentation.

A timetable for completion of the job should be presented at the session and all solicitors urged to complete their calls at the earliest possible moment. Solicitors should be told whether the pledges are payable on a time basis or are being sought only in cash. Obviously, the longer the payment period, the larger the gifts can be; small gifts are expensive to bill and should be collected in cash if possible. Volunteers should be urged to clear any new prospects they know with the office before soliciting.

Volunteers should be given specially prepared envelopes so they can list each contribution on the outside by name, amount pledged, amount paid, and balance due. The completed envelopes are then sent to the section captains, who in turn report them to campaign headquarters for auditing. The central office and each captain must keep a listing indicating the contacts that have been made, the results, and any incompleted calls for follow-up by volunteers. Reasons for not giving should also be posted. If a person has moved, the card should be turned into the central office for reassignment to the area where the donor now resides.

Areas which cannot be successfully organized, or in which there are calls that have not been made, can be solicited by a phonathon of experienced volunteers or by telemarketing, described elsewhere in this book.

Although residential campaigning has declined in importance in recent years, it still represents potential for some organizations and can be conducted successfully if it is selectively organized. It generally does not amount to a major portion of campaign results, but the results obtained may often spell the difference between the success or failure of the total campaign. Its value as an educational tool is also significant. A useful refinement for many institutions is to set up a special-gifts solicitation within their residential program wherein all gifts of $100 or more, for example, are solicited by experienced volunteers carefully selected to conduct this type of campaign.

Finally, it should be remembered that there are still substantial gifts to be obtained in the residential campaign from people with independent incomes and from people who retire and can become generous supporters of the institution.

Telemarketing and Mail Solicitation

Organizations that find it impractical to build a large volunteer force can best solicit residential prospects through telemarketing. The use of telemarketing is described in the discussions of specialized campaigns (Chapters 15–19). Another method gaining popularity is the solicitation of all residential prospects by mail. Mail solicitation is most effective when the letters can be personalized and signed by a volunteer who knows the prospect.

SOLICITING THE PROFESSIONS

Another group that theoretically represents a considerable contribution potential are members of the professions—attorneys, physicians, and dentists. In some campaigns, architects, engineers, and certified public accountants may be added to the professional solicitation.

The approach to professional people will depend on the kind of organization conducting the solicitation. For hospitals, for example, physicians represent a rather natural giving market. Likewise, legal firms would have a natural interest in contributing to law schools; the firms might have only passing interest in other organizations.

Some of the approaches that have been used in soliciting the professions are summarized below. In my experience, the professions are difficult groups to solicit because there is no one easy approach. The most satisfactory solution is to experiment and refine, building on the techniques that best work for your organization.

Attorneys

More and more attorneys today work either in corporate practices or in group practices where they share the same office space and secretarial help. It is, therefore, advisable whenever possible to use these natural groupings for solicitation purposes. To all intents and purposes, law firms that are incorporated or that are partnerships can be approached in the same manner as any other corporation or firm, with a request made for a corporate gift or a gift from the partnership. This is a natural market for

United Ways and most organizations that are dependent upon corporate giving to a large extent to make their campaigns successful.

When attorneys share central services but remain essentially independent operators, the situation is more difficult. Sometimes it is possible to get one of those in the group to accept responsibility for soliciting his or her associates. However, the strong peer influences found in corporate situations do not normally operate in this kind of setting.

Attorneys who are single operators and are not associated with a law firm or a group practice must be solicited by mail, by telephone, or by individual assignment to others. Sometimes a letter from the local Bar Association, signed by the president or by a prominent member, will be sufficient to gain a response from these people. However, campaign statistics show that the number of givers is rather low among attorneys in this category.

The ideal way of soliciting attorneys in the larger firms is to assign them to businesspeople who utilize their services or who have social relationships with them. The most practical approach to the remaining prospects is to solicit through their peers or by mail.

Physicians

Most campaigners have found the solicitation of physicians particularly difficult. Although most are highly intelligent individuals, they are also extremely independent and, with some exceptions, do not seem to have developed a high sense of community responsibility. Physicians are able to achieve dramatic results in their daily work with individual patients. For this reason, perhaps, they do not often recognize the need for community agencies in serving people. Several approaches have been used with physicians with varying degrees of success.

The physicians on the staff of a hospital represent a very natural market for the hospital operating or building campaign. They have a personal stake in the institution and see their contribution as an investment to ensure that the hospital will have the necessary equipment and resources to enable them to do their jobs. Because of this, they are much more approachable in a hospital campaign than in other campaigns, and their average gift tends to be much more generous than to other causes in the community. The solicitation can be handled in hospitals the same as an employee or faculty campaign, with an overall chair and sufficient solicitors to contact all the other doctors. Staff meetings can be used for indoctrination.

Like attorneys, members of the medical profession often work in group practices or in corporate settings in which they are "employed" by the corporation. Some are members of a partnership. When this is the case, they can be approached in the same way as attorneys or any other corporation or partnership in the community, with a request for a corporate or partnership gift to the organization. With physicians who share office and secretarial space in the same building but are otherwise independent operators, one or more of the physicians may be asked to solicit his or her colleagues.

Another approach that has been used by some United Ways is to organize physicians according to hospital staff affiliation. In this situation, a chairperson for *each* hospital is obtained who accepts responsibility for recruiting others to help in the solicitation of colleagues, asking them to make generous contributions. Since most doctors have close associations with one another in a hospital setting, there is an affinity of interest, and this approach often works reasonably well.

In selecting a chairperson for this type of campaign, an internist or general practitioner is frequently the best choice, inasmuch as physicians tend to depend a great deal upon referrals for their practice. Internists and general practitioners are in a paramount position to make referrals to other physicians for surgical, X-ray, pediatrics, obstetrics, and other medical services. These natural referral relationships should be capitalized upon whether the campaign is organized by hospital or not.

When neither of these approaches is reasonable for an organization, the best solution is to organize a mail campaign if possible. Letters should be personalized and signed by a physician with whom the prospect has a personal or referral relationship. Time spent during the year reviewing a list to determine the best person to make the approach is time well spent indeed. Occasionally, the chairperson of the local medical society can be enrolled to send a letter of solicitation to the membership.

In approaching physicians, the case for support is considerably strengthened if the organization can show that its services in some way support or supplement the services of the physician. Doctors are very practical people and will tend to respond more generously when they see some tangible return on their investment.

Dentists

Even more difficult to approach in the professional field are dentists, since fewer share office space or have partnerships or corporate arrangements. Because of this, a mail approach is probably the best. When letters can be individualized from fellow dentists who make referrals, the response may be greater.

The president of a dental association may also be willing to send a letter to his or her professional colleagues. Even in this case, a committee of dentists is needed to follow up on the letter of solicitation because dentists frequently put letters aside, neglecting to reply to them.

Architects, Engineers, and CPAs

To all intents and purposes, architects, engineers, and CPAs can be solicited like any other corporation or partnership. They do not pose the same logistical and geographic problems as other professional groups since they do much of their work for business organizations. Thus it is fairly easy to find someone who does a good deal of business and has influence with these firms. Generally speaking, these groups—because they are similar to other business organizations—are easier to approach and are inclined to be more generous in their giving.

One device that can be used to stimulate all types of professional giving is the giving club. Professional people have a high degree of pride and often can be induced to make more generous gifts if they are included in a group that is recognized in the annual report of the organization. Such clubs are useful in stimulating gifts in the $100, $500, and $1,000 and over categories.

As can be seen from the foregoing, there is no simple and easy way of soliciting the professions. The task is to innovate and try new approaches. Those techniques that work should be continued; those that fail should be discarded and other approaches attempted. However, professional personnel are generally in higher-income groups and do represent a substantial potential market. A year-round program of interpretation is highly important. Explaining the benefits and services of the nonprofit organization can be done through individual mailings, bulletins, and personal visits if possible. Also, personal involvement in the organization is very helpful.

PART II

SPECIALIZED CAMPAIGNS

15

CAMPAIGNING FOR THE ARTS

Nearly every metropolitan area has one or more organizations in the arts that require public support. These include symphonies, chamber orchestras, opera companies, museums, theaters, choral groups, and dance groups.

Experience has shown that it is virtually impossible to support activities of this kind on a self-sustaining basis through the sale of tickets alone, and virtually all arts organizations seek subsidy through the solicitation of special prospects, corporations, and foundations. Symphonies, for example, will typically obtain 35 percent to 40 percent of their funds from ticket sales, with the balance coming from earnings, endowment, and public subscription.

TYPES OF FUND RAISING

In the arts, fund raising takes a variety of different forms.

1. *Annual campaign.* Most organizations will mount an annual campaign of some type in order to build general operating support. The campaign may be fairly limited or it may be quite broad, depending on the institution and the size of the budget.

2. *Special grants.* Arts organizations seek grants from corporations and foundations for specific purposes—for example, the sponsorship of a special concert for children or for an art fair.

3. *Women's activities.* Many arts organizations have women's associations that raise funds through an annual ball, the operation of a gift shop, or some other special activity.

4. *Capital endowment programs.* An increasing number of arts organizations are combining the need for new building with the need to create an endowment by conducting a capital endowment campaign. Even when endowment funds are not sought, capital needs are a very substantial and pressing problem for many organizations in the arts.

5. *Deferred-giving program.* Whether or not capital endowment campaigns are conducted, many arts organizations today have well-organized deferred-giving programs that seek to build an endowment, the income from which will enable them to sustain the organization over a period of years.

6. *General support.* Foundations may lend support to arts organizations on an unrestricted basis for a short period of time with the idea of helping them get started in a new program or assisting them with a financial crisis. However, there is never a certainty that this kind of support will continue beyond a short period. Some arts organizations are reluctant to report such funds in their annual campaign because of the uncertainty of the grants.

CAMPAIGN STRUCTURE AND PROSPECTS— MINNESOTA ORCHESTRA

The kind of campaign that might be conducted by arts organizations can be illustrated by the Minnesota Orchestra's Annual Guaranty Fund, which has an annual goal in excess of $2,000,000. The amount sought would, of course, be much less for an organization in a smaller community, but the principle is the same. The divisional structure used to raise these funds is described below, and illustrated in Figure 15-1.

Major Gifts—Bronze Baton

The orchestra conducts a highly selective solicitation of wealthy individuals, corporations, and foundations that can give $10,000 or more annually in support of the orchestra. Currently, 41 such prospects are solicited by a small, carefully selected committee representing top business and social leadership.

Directors' Division—Board of Directors

The 80 members of the board of directors are solicted by a select group of their codirectors—12 to 15 in number. Some calls are made on prospects through a team of two solicitors rather than one. The presence of two solicitors increases peer influence and emphasizes the need for generous gifts.

Major Businesses

Businesses are selected for solicitation if it is believed they can give $150 to $10,000. A campaign organization is established for each major community that is within the geographic area served by the orchestra. A chairman is selected and enough solicitors obtained to contact five to seven prospects each. Since the orchestra not only serves the central community of the Twin Cities but holds traveling concerts in other cities, it can make a good case for business support.

Figure 15-1. Minnesota Orchestra Association—Guaranty Fund volunteer staff organization.

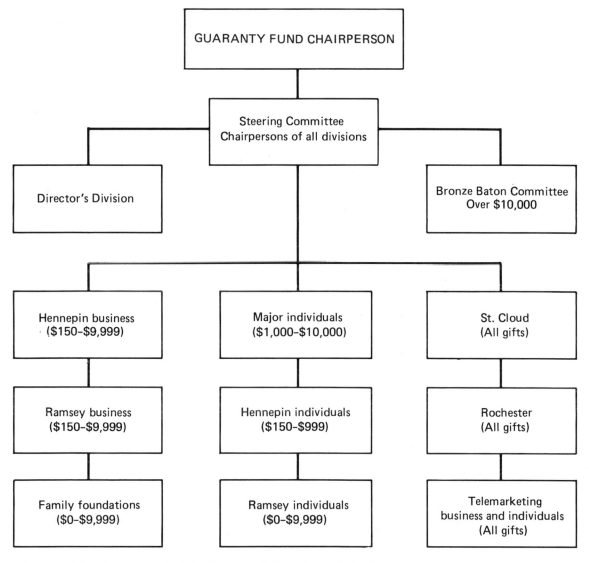

(Courtesy of the Guaranty Fund of the Minnesota Orchestral Association.)

Foundations

A special section of solicitors conducts a separate solicitation of foundations capable of giving a reasonable amount. These solicitors are carefully selected and trained to approach foundations. They prepare specialized case presentations for each foundation, outline the needs of the orchestra, and request unrestricted grants.

Individual Gifts—Maestro Circle

Individuals are solicited who might be capable of giving in the $1,000 to $9,999 range and who live in the metropolitan area. The amounts raised by the higher-level Bronze Baton division from individuals are also later reported through this division.

Small Businesses

Gifts in the range of $150 to $999 are solicited from small businesses through this division.

Telemarketing

Substantial numbers of ticket holders buy tickets either for single performances or for the annual concert series. Although these people are not capable of making large contributions, they represent a substantial potential for raising funds. The Minnesota Orchestra maintains a prospect list of approximately 20,000 people who are current ticket holders, have attended concerts in the past, or have a possible interest in the orchestra. This solicitation is conducted by telephone; the solicitors are paid on an hourly basis with an incentive for all new givers whom they enroll. These solicitors are recruited through ads in the newspaper and are interviewed by the orchestra's personnel department to be sure they have the aptitude and characteristics necessary to do an effective interpretation for the orchestra. A training program is conducted for new solicitors by the development staff.

In its most recent telemarketing effort, the Minnesota Orchestra raised $450,000, at a direct cost of approximately 10 percent. This cost represents salaries only, not the cost of literature and mailings. (The cost is carried by the orchestra's budget as part of its campaign expenses.) After a prospect has indicated an interest, he or she is sent a pledge card and a copy of the orchestra's program for the year.

As part of this effort the organization uses a number of giving clubs in the gift categories of $50, $75, and $100. For example, new members making $50 gifts will be given two tickets to the annual recognition concert held for donors. They are also listed in the annual report of the organization and in the individual concert programs.

Timing

The timing of the arts campaign is generally scheduled in accordance with the organization's program year. When pledges and tickets are obtained in combination, the campaign must be completed by the beginning of the concert year. In the case of the Minnesota Orchestra, most phases of the campaign are conducted between September and the following August.

Leadership

Leadership is obtained by a careful review of board members, patrons, season ticket holders, and chief executive officers of corporations who have shown an interest in the organization.

Prospect Identification

As mentioned in the divisional write-ups, prospects are generally drawn from ticket holders, wealthy individuals, and corporations that have an interest in improving the cultural environment of the community as well as others who have shown an interest.

Sources of Funds

The sources of funds differ from community to community and from organization to organization. In the case of the Minnesota Orchestra, 51 percent of its funds come from corporations, 6 percent from foundations, and 43 percent from individuals.

ARTS COUNCILS

Some communities have satisfied the problem of supporting their arts organizations by organizing united campaigns. These represent a federation of organizations in the arts brought together by interested citizens and contributors to raise funds and do a more effective job of planning and allocating resources.

Such organizations are generally known as arts councils, although their campaigns may be conducted under the name United Arts Fund. Arts councils are becoming more and more prevalent. There were 17 arts councils in 1970, but by 1981 there were 51. They are similar to the United Way in the health and welfare field and, for the most part, satisfy the same objectives, except that their agency membership and their fund-raising market are more restricted. Arts council's may include chamber and symphony orchestras, art museums, theaters, opera groups, choral groups, and dance ensembles.

Like the United Way, the arts agencies present budgets for annual review by a central budget and allocations committee. The committee reviews needs and recommends to the board of directors of the arts council the goals to be set forth. As with the United Way and sectarian federations, it is common practice for the campaign committee of the arts council to review past campaign results, future campaign potential, and the campaign climate in estimating the amounts that can be raised. The Council board then decides the goal for the annual campaign it will conduct.

Market

Generally speaking, arts councils direct their campaigns to the following types of prospects (illustrated in the campaign chart in Figure 15-2):

Foundations. United Arts Funds may get very substantial support from private foundations. For some foundations, supporting the arts is a major priority; others support a broad range of philanthropic activities including the arts. Support may be requested for annual operating expenses or to fund a special program for the arts council or one of its agencies.

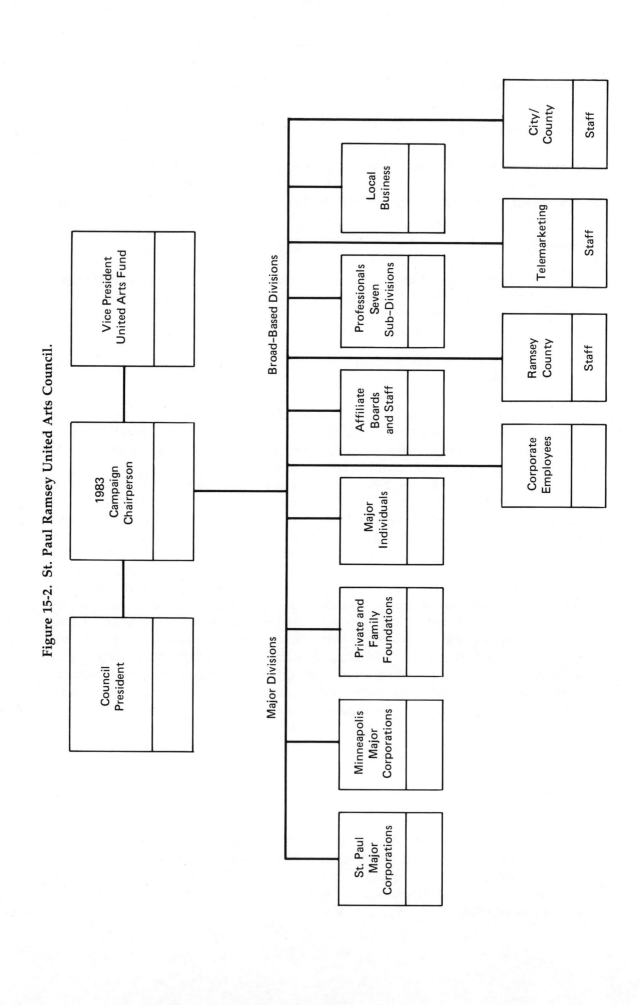

Figure 15-2. St. Paul Ramsey United Arts Council.

Major corporations. Increasing support for the arts is coming from major corporations. In those cities where there are arts councils, corporations may represent the single largest source of contribution income. Generally, a divsion will be formed to solicit gifts from major corporations. It may follow the guidelines suggested in Chapter 11.

Affiliate boards and staff. The membership of affiliated agency boards and their staff also serve as a valuable resource for campaign funds. A chairperson and committee are formed to conduct the solicitation, and each agency is asked to name a chairperson to be responsible for the solicitation of that organization's board and staff. Occasionally agency boards and staff are solicited in advance of the opening of the campaign to serve as pacesetters. Getting the campaign started with substantial increases in contributions from these individuals indicates their belief in the agencies and their willingness to be generous in supporting them.

Professionals. Frequently individual groups of professionals are solicited separately. Typically, physicians, attorneys, dentists, architects, and accountants will be approached through a fellow member of their profession. A chairperson and workers are recruited for each group and the campaign may be conducted through a combination of personal solicitation and a highly specialized mail appeal. Often, in large law, accounting, and architectural firms and in medical groups, a chairperson is sought. He or she accepts responsibility for soliciting colleagues. Others in the profession who do not practice in a group setting are frequently solicited through personal letters from associates who have a close professional relationship with them.

Wealthy individuals. Many arts councils attract a highly devoted group of wealthy individuals who have an interest in the arts and are willing to give generously. These prospects can frequently be identified through membership lists of the participating organizations and will include subscribers to symphony concerts, operas, and other programs in the arts. Wealthy individuals represent a particularly viable source of funds and they should be approached on a highly personalized basis in the manner described in Chapter 12.

Management. In recent years, an increasing number of arts councils have sought support from employee groups in the same way that the United Way does. However, arts councils are usually restricted to soliciting only top management and department heads. Interest in the arts is restricted: The work of the many agencies supported by the United Way is so broad in scope that almost everyone can use the services at some time. Although arts organizations serve a very real purpose in enhancing the quality of life in the community, they do not have the dramatic urgency of programs in health research and care of the physically handicapped, for example. Accordingly, their appeal to many employees is somewhat reduced. For this reason corporations are frequently reluctant to develop another full scale campaign to solicit their employees. However, they may not object to circulating a letter, signed by the chief executive, asking top management to support the arts council.

General Prospects

Specially organized divisions map out a geographic approach to solicit individuals and small businesses. Small businesses are generally approached by volunteers in a business division who hold middle managment positions.

Individuals who may have an interest in the arts, including subscribers of the member agencies, are often solicited through a women's division. These volunteers are recruited from the membership rolls of the agencies and from the general community.

Because of the large number of small businesses and individual prospects, more of this solicitation is being conducted by mail with follow-up by telephone. Some arts councils set aside special days and arrange for phone banks that can be used by volunteers to complete their calls within a specified period. These organized telephone efforts—staffed by volunteers—are frequently referred to as phonathons. Telemarketing, on the other hand, utilizes paid workers.

Telemarketing. The exclusive use of telemarketing is becoming a growing practice in approaching smaller businesses and individuals. Although there is no substitute for personal solicitation, the large numbers of small businesses and general individual prospects have made it difficult for some campaigns to recruit, organize, and train the volunteers necessary to solicit them effectively. Many women who once volunteered in this capacity are unavailable because they work outside the home. Telemarketing is a practical alternative, but it lacks the advantage of involving a large number of volunteers who become ardent advocates because they have learned about the organization's program through participating in the campaign.

Timing

Like other organizations, arts councils will schedule their campaigns to take advantage of the most favorable climate. They will also consider which time of year they are likely to draw the most volunteers. See Figure 15-3 for a sample timetable. Direct conflict with other major campaigns, particularly united campaigns in the community, is avoided if possible.

Source of Funds

A study by the American Council for the Arts indicates that in 1981 arts councils received, on the average, 45 percent of their funds from their top ten gifts. One arts council received 85 percent of its total from the top ten, and the lowest in the range received 19.2 percent from the top ten. Business contributed 72.4 percent of the arts councils' top gift total.

Overall (according to the above study), arts councils received their campaign income from a number of sources. (See Table 15-1.)

Some councils report government grants for general operating support as campaign contributions, even though they do not fit the usual concept of voluntary contributions. In some cities, these gifts from government are used to pay the operating costs of the buildings that house the various arts organizations.

Figure 15-3. United Arts Fund timetable.

Who	When	Task
Staff	January 1	Campaign planned
President	January 15	Campaign chair selected
Staff/chairperson	January 15	Outline of campaign plan presented and approved
Staff/development committee/chairperson	January 15	Goal set: overall and divisions
Chairperson	February 1	Division heads chosen
Staff	February 1	Campaign materials complete
Division heads	February 15	Division captains chosen
Division heads/captains	February 30	Selection of volunteer workers complete
Division heads/captains/ staff	March 15	Begin major corporate solicitation; volunteer assignment complete
Major donors/campaign cabinet/division chairperson/staff	March 15	Orientation for division volunteers begins
Volunteers/staff	March 15–April 1	Solicitations of major corporations Solicitation of corporate employees begins Affiliate boards/staff solicitation Media campaign begins
Chairperson/division heads/staff	April 1–30	Professionals solicitations (7 subdivisions) Local business solicitations Solicitations of family foundations Media campaign continues
Campaign chairperson/ division heads	April 12	Campaign cabinet/report session
	May 1	Major individual solicitations Begin follow-ups
Campaign chairperson/ division heads	May 3	Campaign cabinet/report session
Campaign cabinet/ staff	May 26	Campaign cabinet/report session
Campaign cabinet/ staff	June 1	Celebration to thank volunteers

Table 15-1. Arts councils' sources of campaign funds.

Source	Percent
Corporations and businesses	55.6%
Individuals	27.2
Foundations	8.2
Other	4.1
Government	3.6
Special Events	1.3
	100.0%

Source: *United Arts Fundraising:* 1982 Campaign Analysis, © 1983 American Council for the Arts.

Figure 15-4. St. Paul Ramsey United Arts Council corporate benefits program.

1984 UAF CORPORATE CONTRIBUTION:	$1,000-$2,499	$2,500-$4,999	$5,000-$9,999	$10,000-$19,999	$20,000-$49,999	"Opening Night" $50,000 and over
	All of the following:	One of the following:	One of the following:	One of the following:	One of the following:	Co-sponsorships: All of the following:
	10 complimentary ticket vouchers each to: -St. Paul Chamber Orchestra concert -Chimera Theatre -Minnesota Museum of Art film series	Sponsorship of Schubert Club Sunday chamber series at Walker Art Center. Four dates available	Sponsorship of Schubert Club choral music series at the new Ordway Music Theatre. Four dates available	Sponsorship of a visiting baroque orchestra, Schubert Club at the Ordway Music Theatre. Three dates available	Sponsorship of Schubert Club International Artists series concert. Four dates available	Sponsorship of a Schubert Club's opening International Artists series featuring John Galway October 15, 1984
	One copy of a recent COMPAS anthology of student writing	One day for employees at Minnesota Museum of Art Kidspace—Saturday, free membership for a day. Six dates available	Minnesota Museum of Art loaned artwork from the permanent collection. Five dates available	Sponsorship of a Minnesota Museum of Art exhibition at the Jemne Building. Three dates available	Sponsorship of a Minnesota Museum of Art exhibition at Landmark Center. Three dates available	Sponsorship of the Minnesota Museum of Art's Will Barnet exhibition
		Limited original print by COMPAS artist, Gary Egger. Ten dates available	Sponsorship of a Saint Paul Chamber Orchestra concert. Three dates available	Sponsorship of a Saint Paul Chamber Orchestra baroque series concert. Three dates available	Sponsorship of Saint Paul Chamber Orchestra capital series concert. Six dates available	Sponsorship of the Saint Paul Chamber Orchestra's season opener on September 16 at Orchestra Hall featuring Marvis Martin, soprano.
				Sponsorship of a Chimera Theatre studio series production. Four dates available	Sponsorship of a Chimera Theatre main stage production. Four dates available	Sponsorship of Chimera Theatre's season opener: H.M.S. Pinafore
						Inclusion in the 84-85 COMPAS anthology of student writing as a sponsor through the United Arts Fund

In addition:
Any corporation making a new gift of at least $1,000 or an increased gift of 20% or more will be offered a complimentary use of a courtroom in Landmark Center.

Table 15-2. Arts councils' allocation of campaign funds to various arts organizations.

Type of donee	Average percent allocated
Orchestras	32.2
Theaters	20.8
Museums	19.6
Operas	14.5
Dance companies	14.5
Visual arts groups	9.7
Youth Groups	6.8
Miscellaneous educational organizations	9.7
Miscellaneous cultural organizations	10.4
Miscellaneous music societies	12.2
Arts councils and arts centers	8.5
Other	7.4
Groups funded by discretionary funds	20.5

Source: *United Arts Fundraising:* 1982 Campaign Analysis, © 1983 American Council for the Arts.

Allocation of Funds

The largest beneficiaries of arts councils are orchestras, followed by theaters and museums. According to the American Council for the Arts, arts councils allocate their funds as shown in Table 15-2. (Note that since each of the arts councils surveyed serves a somewhat different constituency, the total of allocations in the table adds up to more than 100 percent.)

The average arts council spends 19.9 percent for its own administration, 5.8 percent for reserves for losses, and 4.9 percent for other purposes.

Packaging an Approach

It is increasingly common for some arts councils to suggest to corporations that, in return for their contribution, they will offer the corporation the opportunity to underwrite an event. Arts councils also offer corporate benefits programs (see Figure 15-4 for an example) or special services. Using this approach, arts councils ask corporations to make a contribution of a specific amount—$1,000, $5,000, $10,000, or $20,000. In return the corporation may select certain events with which their names will be associated as sponsors. A $1,000 giver might have the choice of sponsoring one performance of a dance ensemble or one presentation of an amateur theater group, for example. A $5,000 contribution might sponsor one performance of a symphony orchestra or a special showing at an art museum. The concept of tying direct recognition to financial support not only provides an incentive to upgrade its giving to higher levels, but also allows companies to disburse their gifts among several arts organizations and gain visibility.

16

COLLEGE AND UNIVERSITY CAMPAIGNS

The rapidly changing economic situation, declining enrollments, and increasing costs have created major problems for nearly all colleges and universities throughout the United States. Even those which have been economically secure in the past must now give more time and attention to developing new outside sources of revenue.

Today college support is drawn from a broad base. Data collected by the Council for Financial Aid to Education (CFAE), in a study of 1,101 colleges and universities, showed the following sources of income for 1981–1982:

Source	Percent of total
Alumni	25.7%
Non-alumni (individuals)	22.4
Foundations	20.6
Corporations	20.1
Religious denominations	3.6
Fund-raising consortia	2.1
Other sources	5.5

Note that 48.1 percent of gifts to higher education came from individuals, both alumni and non-alumni. Sixteen percent of that income came from bequests and life insurance contracts. The amount private universities received from deferred gifts was even higher—21.3 percent. This underscores the growing importance of deferred-giving programs for colleges and universities. Despite the fact that the largest amount of money received by universities comes from individuals, corporations have become an increasingly important source of support for higher education. Of the corporate dollars contributed in 1983, 37.8 percent was given to education, the bulk of it in the field of higher education, according to The Conference Board, a business information service.

Data in the CFAE survey indicate that gifts received by colleges and universities were used for the following purposes:

Purpose	Percent of total
Unrestricted (general purpose)	27.6
Physical plant	15.3
Basic research	13.9
Student aid	13.4
Faculty compensation	5.8
Other purposes	24.0

Private universities received three times as much money in unrestricted gifts for faculty and physical plant as was received by tax-supported colleges and universities for these purposes. Most of the funds received by tax-supported institutions are for scholarships and research. Research alone commands 55 percent of such contributions in the tax-supported schools.

THE COLLEGE CAMPAIGN

The major sources of income usually determine the structure of a college or university campaign. Today, most colleges conduct an annual campaign for sustaining purposes. Periodically, they conduct sizable campaigns for both capital improvements and endowments. Over the past decade, it has become more and more common to include an appeal for endowment funds with the capital campaign. (See Chapter 20.)

Typically, the annual campaign is organized to target several groups.

Large Individual Gifts

Wealthy alumni, wealthy parents of students, and selected individuals of means who, over a period of years, have demonstrated an interest in the institution are natural prospects for major gifts. The solicitation is generally conducted by a group of carefully selected volunteers in the manner described in Chapter 12's discussion of solicitation of the wealthy individuals.

Corporate Gifts

Corporations may be included in the same division organized to solicit wealthy individuals or they may be solicited through a separate division. Generally the solicitation is directed toward corporations located in the college's community and likely to hire employees who are graduates of the school. Occasionally corporations in other cities which are headed by prominent alumni are solicited. Some universities solicit major national corporations regardless of where they are headquartered.

The United Negro College Fund solicits a broad gamut of national corporations throughout the country on behalf of its member colleges. In other cities and states private colleges may unite and agree to seek annual support by approaching corporations together. Such joint campaigns are organized to realize a more effective solicitation of corporations, and to reduce the irritation that competitive solicitation might bring. Where combined approaches to corporations are used, the campaign results are usually distributed on the basis of an equal split of the money to the participating colleges. Another practice is to split 50 percent of the corporate contributions on an equal basis. The remaining 50 percent is divided among the schools on the basis of proportionate enrollment.

Employee Matching Gifts

A growing number of corporations have matching gifts programs: Employees give to their alma maters and have their gifts matched by the corporation. There is a growing tendency to include retired employees and board members among those eligible to participate. A fairly common matching maximum for a gift is $500, but some of the larger corporations match gifts which are substantially larger—some as high as $2,500 or more. Some corporations match the employee's gift with an equal sum, but others will give twice or three times as much. Although the company doesn't conduct a campaign to get employees to give to educational institutions, the employees are given the pertinent information about the matching gifts program. All the employee must do is complete a short form giving the information about the college or university of his or her choice, its location, and the amount of the gift. Generally the employee's check will be forwarded to a designated company department and the company sends its matching check to the recipient institution in the name of the donor. Promoting the matching gifts program among alumni and friends of the college is the responsibility of each individual institution. The program is valuable because it permits colleges and universities to gather support from corporations which would otherwise be unavailable. The matching gifts program also serves as an incentive to employees because they know their gifts will be doubled or even tripled. In 1981, the CFAE surveyed 404 companies and found out that 15.6 percent of their support to higher education ($45,417,756 out of $290,517,976) came from employee matching gifts programs.

A sample matching gifts policy statement for employee gifts to higher education is shown in Figure 16-1. (It is a folding brochure.)

Foundation Gifts

Foundation funds may be sought for special purposes of a noncapital nature, such as the initiation of a new educational program, the development of special faculty positions, or the conduct of special research programs. Foundations are also a prime prospect for capital gifts.

Faculty Gifts

Soliciting faculty on an annual basis is a means of demonstrating the support of faculty and staff for the university, and serves as an example for other contributors to

Figure 16-1. Northwestern Bell's matching gifts program.

The Program

The employee Educational Matching Gift Program of Northwestern Bell supplements the Company's program of financial assistance to higher education.

Its purpose is to encourage active and retired employees and directors of Northwestern Bell to join the Company in the financial support of educational institutions.

Under the program, gifts by eligible persons ranging from $25 to $3,000 per annum will be matched by the Company subject to conditions of the plan. "First time" gifts to a qualifying institution will be matched on a two-for-one basis up to a maximum Company gift of $3,000 per individual donor per calendar year.

Eligible Individuals

Regular full or part-time employees of Northwestern Bell, retired employees receiving a service or disability pension from the Company and directors of the Company are eligible. Individuals need not have attended the educational institution to which they contribute.

Eligible Institutions

Degree-granting graduate and professional schools, universities, four-year and two-year colleges, seminaries and theological schools and technical institutes which are located in the U.S. or one of its possessions, are regionally or professionally accredited, as appropriate, and are recognized by the Internal Revenue Service as tax-exempt, contributions to which are deductible for income tax purposes.

The individual can also give to an alumni fund, foundation or association that has a tax-exempt status and collects funds for an eligible institution. (NWB's corporate matching gift will be an unrestricted grant paid to the institution.)

Tax-exempt educational fund (e.g. United Negro College Fund) if its sole purpose is to raise money for its constituent member colleges which individually are eligible under the program.

Eligible Gifts

The contribution must be a personal gift of the individual. It must not be a payment for which reimbursement of any kind is made by another individual or organization. It must be paid, not merely pledged, and may be a payment by check, in cash, or in securities having a quoted market value. Northwestern Bell will match the total contributions of any eligible individual to eligible institutions or funds up to a maximum of $3,000 per individual donor per calendar year. A "first time" gift to an eligible institution will be matched on a two-for-one basis subject to the same limits. An individual who has previously contributed to an eligible institution cannot qualify as a "first time" giver to the same institution under the matching gift plan. No single gift of an individual will be matched unless such gift is $25 or more.

The Northwestern Bell Matching Gift Coordinator must receive certification of the gift from an authorized financial officer of the institution within 90 days of the date of the gift.

Ineligible Gifts

Gifts to elementary and secondary schools.

Dues or gifts to alumni groups which are not distributed to affiliated eligible educational institutions.

Amounts payable as subscription fees for publications.

Insurance premium payments.

Payments in lieu of tuition, books or other student fees.

Gifts for non-scholastic programs such as athletics, ticket purchases, parking privileges, etc.

Additional Terms

The Company may suspend, change, revoke, or terminate this program at any time. No individual and no eligible institution or fund will acquire any rights against Northwestern Bell or any of its employees by reason of the Company's failure to make a matching contribution, the suspension, change, revocation or termination of this program, or otherwise.

Intentional abuse of the plan could result in future disqualification of the donor and/or the recipient.

The interpretation, application and administration of the program shall be determined by Northwestern Bell and its decision shall be final.

Application Procedure

Donor—Fill out Section One and Two. *Send the entire folder* to the institution with your gift.

Educational Institution—Complete Section 3. *Return the entire folder* to *Northwestern Bell Educational Matching Gifts Coordinator, 1314 Douglas On-The-Mall, 5th Floor Omaha, Nebraska 68102.*
Questions on the program should be directed to the Matching Gift Program Coordinator, 402-422-3479

 Northwestern Bell

---

Educational Matching Gift Program

No influence in America holds greater promise for an improved quality of life than education, nor is any basic institution more interdependent with business. Thus Northwestern Bell's contributions program is heavily oriented toward support of higher education, and matching gifts are an important part of the overall program.

Through this matching gift, we are pleased to join with you in contributing to the strength and effectiveness of our nation's educational system.

Matching Gift Program Coordinator.

follow. Generally a member of the faculty is asked to serve as chairperson and will in turn recruit other faculty members for personal solicitation. In some cases the faculty may be solicited by a letter from the faculty chairperson with follow-up from the faculty campaign committee.

Parents

Parents of current and former students provide another possible source of support for university campaigns. Those who represent substantial worth will, of course, be included in the campaign section directed to wealthy individuals. However, many less-than-wealthy parents who appreciate the education their sons and daughters received often respond to campaigns with annual pledges. Because this group represents a considerable number of people, solicitation is generally done by mail. Giving clubs set up according to size of contribution—Century Club, Presidents Club, etc.—are devices frequently used to avoid a minimal gift and stimulate more generous giving. Where mail is used, personalized letters are highly desirable. There are mechanical means of producing and personalizing such letters that aren't too costly.

Alumni

Most colleges and universities have sizable numbers of graduates who represent a considerable potential for support. A major problem in reaching alumni is that it is difficult to keep track of such a large number of individuals, especially when they are spread across all geographic regions of the country. Because we live in a mobile society, universities find that their graduates move to many different cities and states. Keeping a reasonably up-to-date prospect list of such graduates is a time-consuming, but important part of the campaign function.

Geographic solicitation. There are two methods of soliciting alumni—according to the year they graduated and by geographic region. For many years the more popular method was to work through alumni associations in major cities. They provided a forum to explain the university's financial needs and solicit funds. When possible, the president, campaign chairperson, or development director attends a meeting of the alumni association and makes a formal presentation of the university's progress, programs, and needs. In this approach, there is an alumni chairperson for each major state and city, depending upon the number of graduates residing there. That chairperson is responsible for communicating with alumni, usually by mail because of the large numbers to be reached. Sometimes there is a selective personal follow-up.

Organization by graduating class. Of recent years it has become more commonplace to organize solicitation of alumni by graduating class. In this type of campaign structure, a volunteer is responsible for contacting members of his or her class, and asking them to contribute. Contact is generally made through mechanically processed personalized letters. Each class chairperson signs the letter for his or her class. In some cases, the letter may be signed jointly by the class chairperson and the chairperson of the campaign.

Soliciting alumni is problematic. These data from the CFAE illustrate the difficulty of obtaining gifts from former students:

Type of institution	Percent of alumni who contribute
Private colleges and universities	24.8%
Public universities	13.6
Two-year institutions	11.8

Only 18.9% of former students of all post-secondary schools contribute to their alma maters.

Phonathons and telemarketing. Recently, a new method of reaching alumni has been developed—telephone solicitation. This is done in one of two ways: Some universities are able to obtain the use of corporate telephone lines in off-duty periods. A staff of volunteers or students call alumni, give a short résumé of the needs of the university, and ask them whether they would like to contribute. The volunteers are carefully briefed and are generally given a prepared statement or pitch to read to the prospect. Answers to commonly asked questions are also provided.

A second way uses a commercial enterprise that specializes in raising funds by telephone solicitation. Typically, the college or university negotiates the fee, and then the commercial institution assumes responsibility for contacting the large number of alumni whether they live in the vicinity or are located in other cities. Students or other persons are hired and paid an hourly wage. They use the university's prospect lists to make the telephone solicitation, and each caller keeps an account of the attempts he or she has made to contact prospective alumni. (See tally sheet in Figure 16-2.) Where it has not been possible to reach the prospect, the names are reassigned to another caller for recontact. Gifts are recorded and are followed up with a thank-you note and a request to sign a pledge card. Because these calls are made in the evenings, long-distance rates are lower and, therefore, the telephone bills can be kept reasonable.

Telemarketing incurs a fund-raising expense of at least 25 percent, but, as all campaigners know, fund-raising costs consume a higher percentage of the whole when gifts are small. The cost also increases when the targeted group is difficult to reach. More time, organization, and attention are required. In the same way, the costs of conducting a residential campaign, or a campaign among small businesses, will be, proportionately, many times higher than the solicitation of large gifts from corporations and foundations.

THE BUILDING ENDOWMENT CAMPAIGN

In terms of the structure of the campaign divisions, the building endowment campaign will generally be similar to that of the annual giving program. However, the amounts sought will be substantially greater. In the general capital solicitation, funds for building purposes may be related to annual giving—that is, givers may be asked to double or triple their usual gift for capital purposes. In some cases, giving may be related to the

Figure 16-2. Sample caller tally sheet for telephone solicitors.

PHONE/MAIL PROGRAM
CALLER TALLY SHEET

Caller's name: _____   Date: _____

Caller's number: _____

(Indicate as follows: ⊤⊬⊥ III, ETC.)   DO NOT WRITE IN
                                                        THESE BOXES

CARDS USED		
CALLS DIALED		
PROSPECTS NOT REACHED		
NO ANSWER		
CALL BACK		
PROSPECTS REACHED		
NO PLEDGE		
HANDLE BY MAIL		
CALL BACK		
PLEDGE		

DO NOT WRITE BELOW THIS LINE

HOURS WORKED: _____   _____ / _____ / _____ / _____

OF   TOTAL   AVERAGE   TOTAL
PLEDGES   PLEDGED   PLEDGE $ PER
                                       PROSPECT
                                       REACHED

number of years that have passed since the alumnus graduated from the university—for example, $10 or $25 for each year since the person has graduated, payable over a three-year period. Giving clubs are also widely used.

The solicitation of the top ten and the next 200 largest gifts, however, should be carefully rated, assigned, and approached in the manner described in Chapter 7.

The college's needs can generally be presented in summary form. The "St. Thomas: Priorities for the 80's" program, which successfully oversubscribed its campaign by raising $14,403,000 for a variety of purposes, did it this way:

Endowed professorships	$ 4,200,000
Distinguished fellows	375,000
Faculty professional development	300,000
Student financial aid	2,375,000
Toward construction and modernization of facilities, recycling, and improvement of physical plant and grounds	4,038,000
Annual alumni fund and other gifts for current use	3,115,000
	$14,403,000

As mentioned previously, the capital campaign will seek to raise from 33 to 50 percent of its money from the top ten givers and another 33 percent from the next 100 to 200 givers. The balance of the campaign will be sought from other divisions. Gifts for designated purposes are fairly common. Sponsorship of a chapel, the endowment of a chair or faculty position, and the establishment of a scholarship in the name of an individual are all devices that permit the individual to make a substantial gift and become associated with the institution in a personal and visible way.

Although colleges and universities have had increasing financial problems, they have shown the kind of financial vitality that enables them not only to persevere, but, in many cases, to increase their enrollment; this, in spite of increasing costs and a diminishing availability of potential students.

Timing

Colleges and universities generally gear their campaign periods so that they interfere as little as possible with student registrations and other periods that require the attention of the president and other essential officers. Otherwise, timing considerations are the same as for any other organization contemplating a campaign.

Giving Clubs

Annual giving tends to stay the same year after year unless the prospect is challenged to increase his or her gift. Like other institutions, colleges and universities have found that giving clubs do achieve increased giving. (They were mentioned earlier as a way to solicit parents.) Various gift classifications are used to identify donors who give certain specific amounts. Accordingly, gifts of $1,000 or more might be termed the

"$1,000 Club," or the club might be named after a prominent alumnus or past president of the college. Generally the recognition for these donors would include listing their names in the annual report or alumni news, a special letter of thanks, and possibly issuing a certificate or small token of appreciation.

An annual dinner and a special program with a prominent outside speaker is arranged for contributors of larger gifts. The president of the university and the chairperson of the campaign can use this occasion to thank the contributors and to give them an insider's review of what is happening at the university.

PRIVATE SECONDARY AND PRIMARY SCHOOLS

Support of higher education has been a major objective of corporations for many years, but matching gifts programs are now being extended to private, secondary, and elementary schools. The CFAE, in its survey of national corporations, found that approximately 40 percent of those that responded now permit matching gifts to private secondary and primary schools. However, very few corporations include public schools in their programs.

To determine eligibility the CFAE defines independent schools as "basically those operated and controlled by a board of trustees." Parochial schools operated and supported by a parish or diocese sometimes do not qualify as independent schools, but there is an increasing tendency to include even those in matching gifts programs.

Campaign Organization

The data that follow show that private primary and secondary schools draw their support from the same sources as colleges and universities, although the amount and the way it is allocated differ somewhat. Accordingly, the campaign structure organized to solicit gifts for these schools is very similar to that used by the institutions of higher learning. (See Figure 16-3).

Table 16-1. Voluntary support of independent schools by source, 1981–82.

Source	Current operations	Capital purposes
Business corporations	$ 4,669,423 (414)	$ 6,546,241 (244)
Religious denominations	1,559,788 (62)	211,799 (19)
Alumni	31,145,041 (434)	60,321,452 (332)
Non-alumni	42,873,717 (472)	84,801,745 (404)
Foundations	10,336,082 (360)	41,808,922 (313)
Fund-raising consortia	903,532 (52)	320,362 (15)
Other	5,095,752 (181)	4,449,905 (105)
Grand Total (486)	$96,583,335	$198,460,426

(Figures in parenthesis show the number of schools reporting.)
Source: Council on Financial Aid to Education.

Figure 16-3. Organization chart for a university campaign.

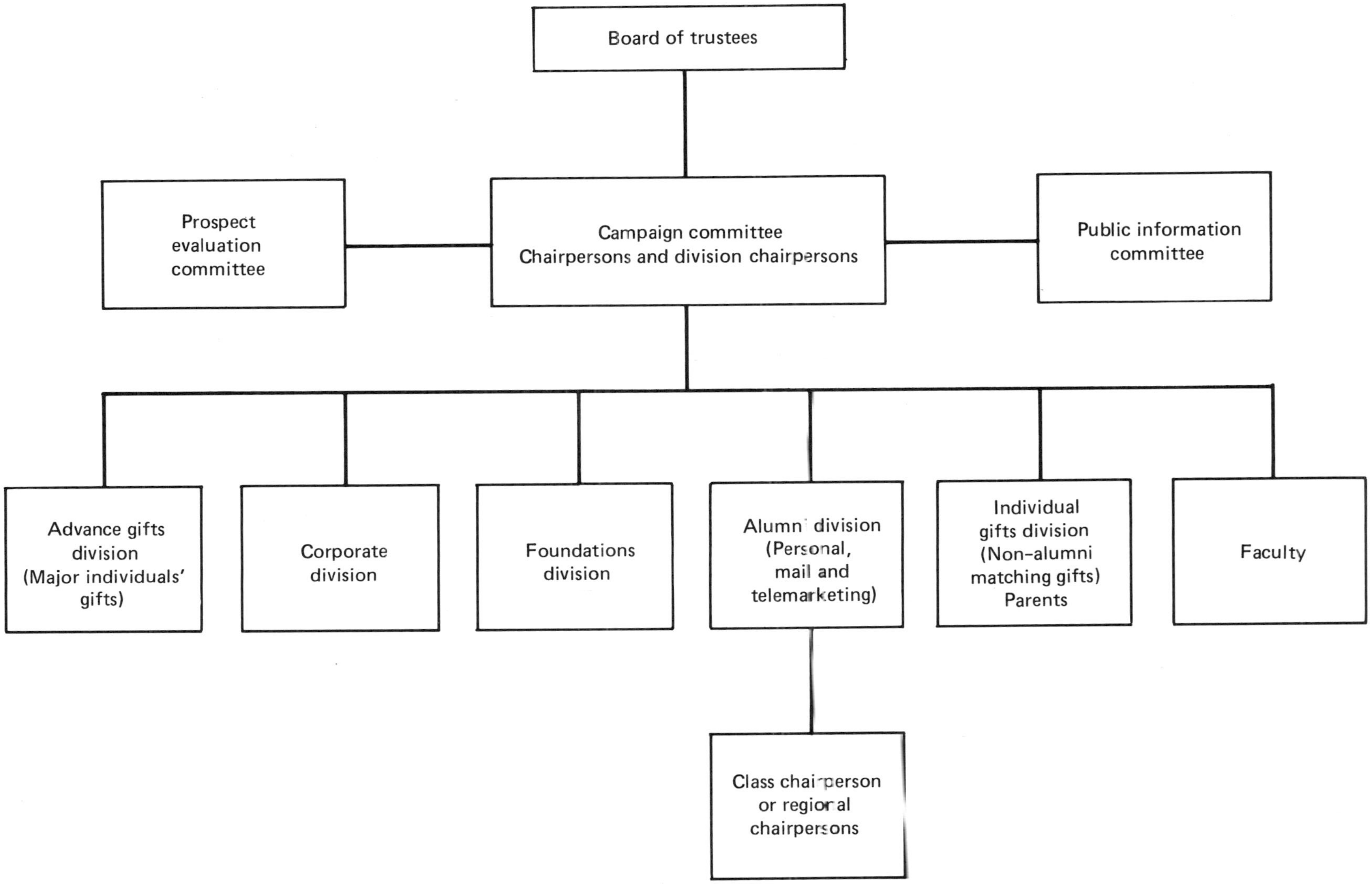

Table 16-2. Corporate support of independent schools by purpose.

Purpose	1980–81	1981–82	
Unrestricted	$3,886,237 (55.8)	$ 5,958,830 (53.1)	
Physical plant	1,943,673 (27.9)	3,820,430 (34.1)	
Student aid	659,332 (9.4)	648,979 (5.8)	
Faculty compensation	117,773 (1.7)	180,622 (1.6)	
Other	362,863 (5.2)	606,453 (5.4)	
Grand Total			
All institutions	$6,969,878 (100.0)	$11,215,314 (100.0)	
Core institutions	6,000,377	7,398,573	+23.3%

(Figures in parentheses show percent of total in each column.)

Note: Research grants of $5,091 in 1980–81 and $350 in 1981–82 are omitted.

Source: Council on Financial Aid to Education.

Support from all sources. The CFAE reported that private independent schools received voluntary support from a number of sources in 1981–1982. (See Table 16-1).

Gifts from non-alumni represented 43.3 percent of all support, and corporations gave 3.8 percent. Gifts for capital purposes were twice as large as those for current operations, according to the CFAE. Corporate support was mostly unrestricted (53.1 percent), although 34.1 percent was given for physical plant.

Table 16-2 shows how corporate support was allocated in gifts to private, secondary, and elementary schools. The figures cover the years 1980–1982, and include matching gifts programs.

17

HOSPITAL CAMPAIGNS

Fund raising for hospitals is complicated because of the nature of the health care industry today. Health care costs are always rising, but most hospitals are reimbursed by third-party payers, including private insurers, medicare, medicaid, and welfare departments. Third-party payers have substantially changed the financial position of hospitals over the past several decades. Still, increasing health care costs represent a special barrier to successful fund raising.

Understanding Hospitals' Expenses

Government and third-party payers are alarmed that the persistent increases in health care costs generally outstrip the rate of inflation, although the regulations imposed on the health care industry by government itself account for a substantial share of the expense. A required series of review processes—including peer, utilization, certificate-of-need, and rate reviews—impose costs upon hospitals and add to the charges made to patients. In addition, a number of environmental regulations necessitate the purchase of expensive equipment to provide protection against possible radiation or contamination. Certification requirements for professional staff to operate the new technology pose another expense. Hospitals must also bear the same increases in costs as private industry, including worker's compensation, increased Social Security contributions, and compliance with the Employee Retirement Income Security Act (ERISA).

Unrecognized is the fact that the improved quality of medical care increases hospital expenses. In the last ten years, there has been a substantial reduction in heart diseases because of new medical knowledge, better equipment, and improved surgical techniques. Unfortunately, benefits resulting from better medical practice have their price and that, too, is one of the important factors in the increase in medical costs.

Another expense that must be taken into account is the growing number of law suits brought against hospitals. Some of the suits may be attributed to unrealistic expectations on the part of patients. Tremendous increases in premiums for professional liability insurance add an additional burden.

The passage of medicare and medicaid legislation in the 1960s established access to quality medical care as a right of all citizens. For the first time, the government guaranteed medical care for all. This action, together with the growth of private insurance plans, provided improved coverage of medical costs and better access to health care than ever before. It also imposed more demands on hospitals to purchase expensive technology, enlarge and expand physical facilities, and add to the technical-medical staff.

As costs increase, the government has taken measures to reduce reimbursements to hospitals for services rendered. Historically, the government has not paid hospital charges or even an amount that approximates hospital expenses. With the passage of the Social Security Amendment Act of 1983, the reimbursement picture for hospitals has become even more difficult. The federal government has dramatically changed the basis of payments for services provided to medicare recipients. Hospitals are now paid on a fixed rate per discharge, based upon each patient's illness. This fee is established prospectively on a predetermined basis according to related diagnostic groups, i.e., illnesses that are similar in nature are bracketed into payment groups and a fixed amount is paid for the service based on average costs, regardless of the actual expenses borne by the hospital in caring for the patient.

Some private industries are taking corrective action to ensure that they are obtaining hospitalization for their employees at the lowest cost possible. Business coalitions are monitoring costs and are refusing to assume the charges for medicaire and medicaid patients declined by the government. Preferred providers, or selected hospitals, are designated by the employer to be used by employees in return for a discount on charges. In addition, interest in Health Maintenance Organization (HMO) contracting has increased notably.

These circumstances create a particularly unreceptive atmosphere which must be countered by hospitals in their fund-raising programs. It is difficult to ask a corporation for a substantial gift when its costs for employee hospitalization coverage are already high. A great deal of explaining and "selling" is necessary to convey an understanding of the problems and needs of hospitals.

Another challenge hospitals must face is demonstrating that, even in a community where there are a number of hospitals, theirs deserves special support. Each hospital must explain the unique role that it performs.

The Review Process

Many hospitals today have to present their budgets for review to some type of state rate-setting process. Because such review boards are interested in lowering patient costs, review boards often try to reduce the hospital's bottom line. This means hospitals are left with little uncommitted money to purchase new equipment, modernize existing facilities, and undertake new programs. (In addition, some courts and other agencies force hospitals to use unrestricted contributions toward the reduction of the per diem costs for patients. In 1972, the American Institute of Certified Public Accountants, through its hospital audit guide, stipulated that unrestricted charitable gifts and bequests must be reported in the hospital statement of revenue and expenses, and applied toward the cost of patient care.)

These conditions impose a double whammy on hospitals: They receive less income from federal reimbursements while at the same time review boards are pressing them to reduce costs.

HOSPITAL FOUNDATIONS

Because of these circumstances, some hospitals have found their salvation in the formation of hospital foundations. A hospital foundation, because it is a separate corporation, can accept gifts, bequests, or other contributions without the funds being included in the hospital's financial statement. Hospital foundations are separately incorporated groups qualifying under Internal Revenue code section 501(c)(3), which does not define them as private foundations. There may be a misunderstanding here since the word *foundation* is used; however, because the funds come from multiple sources, they are, technically, public charities. Such foundations may disburse funds solely to the hospital or to a variety of health care facilities. Typically, they are tied to the hospital through overlapping board memberships and through their association with the hospital medical staff and administration. The structure of a typical hospital foundation (and its relationship to the hospital) is illustrated in Figure 17-1.

As a separate corporation, a hospital foundation can entertain requests from the hospital for special-project funding and the purchase of special equipment. Since the funds come from the foundation and the expenses are paid by the foundation, the grants are not included in the hospital's financial statement and do not have to be taken into account in determining patient fees.

Another point to consider is that a hospital foundation's board of directors is generally composed of individuals of considerable prestige in the community; their involvement is very helpful in fund-raising efforts.

When hospitals elect not to use a foundation, their best strategy is to try to obtain contributions and bequests which are restricted in some way by the donor—such as funds for the purchase of specific equipment. In this way, the income does not have to be used for general operating purposes.

Advantages and Disadvantages

When considering the usefulness of a hospital foundation, weigh the advantages and disadvantages. In its favor, a hospital board:

1. Builds a highly reputable and effective volunteer board for fund-raising purposes.
2. Assures that contributions will be used for the specific purposes intended, and not go into general operating income.

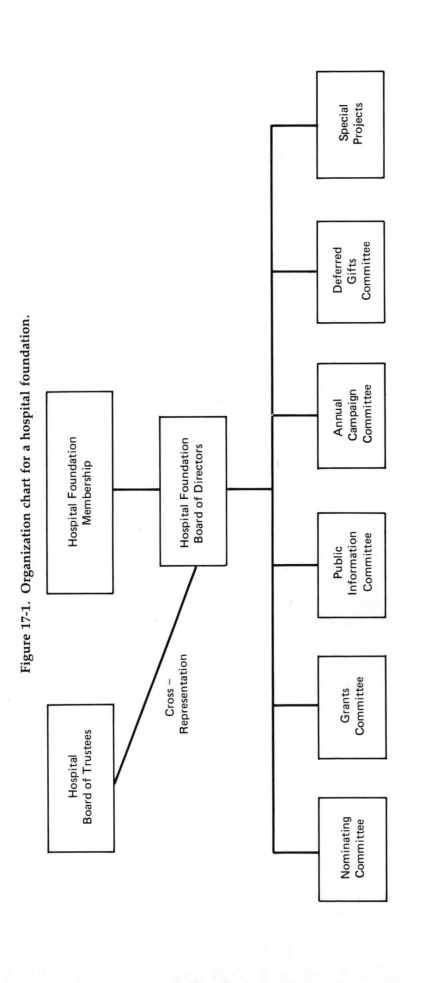

Figure 17-1. Organization chart for a hospital foundation.

3. Provides a better vehicle for the promotion and investment of charitable gifts, and for the management of an endowment and deferred-gifts program.
4. Protects the hospital from lawsuits involving contributions or gifts.

Consider the disadvantages as well:

1. There is the possibility of a conflict of goals between the foundation and hospital board.
2. The foundation board could become isolated from the hospital's main activities.
3. A strong foundation board may be perceived as a threat to the existing hospital board.

Policy Decisions

In deciding whether to establish a foundation to conduct a hospital's giving program, a number of policy decisions need to be made. The purposes and objectives of the program must be taken into account. Are efforts to be directed toward developing an endowment, conducting research, providing money for much needed equipment, or obtaining funds for new programs? In this connection, policies should recognize some of the difficulties likely to arise with regard to medicaid reimbursement. Recent court decisions have provided that hospital endowment income must be applied to offset the cost of medicaid patients.

Types of hospital foundations. Such conditions necessitate a decision as to whether to solicit contributions directly or through a foundation. If it is decided to form a foundation as the vehicle to receive gifts, further decisions need to be made concerning its structure. Should the foundation be a completely separate corporation or should it be tied to the parent organization? The manner in which the foundation's board of directors will be elected—by the hospital board or by the general membership—is a key question to be addressed. Authorities in the field of fund raising generally recommend that the foundation not be tied in a formal way to the parent corporation to avoid an implied conflict of interest or control which later can be challenged by the Department of Health and Human Services.

If this course is followed, approval should be sought from the IRS to qualify the foundation as public charity under its code section 501(c)(3). This section provides that a public charity is one that receives at least 10 percent of its total support from government and the general public (rather than one individual or family) and that maintains a continuous and bona fide program of solicitation from the general public.

Articles of incorporation and bylaws describing the purposes of the organization and its manner of operation need to be drawn to conform with all IRS requirements.

If the foundation is "independent" from the hospital, establish a policy about whether the foundation will consider making grants to organizations other than the hospital. Theoretically, the ability of the foundation to make grants to other organizations establishes its independence from the hospital and may protect it from challenges by government agencies.

An alternative to the independent foundation is the establishment of a foundation which is considered a supporting agency to the parent organization only. This can be accomplished through IRS code section 509(a)(3). However, as I pointed out earlier, this course is not generally recommended by authorities in the field.

An additional consideration in a multi-hospital system is whether the foundation will be formed at the corporate level or separately in each hospital. A major factor to keep in mind is that the corporate-level foundation is likely to have a better budget and staff than each individual hospital. Some of the smaller hospitals probably could not afford any staff. The corporate-level foundation could automatically hold any gifts in the event that one hospital is sold or goes out of business.

Other policy decisions. Consideration should be given to transferring any existing gifts or bequests to the foundation. The income would thereby be removed from the operating budget.

Another matter to be resolved is the relationship of an already existing hospital auxiliary to any foundation that is formed. Should the auxiliary continue to raise money through special events and make separate grants from the proceeds? Many hospitals have a cadre of hard-working women volunteers who raise funds by conducting an annual charity ball, staffing a gift shop, or running a coffee shop. The efforts of these dedicated volunteers should not be lost. The auxiliary might prefer to remain independent and retain its identity. On the other hand, the auxiliary's fund-raising efforts could be channeled through the foundation, with the auxiliary represented on the board. This would allow for better coordination of grant-making and fund-raising activities.

Finally, the board should adopt an adequate budget that will allow for proper staffing and provide the necessary public relations and systems support. The cooperation of all hospital departments is necessary if the program is to be successful.

STRUCTURAL RELATIONSHIP OF FOUNDATIONS TO HOSPITALS

Several years ago, I reviewed a number of hospital bylaws and found the following types of structural relationships between foundations and the hospitals:

1. All hospital foundations were organized as separate corporations but the degree to which the hospitals controlled the foundations varied widely.
2. Two major factors determined the relationship of the foundation to the hospital: the type of foundation membership and the way in which the directors and representatives of the hospital were elected.
3. All bylaws made provisions for several types of membership:
   (a) A single corporate member—the hospital or religious order which sponsors the hospital.
   (b) Membership and board of trustees of the foundation are essentially one and the same, although bylaws provide that additional classes of members may be established. The board and membership are self-perpetuating.
   (c) Membership determined by contributing members—sometimes by class

(size of gift). For example, all donors of $100 or more are members and have the right to vote for members of the board.

   (d) All foundation board members are board members of the hospital as well.
   4. Directors are always elected by the membership, either the single corporate member, contributing members, or some combination thereof.
   (a) According to many bylaws, certain members of the foundation board automatically become members, such as the hospital president, the chairman of the hospital board, and the chief of the medical staff.
   (b) Generally, bylaws specify a minimum and maximum number of directors, e.g., neither less than nine nor more than 45.
   (c) Length of service is generally in rotating terms of three years.
   5. Purposes stated in the bylaws are worded in general terms but usually specify raising funds for the hospital.
   6. Other bylaw provisions are fairly standard, but some are quite detailed.

Implementation

The following steps should be taken by the hospital board to establish a hospital foundation:

   1. Approve the appointment of a small pro tem committee (not more than three or four persons) to outline the foundation's program and establish guidelines.
   2. Seek the advice of legal counsel and the help of a public accounting firm.
   3. Draft articles of incorporation and bylaws, to be approved by the hospital's board of trustees, and later by the foundation board itself.
   4. Register the foundation with the state's secretary of state and seek qualification as a 501(c)(3) organization from the IRS.
   5. Adopt a budget to cover necessary operating expenses and staff salaries.
   6. Formalize purposes, policies, and procedures. (This should be done by the foundation board.)
   7. Develop a solicitation plan and put it into effect.

The foundation board should appoint a grants committee to recommend allocations for various projects.

TYPES OF FUND RAISING

There are five basic kinds of fund raising carried out by hospitals, either through foundations or as part of their own program.

Annual Giving

Annual giving programs are a combination of mail and personal solicitation of corporations, foundations, wealthy individuals, former patients, and others. (See Figure

Figure 17-2. Organization chart for an annual giving campaign.

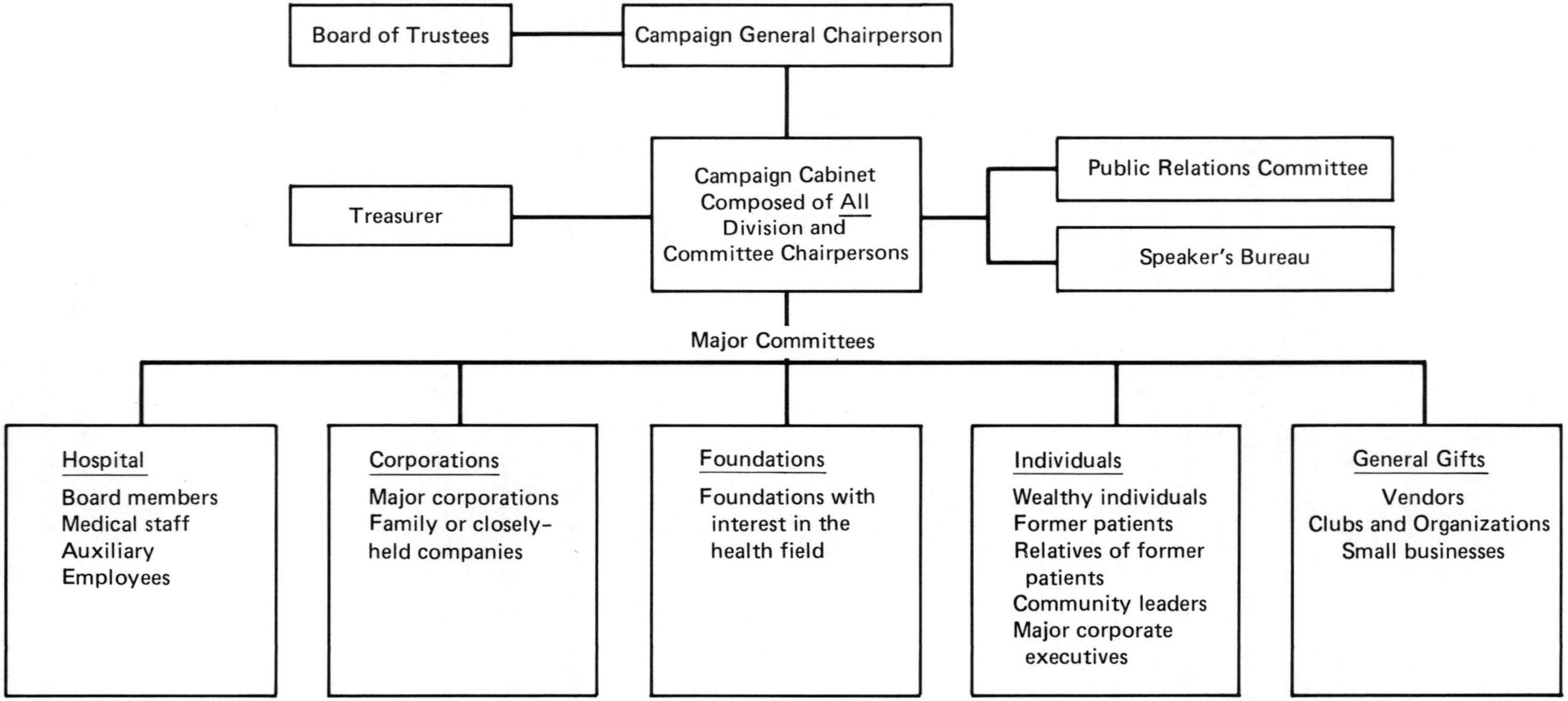

Board of Trustees

Campaign General Chairperson

Treasurer

Campaign Cabinet Composed of All Division and Committee Chairpersons

Public Relations Committee

Speaker's Bureau

Major Committees

Hospital
Board members
Medical staff
Auxiliary
Employees

Corporations
Major corporations
Family or closely-held companies

Foundations
Foundations with interest in the health field

Individuals
Wealthy individuals
Former patients
Relatives of former patients
Community leaders
Major corporate executives

General Gifts
Vendors
Clubs and Organizations
Small businesses

17-2 for an organization chart for an annual giving campaign.) Most hospitals depend upon a highly selective mail campaign directed to former patients and friends who live in higher-income areas. Generally, such letters are personalized and signed by the president or chairperson of the hospital or its foundation. The letters are designed to point out the needs of the hospital as succinctly and dramatically as possible. (See Figure 17-3 for a sample format.) Mass-mailing programs have been promoted by some commercial mail organizations. These organizations depend upon computerized letters addressed to large numbers of prospects. An analysis of these mailings, however, shows

Figure 17-3. Sample format of a solicitation letter for a hospital campaign.

MEMORIAL HOSPITAL

Anywhere, USA

Dear Mr. Blake:

It was six months since Jane Allison was married and the world couldn't have seemed rosier—her wonderful husband had just received a promotion and they had moved into their new home. Plans were already under way for an addition to the family. Yes, life was perfect!

Jane had noticed the swelling in her neck, but "it was just one of those glandular things" that would go away. When it didn't, Jane thought she had better have her doctor check; some medication would probably resolve it in a few days.

The general physical exam was good and lab tests were all negative, but further testing was advised. X-ray clearly showed a tumor mass in the upper chest. A biopsy was performed upon the lump in her neck and the results were positive. Diagnosis: Hodgkins disease, a form of cancer. Jane was devastated; the world that had seemed so bright was suddenly dismal indeed. The doctors, however, encouraged Jane. It was a form of cancer that, if treated early, could be arrested.

A course of radiation therapy was prescribed for Jane that took four weeks and included treatments with a high-energy linear accelerator. This machine focuses on tumors and minimizes damage to healthy cells. A three-week rest period followed. Follow-up x-rays over the next two months showed that the tumor mass had shrunk. Jane's outlook for cure are now excellent.

Jane's life returned to normal and today she has two wonderful children. Fortunately, skilled doctors and nurses and the linear accelerator—though expensive—had saved her life.

Jane is only one of thousands of patients who use Memorial Hospital's facilities each year. But it is getting more difficult to be certain that the proper equipment will be available to provide the best in medical treatment. Inflation and regulations are making it increasingly difficult to improve programs, demonstrate new procedures, and buy the expensive equipment so necessary.

For this reason, the Memorial Hospital Foundation has been established to raise funds so that the highest quality of medical care can be continued.

Your help is greatly needed. We would appreciate your reading the enclosed material which describes the program more fully, and then sending your gift to ensure that the facilities and equipment will be there to serve you and your family, as well as others in the community, when needed.

Thank you for your help.

Yours sincerely,

James Jones
President
Memorial Hospital Foundation

---

that not only are they impersonal, they are not very effective either. The cost of the mailings frequently absorbs the total income received for several years. About the best that can be said for them is that they do help develop a list of names of people who have an interest in the hospital. A more selective mailing prepared by the hospital development department, and directed to high-potential contributors, makes much more sense.

Personal solicitation is often conducted among major corporations and wealthy individuals. Here the possibility of special gift opportunities can be emphasized. In this way, a corporation or wealthy individual might be asked to sponsor a particular piece of badly needed equipment. Generally speaking, such gifts are given public recognition. At the very least, they are mentioned in the annual report. If the gift is particularly significant, a plaque may be put up in the hospital.

Special Projects

In addition to the purchase of special equipment (see Figure 17-4), opportunities exist to invite donors to fund special new programs. These projects can include seed money for a new outpatient program or a special chemical-dependency program. Contributions may be requested for demonstration funds for a home health care program, one-day surgery experiments, ambulatory care, and the support of satellite clinics.

Formal proposals for such projects should be prepared and sent to foundations as well as corporations, with follow-up visits wherever possible.

Deferred Gifts

Because many people have had satisfying and dramatic experiences with hospitals, an excellent opportunity exists for the development of bequests and other forms of deferred gifts. The development of such a program is described in Chapter 21. Since deferred gifts are often received only after the death of the donor, it is important that an approach to prospects be conducted with great sensitivity and a full knowledge of the prospect's medical condition.

Capital Gifts

Most hospitals plan major capital campaigns every decade or so, depending on their needs. Typically, they are structured as most other organizations' capital campaigns only they have particular audiences, such as the medical staff. The medical staff is often an untapped resource of considerable potential.

Special Events

Charity balls, fashion shows, and bazaars are often sponsored and organized by the hospital's auxiliary.

Figure 17-4. Selective listing by department of major gift opportunities for a community hospital.

Department	Item and quantity (each)	Cost	Description/explanation
Nursing—Surgery	Opthalmic lasar (1)	$80,000	Unit used for traumatic eye injuries allowing rehab surgery; used for extra capsular cataract removal on children.
Laboratory	Spectrophotometer (1)	4,990	Used in obtaining preliminary drug serums and in therapeutic drug monitoring.
Nursing—Psych	Dinamap monitor (1)	2,065	Unit automatically operates and provides data on patient's blood pressure, mean arterial pressure, and heart rate.
Nursing—Pediatric Care Unit	Telemetry units with arrythmia detection (6)	43,865	Cardiac surveillance capabilities improved with use of computerized arrythmia detection units.
Nursing—Cardiac Care Unit	Monitor and defibrillator (1)	7,350	Monitor used to evaluate patient's cardiac rhythm. Documentation provided by strip chart recorder.
Nursing—Cardiac Care Unit	Apnea monitor (1)	2,000	Unit used on patients who are being weaned from mechanical ventilator or who are in danger of respiratory depression.
Nuclear Medicine	Thyroid uptake system	8,000	Unit is smaller with more up-to-date features and replaces obsolete thyroid uptake equipment.

IMPLEMENTING THE PROGRAM

Because they rely on a mail campaign and selective solicitation of individuals, corporations, and foundations, hospital development programs generally do not require an extensive volunteer organization.

The foundation board usually appoints a development committee responsible for the annual fund-raising effort. The deferred-gifts program may be carried on by a separate committee.

Hospital solicitation prospects will be determined primarily from the list of former patients, a careful analysis and evaluation of major corporations and foundations in the community, suppliers, its own medical staff, previous givers to the institution, and individuals of means who may—with proper attention—develop an interest in the hospital.

A corporate luncheon, with a tour of the hospital, is an excellent way of acquainting potential major givers with the hospital and its needs.

18

CAMPAIGNS BY SECTARIAN FEDERATIONS

Many institutions under religious auspices depend on annual campaigns conducted by sectarian federations for major funding. The services supported by such campaigns include diocesan seminaries in the Catholic community, highly specialized human services agencies, and overseas support of services in Israel by the Jewish community.

The two major types of sectarian federations that we'll examine in this chapter are the Catholic federation, often called the Annual Diocesan Appeal, and the Jewish federation, whose campaign is known as the United Jewish Fund. Both of these federations are locally organized and controlled. Decisions on the kinds of services their fund raising will support are made locally. Generally they support both local and national services for their respective organizations and, in the case of the Jewish community, services in Israel.

FUND RAISING IN THE CATHOLIC COMMUNITY

There are two basic sources of funds for Catholic institutions in the diocese:

1. The parish assessment, which is levied on each parish for the support of certain diocesan regional activities and programs approved by the Vatican.
2. The annual diocesan appeal, also called the annual appeal, which raises money on a voluntary basis for the support of Catholic institutions.

The annual diocesan appeal is a cooperative campaign. Philosophically, it represents a partnership between the diocese or archdiocese and the parishes within it. It relies on the cooperation of the parishes and the parishioner donors.

The organization of the annual appeal—and the member agencies that participate—are determined at the diocesan level. The annual appeal frequently includes requests for funds for seminaries and other religious vocational training, funds for priests' retirement, support for the parochial school system, and a wide range of human services. The services each federation helps differ from diocese to diocese, depending upon the needs of the diocese and the programs that the federation decides to support.

Individual institutions present a budget and a request for funds to the diocese, which reviews the programs and budgets and decides what portion of the annual campaign will be allocated to them. Frequently, the goal established is a compromise between what the institutions perceive their needs to be and the amount the diocesan campaign organization thinks can be raised.

The Parish Assessment and the Annual Diocesan Appeal

Some dioceses make no clear-cut distinction between the assessment and the annual appeal. Historically, most diocesan activities were once supported through parish assessments, but in recent years many dioceses are reluctant to increase the assessment which the parishes have to pay because of budget constraints and the increasing expenses of supporting parish schools. Many dioceses organized annual appeals to raise additional funds on a voluntary basis, even though the funds came from some of the same parishioners who had paid their share of the parish assessment.

More recently, some parishes are asked to raise all they can from voluntary gifts through the annual campaign. If the parish cannot achieve its goal, it is charged with an assessment drawn from its operating budget. On the other hand, if the campaign exceeds its goal, the parish can retain the overage. This arrangement is rather new and is not used often. A more common arrangement is for the assessment to be levied on the basis of a formula which takes into account each parish's weekly collections as well as the size of the parish membership. The appeal then raises as much as it can on a voluntary basis, but the parish does not have to make up the difference through an assessment if it falls short. In some cases, the annual appeal is organized so that a percentage, say 25 percent, of the amount raised in the appeal stays with the parish for it to use to meet its own needs. This "refund" serves as a powerful incentive for each parish to meet its goal.

THE ORGANIZATION OF THE ANNUAL APPEAL

In theory, an annual appeal is conducted so that parishes can band together to provide services needed by the Catholic community which no parish could afford to support by itself. Although the parishes do run the campaign, the annual appeal organization and staff at the diocesan level take part in carrying out the campaign in a number of different ways. The bishop or archbishop is usually the honorary chairman of the appeal. He, in turn, appoints a lay person to serve as campaign chairperson.

In some campaigns, the chairperson and staff at the diocesan level appeal directly to the parishioners through each pastor. In these cases, the appeal depends upon the success of the mailings and personal contact between the chairperson and staff at the diocesan level and each parish.

Organization by Deanery

A new structure is used in the Archdiocese of Saint Paul and Minneapolis. The archbishop serves as honorary chairman of the appeal and a lay person serves as overall chairperson. Each diocese is divided into deaneries, basically geographic divisions of the diocese that comprise anywhere from 7 to 25 parishes. The parish priests elect a priest as representative to the deanery and they serve as an advisory committee to the bishop. In Saint Paul and Minneapolis the deanery structure is used as a way of conducting the campaign. The lay chairperson of the campaign selects a lay representative for each deanery. He or she serves as what might be termed a division chairperson.

Each deanery is divided into a prescribed number of areas and each area has an area representative. The area representative is responsible for two to seven parishes and will make contact with the pastors in those parishes and assist them in setting up the campaign organization. Generally the pastor will recruit the lay chairperson in his church. In some cases this may be an individual, in others it may be a married couple. In many cases, the parish will also select chairpersons to take on the chairmanship the following year. (See Figure 18-1 for a representation of this approach.)

The Campaign Within Each Parish

Whether or not the deanery structure is used to organize the campaign, church campaigns generally tend to follow one of several patterns:

1. A particular Sunday—Annual Appeal Sunday—is selected as the kickoff for the campaign. Generally, a letter from the bishop is read to the congregation. The letter outlines the needs of the institutions and requests the parishioners' support.
2. Either on Annual Appeal Sunday or on the following Sunday a tape prepared by the bishop may be played or a slide presentation made that shows the services that will benefit from the proceeds of the appeal and the amount of funding that is needed.
3. The pledging process may be handled on an individual or group basis. In some parishes workers organized by the parish chairperson solicit all the parishioners personally. In other parishes, donors of larger gifts are solicited personally, while the other parishioners are solicited by mail.

    In some parishes the congregation is asked to sign pledges after the tape or slide show has been presented. This method of group solicitation has been adopted in recent years and has the advantage of obtaining pledges from a very high percentage of the congregation in one day. In other parishes, after the formal presentation has been made at mass, the congregation is invited to the church hall to formalize their pledges. Another possibility is to ask the congregation to return their pledge cards within a prescribed time period.

Payment period. Nearly all annual appeal programs are set up on a time payment basis. Some attempt to have payments made over a six-month period while others will allow a full year for payment.

Figure 18-1. Organization chart for annual Catholic appeal.

A. Organization by Deanery.

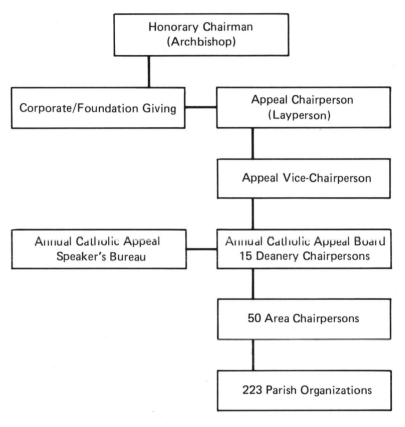

B. Organization by Parish.

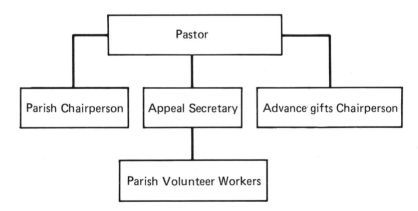

Timing. The timing of the annual appeal will differ from diocese to diocese depending to a large extent on climatic conditions. The spring is a good time in the north and the winter is favored in the south. Others will hold their campaigns in the fall.

Promotion. In addition to the presentation at mass, special articles will appear in the Catholic newspaper and church bulletins. Some coverage is also obtained from the local newspapers. Throughout the campaign, bulletins are sent to each parish to report the status of the campaign and give updates for each parish. The articles in the Catholic newspaper frequently include the opening campaign story and later run special features about the individual institutions that will benefit from the campaign.

GOAL SETTING

The way in which annual appeal goals are set for each parish differs from diocese to diocese. In some dioceses, the individual parish's offertory income is weighed against the total offertory income in all parishes. In other words, if the offertory in a particular church represented 3 percent of total offertory income in the diocese, that parish would be asked to accept an annual appeal goal equal to 3 percent of the total annual appeal in the diocese.

In other parishes, the formula may be based on the number of family units in each parish. In this situation, a parish's goal would be determined by multiplying a per-family amount for each parish. Larger parishes would be expected to meet larger goals while considerably less would be asked of the smaller ones.

Some dioceses set parish goals by considering both the number of family units and the past performance of the parish. If, for example, the parish has a history of meeting or exceeding goals, that will be taken into account. Parishes that have had considerable difficulty in reaching goals, perhaps because the membership is from low-income areas, are given proportionately lower goals.

Finally, the diocese asks individual parishes to set goals equal to a percentage of their offertories. The diocese knows the offertory income of each parish, so it can determine what percentage of that offertory would bring in sufficient funds to meet the annual appeal goal.

THE UNITED JEWISH FUND

The Jewish federation conducts a federated appeal in the Jewish community (known as the United Jewish Fund) that is similar to the United Way campaign. There is a dimension, however, to this campaign that the United Way does not have: A very substantial part of the funds raised—sometimes as much as 50 percent or more—goes for overseas social, health, and welfare agencies in Israel and to Jewish communities throughout the world.

Typically, agencies in the Jewish community submit their budget requests on an annual basis to the Jewish federation, which provides a review process through specially selected panels of volunteers in the fields of aging, group work and education, community relations, campus services, and working with national agencies. A preliminary review of the agencies' budgets is done before the campaign and estimates for local and overseas needs are made. Meanwhile, the campaign committee makes some tentative estimates about the amount that might be raised after considering the contributions likely to be made by the major prospects. Its report, together with that of the budget committee, goes to the board, which establishes the campaign goal. When the campaign is nearly complete, the panels, which know approximately how much is available for allocation, consult with the agencies, review their needs in detail, and make recommendations about their allocations.

In some cities, Jewish agencies may be supported jointly by the Jewish federation and by the United Way, and occasionally there are pre-arranged agreements as to the proportions of support that may be requested of each.

In deciding upon the campaign potential, the campaign committee reviews each division's productivity in the prior year. A detailed review is made of each division's key givers and tentative targets are set—including decisions about who may be asked to give substantially more. These targets are used to set potential goals. If the board of directors feels that the figures presented by the campaign committee are not high enough, it may ask the committee to accept a "stretch goal" which is generally considerably higher than what the committee thought was achievable. A re-evaluation of the major prospects is necessary.

It is also commonplace for the representatives of the budget and campaign committees to meet with representatives of the agencies and to share with them their thinking about the goal and the reasons for it being set at a certain level. The meeting keeps the agencies informed and involved. This participation is important since many of their board members will be asked to serve as solicitors.

Solicitation

Typically, campaigns by Jewish federations in medium-size communities depend primarily upon solicitation of individual gifts. Foundation and corporate gifts are made when an individual decides to contribute through his or her corporation. Individual solicitation is particularly effective in the Jewish community because the numbers involved are generally not large and the community identifies very closely with its interests.

In larger cities, divisions are generally structured according to the size of the gift. Smaller cities could use the same structure but the amounts requested would be lower. Such a structure might be organized as follows:

Division	*Prospects*
Top gifts	Prospects might be expected to give $10,000 to $20,000, or more. Their giving represents a very substantial part of the campaign goal.
Advanced gifts	Givers might be expected to give $5,000 to $10,000.
Major gifts	Prospects give in the $1,000 to $5,000 range.
Other	Other prospects might be expected to give less than $1,000.

Separate men's and women's divisions are organized. All women are encouraged to make a separate gift from their husbands' and are solicited by other women in the community. Men in this prospect range are solicited by men of approximately peer status.

Most solicitation is made on a personal, face-to-face basis, especially if the giver is in the top-prospects level, and to a lesser degree if the giver is in the lower category. However, an effort is made to encourage face-to-face solicitation at all levels of the campaign.

Card Calling Meeting

A technique used by the Jewish federation, particularly in appealing to those in the higher-gift categories, is to invite donors to a dinner meeting where a presentation of the needs is made. Generally speaking, an outside speaker of national reputation is invited and his or her presence serves as an incentive to attend the meeting.

Some of the people invited have been solicited in advance and have made a commitment to the campaign. At the dinner meeting, a presentation is made and the chairperson, who is particularly well qualified to handle the card calling function, asks the donors to rise and announce their gifts. The caller has the opportunity to make some grateful remarks about each of the prospects and commend the giver if the gift is being increased substantially. Frequently the meeting will be started by calling upon pace-setter givers who have already committed themselves to a very generous gift representing a substantial increase over the prior year. The gifts of others may be called in rotation and placed between some of these major gifts. This provides the opportunity for a person to see what his peers are doing and exerts a subtle influence that encourages generosity.

Follow-Up

A phonathon Sunday is organized; volunteers call those who have not responded, with special attention to the givers in lower categories. A young men's division is organized for those in the 21 to 40 age bracket. Their gifts are not expected to be more than $1,000, but it is felt that their contributions mark the beginning of a lasting association with the Jewish federation. Their starting experience is a training ground. They are potential future leaders in the federation's divisions.

In larger communities, in addition to the specialized approach to generous givers, the solicitation may be divided according to trades and professions, synagogue affiliation, or geographic area. In some cases, solicitation is also conducted by country club or even high-rise building.

Training

Because such a large proportion of the Jewish federation's funds is given to services overseas, it is absolutely essential that leadership understand the needs. It is not uncommon to take a group of top leaders on a "training mission" to Israel so they have an opportunity to see the problems and what is being done to resolve them. This way the leaders can bring back a first-hand account of what is needed from the American Jewish community.

Timing

The conduct of the annual campaign will vary from community to community, depending in large part on climatic factors. The kickoff may be timed to coincide with one of the Jewish holidays.

Leadership Development

It is not uncommon for the United Jewish Fund to plan its leadership needs for five years in the future. Typically, they will at least arrange a two-year cycle with a chairperson and a vice chairperson. The chairperson is responsible for the overall leadership of the current campaign and the vice chairperson usually supervises several divisions. This gives him or her an opportunity to observe the campaign and move into the top role the following year. Although the long-range leadership plan may cover five years, it may have to be adjusted subject to the availability of Jewish leadership.

Promotion

Most United Jewish Funds produce their own newspapers which are circulated among givers and prospective givers. They also conduct an extensive direct-mail campaign to people's homes to keep the community informed about the campaign and its progress.

The Jewish federation campaign is generally highly selective, well-executed, and extremely successful. Because the Jewish community is very close-knit and identifies with its needs, it is possible to use certain campaign techniques (such as the card calling meeting) that probably would not be appropriate in other communities or groups.

19

UNITED WAY CAMPAIGNS

The first attempt to combine fund raising for health and welfare agencies occurred in Denver in 1882. Led by a priest, a rabbi, and a minister, the effort mobilized community leaders to give more generous support to organizations serving the poor, the ill, dependent children, the aged, and the youth. Another major effort to establish a local federation came about in Cleveland in 1913. Later, stimulated by concern over the large number of organizations raising funds for war-related causes (during World War I), the federated movement took hold. Its aim was to help the many local charities that were having difficulty raising funds and to develop a better system of planning and budgeting to meet community needs. The federated movement has been known by a variety of names: the Community Chest, Community Fund, War Fund (during World War II), and United Fund. Finally in 1971 the name United Way was to symbolize the organization's major purpose: to provide a united approach to fund raising, budgeting, and planning. Each United Way is completely autonomous and policy decisions are made by individual communities. There is a national association called United Way of America. In 1984, over 2,000 United Ways raised a total of more than $2 billion, making it the largest voluntary fund-raising movement in the country. In small communities, United Ways are often run entirely by volunteers without any paid staff.

Today the United Way is an organization of contributors who work together to serve the community by giving generous support to worthy health and welfare services. These comprise a large number of local health and welfare agencies, as well as local offices of national organizations such as the American Red Cross and the American Cancer Society. Some United Ways also include a number of state-wide agencies. An allocations committee reviews which agencies will be included and the amount to be given to each and makes its recommendations to the board of directors of the United Way. The aim of the budgeting process is to allocate funds according to the *needs* of the agency rather than according to its ability to raise money.

Member agencies retain certain rights, including the right to decide their own programs and the right to appeal their allocation to the board of directors if they think their case has not been properly considered. There are a number of arrangements used by United Ways to determine how to support agencies including deficit financing (that is, making up the difference between the income of an agency and its total expenditures), purchase of services, block grants, and allocations for specific programs. These arrangements differ from city to city and agency to agency and depend upon the policies determined by the board of directors.

The agencies must agree to meet certain standards including an annual audit of their accounts and submitting monthly or quarterly financial reports to be reviewed by United Way staff and committees. They must also agree not to make solicitations during the year except with specific approval of the United Way, and they pledge to cooperate in the coordination of programs with other agencies. United Way agencies are also requested to submit their budgets and programs for review by an impartial citizens committee.

CAMPAIGN ORGANIZATION

Unlike most philanthropic organizations, which have selected markets of potential contributors, United Ways have very broad markets. Because they represent annual campaigns of sizable proportions that support many agencies which serve the entire community, they must conduct saturation campaigns to present the need to every potential contributor in the areas they solicit. A very large part of this market are the many employee groups in business, government, and nonprofit sectors.

United Way campaigns will generally be structured to approach the following types of prospects.

Corporations

Corporate giving to United Ways accounts for an average of approximately 25 percent of the total raised. The solicitation of corporate gifts is a highly-developed practice and has been very successful. Much of this is due to the participation of top business people in the campaign and on the boards, and their willingness to act on their conviction that the United Way is the best and most efficient way to raise money for health and welfare services.

United Ways have experimented with a number of corporate giving formulas. These formulas are described in Chapter 11, and include methods based on profits, number of employees, and trade group contribution averages.

Foundations

Foundations normally do not represent a very large source of support for United Ways except in a few cities. This is due to the fact that basically United Ways seek annual, repetitive support for their agencies and many foundation grants are short term. However, there are a number of private foundations which do make annual United

Table 19-1. Sources of funds for the United Way—1982.

Source	Percent of total
Corporate gifts	25.2%
Employees—corporations and small business	49.9
Nonprofit and government employee gifts	10.9
Professional gifts	2.5
Small business gifts	2.8
Noncorporate foundation gifts	1.8
Other	6.9
Total	100.0%

Source: United Way of America.

Way gifts and other foundations which make grants for short-term demonstration projects, or to support agencies on an interim basis before their membership in the United Way has been finalized.

Employee Giving

Gifts from individuals through employee giving programs represent the largest source of support for United Ways. Generally, United Ways are the only organizations given the privilege of soliciting employees at work. The privilege of conducting internal company campaigns is based upon the premise that the participating organizations are willing to submit to certain standards in the interest of serving the community. They agree to participate in the United Way effort and give up separate campaigns, they submit their budgets for impartial review, and they pledge to coordinate programs with other agencies. Companies feel they can justify a combined campaign among their employees on behalf of a number of agencies which accept these disciplines, but they could hardly justify separate campaigns for individual agencies, federations which do not meet these standards or do not serve the total community, or single-issue organizations which serve narrow or sectarian constituencies.

Large Gifts from Wealthy Individuals

Top corporate executives of substantial means may be solicited either outside the firm or as part of the internal employee solicitation. Other wealthy individuals who are not employed but have independent sources of income from investments represent another source of large gifts. Typically, they are solicited through a separate individual-gifts division, or along with major corporations through an advance-gifts division. In that case, corporate executives are organized through separate employee groups.

Professions

The professions—doctors, lawyers, and dentists, and in some cities, architects— are major prospects. Because of the large number of individuals involved, the scattered location of their offices, and the tight appointment schedules they follow, they are quite difficult to solicit. The types of solicitation used are described in Chapter 14.

Small Businesses

There are literally hundreds—and in some communities, thousands—of small businesses employing fewer than 25 people. They constitute a very substantial part of the business community. Organizing to cover these prospects is a very major effort. Although the amount obtained from small businesses is not large, the prospects for future funding are sometimes considerable because many eventually grow to be sizable enterprises. Looking to the future, economists project that more and more of our enterprises will be small, rather than large firms with major employee groups. Therefore it is important to learn how to approach these companies.

Other Individuals

United Ways usually attempt to contact people who work out of their own homes, are retired, or are housewives with independent incomes. At one time, they were solicited through residential divisions involving many hundreds of volunteers. More recently, this solicitation is often made only to prospects whose gifts are in the medium to larger ranges in order to reduce the number of volunteers needed and save time.

With an increasing number of women working, it is difficult to obtain the volunteers necessary to staff large residential campaigns. Because of the fear of crime, homeowners and apartment dwellers are reluctant to respond to solicitors. Accordingly, many United Ways approach these prospects through mail or telephone solicitation.

ORGANIZING EMPLOYEE CAMPAIGNS

United Ways are among the few organizations which have the privilege of soliciting employees at their place of employment. (United arts campaigns and, in some cases, community-based combined building campaigns may also be permitted to solicit at the office.) To be eligible, a joint building campaign would have to be able to demonstrate that it gives essential services to a large number of employees. For example, a campaign on behalf of the only two hospitals in a community might qualify.

United Ways campaign either by approaching corporations and their employees through separate divisions, or by making a single approach wherein the corporate gift and the employee solicitation are established in one call by the same solicitor. In approaching corporations for both corporate and employee support, two established methods are widely used.

The Single Corporate-Employee Approach

Under this plan, the company is approached by a campaign volunteer and is asked to make a corporate gift and to set up the necessary facilities for in-company solicitation of its executives and employees. The volunteer calls on the chief executive officer of the corporation and requests a corporate gift (in the manner described in the section on the solicitation of corporations in Chapter 9).

Once the corporate gift has been discussed and established, the CEO is asked to make arrangements for the solicitation of the company's executives and employees by appointing two chairpersons within the company—one to head up the executive solicitation, the other to be responsible for the solicitation of all other employees. The CEO is also asked if he or she would permit the campaign to hold employee meetings during office hours, arrange a tour of the United Way agencies for solicitors, and possibly hold a company rally. Promotion plans for the campaign are cleared in a general way, and the chief executive is asked to give tentative approval to the goal suggested for executives and employees. An organization chart illustrating the single corporate-employee approach is shown in Figure 19-1. The strength of this approach is that it requires only half as many volunteers as the separate corporate-employee campaign. It also gets the CEO more involved in the internal campaign.

Separate Corporate-Employee Campaign

Corporate gifts are handled through one division and the solicitation of employees through another in the separate corporate-employee approach. A volunteer from the corporate division calls on the CEO and asks for a generous corporate gift. Once that is done, the corporate solicitor has completed his or her assignment.

A volunteer representing the employee division makes a separate appointment with the CEO and asks for cooperation in conducting the campaign among executives and employees. The requests for assistance are much the same as in the single approach. Figure 19-2 illustrates a campaign using the separate corporate-employee approach.

Differences between the two campaigns. The two approaches represent different points of view. Some campaigners believe that a corporation has a responsibility to support the community's nonprofit institutions regardless of what its employees might do. They feel that mixing employee and corporate gifts may, over a period of time, dilute one or the other and therefore separate campaigns should be maintained. Historically, many campaigns formerly used what is called a unit approach. A corporation was asked to accept a certain goal, and although proportions for the corporate gift and employee giving were suggested, the soliciting organization in effect said, "We don't care where the money comes from as long as you meet this goal." The weakness in this approach is that very generous employee gifts often meant that the corporation gave far less than it should have. In other cases, a very poor job of employee solicitation was concealed by a very generous corporate gift. Under the unit plan, the campaign seldom receives the benefit of an oversubscribed goal.

A strength of the separate corporate-employee approach is that the corporate division is an excellent place to use past presidents, past campaign chairpersons, chief executive officers, and past division chairpersons. Frequently they can be enrolled to handle a few select corporate calls although they might not want to become involved in the employee campaigns. However, regardless of the approach, the CEO should always be contacted by a high-level business volunteer.

Figure 19-1. Sample campaign organization when the single approach to corporate and employee gifts is used.

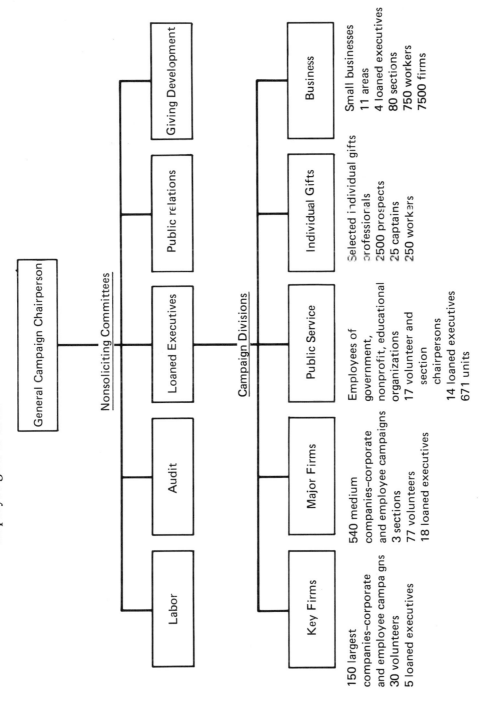

General Campaign Chairperson

Nonsoliciting Committees

Labor | Audit | Loaned Executives | Public relations | Giving Development

Campaign Divisions

Key Firms | Major Firms | Public Service | Individual Gifts | Business

150 largest companies–corporate and employee campa gns
30 volunteers
5 loaned executives

540 medium companies–corporate and employee campaigns
3 sections
77 volunteers
18 loaned executives

Employees of government, nonprofit, educational organizations
17 volunteer and section chairpersons
14 loaned executives
671 units

Selected individual gifts
professiorals
2500 prospects
25 captains
250 workers

Small businesses
11 areas
4 loaned executives
80 sections
750 workers
7500 firms

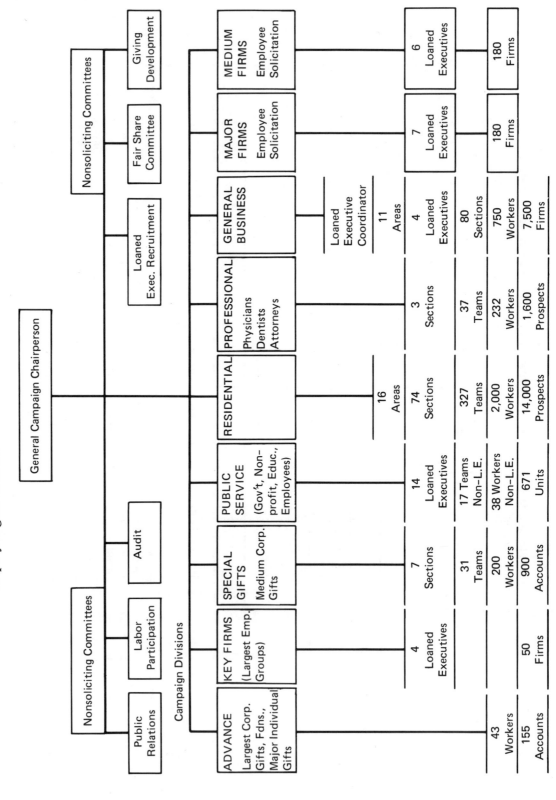

Figure 19-2. Sample campaign organization when the separate approach to corporate and employee gifts is used.

Even when a single approach is used, considerable effort should be made to distinguish and keep separate the corporate gift from those of the executives and employees. For this reason the corporate gift is generally requested and committed on the first call before the employee campaign begins.

Many United Ways today use volunteers in key leadership roles—division, section, and group chairpersons—and supplement their efforts with loaned executives recruited from businesses. They carry the major responsibility for employee campaigns, thus reducing the number of volunteer workers needed. Even when the firm has volunteers only in key leadership roles, it is possible to team the loaned executive with the United Way's corporate solicitor in the initial call. This ensures that the CEO will be seen personally, and that his or her assistance will be obtained in conducting the employee campaign.

Since the corporate solicitor is generally a top businessperson who has a good relationship with the chief executive officer, he or she can present the loaned executive and clear the necessary arrangements within the company. Then the loaned executive works with the employee chairperson in organizing and carrying out the campaign. If there are any difficulties, it is always possible to ask the corporate solicitor to intercede and clear any problems with the CEO.

Noncorporate Employee Groups

The campaign must also include a plan to solicit nonprofit organizations with sizable employee groups. These will include federal, state, and local government offices, private and public school systems, colleges and universities, nonprofit charitable organizations, and hospitals and nursing homes. Together these prospects have considerable potential.

In these situations, of course, no corporate gifts are solicited. However the chief executive or manager of each institution should be approached in the same manner as corporate CEOs. Plans for employee solicitation are made in much the same way as they are in profit-making companies.

Conducting the Internal Campaign

The meeting with the CEO will have cleared the important issues so that the campaign can be implemented. From that point on, the campaign volunteer (or loaned executive where one is used) works with the chairperson of the executive and employee campaign, and establishes an internal campaign committee. Minimally, this committee includes representatives of the firm's public relations, personnel, accounting, and data processing departments, and organized labor, if the firm is unionized. The campaign committee formulates a campaign plan which includes the following agenda:

Timing. The committee establishes the time period over which the campaign will be conducted—generally as short a period as is feasible to get the job done. Included in this schedule will be a plan for precampaign promotion, the enrollment and training of solicitors, and follow-up directed toward those who have been missed or did not give.

Goal for employees and executives. The volunteer (or loaned executive) works with the campaign committee to establish a formal goal for executives and employees. This may be based upon a percentage of total payroll, the use of suggested minimum gifts, the estimated number of employees who will participate, or the previous year's results with a percent increase.

Promotion. Specific plans for promoting the campaign within the organization are finalized. Promotion plans usually include precampaign mailings to employees, a letter of endorsement from the CEO and the union leader (if there is one), posters on the bulletin boards, and an audio-visual presentation.

Payment plan. A payment plan utilizing payroll deduction is decided upon. If the payment plan includes a number of deductions, each one will be for a smaller amount. That makes it easier for employees to give generously. A firm which provides a plan for weekly or semi-monthly deductions will find that it is easier for employees to respond than if they have, for example, only three deductions in total.

Enrollment and training of solicitors. A specific plan to enroll and train solicitors is established. The plan should specify the content and materials to be used and determine who will make the various presentations. If there is a union, its cooperation should be sought. Solicitors may be given an opportunity to visit the United Way's agencies so they can give a first-hand account of their needs and services.

Records and auditing. An auditing committee is responsible for finalizing the campaign results and turning them over to the payroll department to computerize and collect the pledges. Records of each department's contribution should be kept. A list of people who might have been missed the first time should also be kept to facilitate the follow-up.

Follow-up. To ensure that everyone is given an opportunity to contribute, a plan to follow up on those who have not responded or prompt departments that are slow needs to be arranged. Occasionally a solicitor cannot complete the follow-up. Plans to find a substitute need to be made.

CONDUCTING THE SOLICITATION

The solicitation of employees can be accomplished either through a system of group solicitation (described later in this chapter) or by the solicitation of each individual employee.

Individual Solicitation

With individual solicitation, it is important to stress to solicitors that they should always approach the most generous and responsive employees first. The best prospects are those who have given generously in past years to other campaigns, or who are known to have a positive attitude toward the charitable cause. As I've noted, giving is largely a follow-the-leader concept. Even when guidelines are given, people often do not know how much to give. The tendency is to want to do what others do, and give neither more nor less. Therefore, it is important that the first gifts be generous so that others in the department will respond in kind.

Solicitors should also explain the payment plan that is being used and note the reasonable deduction being asked each pay period. It is also important to point out the services the United Way has provided for fellow employees and that are available when the need arises.

Department goals should be established. They give each department something to strive for and stimulate competition among the departments and solicitors. Some organizations use rewards as incentives to stimulate participation, for example, a drawing in which all employees who have given are eligible to win prizes. I have never been a strong advocate of giving prizes to employees for responding to a community need, but I have to admit that they seem to be effective, at least with those who would not otherwise be responsive.

Solicitation should always be personal and face-to-face. This way, each employee has the opportunity to hear the sales case pitch and ask questions. Some solicitors drop pledge cards on desks without a personal appeal. This should be avoided because it often results in small, casual cash gifts.

Solicitation—nonsupervisory versus line. In soliciting individuals some firms prefer to use their line organization: They use their supervisors and foremen as solicitors. Other companies prefer to use nonsupervisory employees entirely. They feel it is more democratic and that there is less perceived pressure. For some employees, merely the fact that the supervisor is doing the solicitation is intimidating. However, supervisors and foremen generally have duties and schedules which make it more convenient for them to perform this function.

In some manufacturing plants, the solicitation is carried out jointly by the foreman and the steward. This demonstrates to the workers that both union and management are solidly behind the campaign. The presence of the union steward also assures the workers that there is no undue pressure.

Generally, research has shown that pressure is perceived in firms where management-labor relations are poor and when a good job of public information has not been provided. A study of the solicitation of federal employees done a number of years ago showed that when they were well informed, employees gave more generous gifts, participated, and perceived less pressure associated with the campaign. Among poorly informed employees, the exact opposite was the case. Employees need not be pressured. They will respond generously if they are properly informed and understand the need for generous giving.

Employee Goals

Employee goals may be established in a variety of ways. Since World War II, the most commonly suggested guide for giving has been one hour's pay per month. However, because of inflation this may be unrealistic and unattainable in many companies.

However, the employee goal can be computed as shown in Table 19-2.

Another way to estimate is to use the number of employees and hourly payrates as shown in Table 19-3.

Note that the potential is modified by making allowance for the fact that not everyone will give according to the giving guide. The goal is reduced by some agreed-upon figure. Here it was estimated that 80 percent of the employees would comply. The employee goal may be established separately or combined with the executive estimate as a composite for the entire group.

Campaigning by potential. More and more United Ways are campaigning by potential. Rather than establishing a goal for a corporation at campaign headquarters and attempting to sell it to the CEO, the CEO is asked to examine the potential among the employees.

The CEO is asked to estimate what the executives would give if they followed the guides for giving. The CEO is also asked to review the total payroll and estimate what could be raised if participation and adherence to giving guides were followed. He or she follows the procedure already described, but the approach is different in that the CEO is relied upon to suggest the goal. The CEO might decide to try to increase participation from 50 to 60 percent in a given year. When campaigning by potential is used, the soliciting organization must be cautious that the goals are at least as high as, or higher than, the campaign increase. Otherwise the effort will fall short.

Obviously, any formulas used to establish company goals will be modified according to the total community goal and past levels of giving. In general, goals should be high enough to challenge people to give more, but not so high as to completely discourage both the giver and the solicitor. However, when the goals of the various employee groups are added up, they should be 10 to 25 percent higher than is required to make the division goal; otherwise, the division will fall short.

Soliciting executives. While the solicitation of employees is being conducted, a separate solicitation of management personnel is held. A meeting of the executives with the CEO presiding provides a good beginning. The CEO may offer his or her personal endorsement—and the endorsement of the firm—to the campaign and explain why executives should respond generously. The CEO's own gift is very important in that it sets an example for others to follow. The chairperson for executive solicitation is responsible to follow through.

In some cities, the solicitation of executives is still carried on through external solicitation rather than from within the company. In that case, executives are included

Table 19-2. Determining the employee goal based on percentage of payroll and compliance.

Annual company payroll	$5,000,000
Multiplied by ⁶⁄₁₀ of 1 percent (one hour's pay per month)	× .006
Employee goal	$ 30,000
Multiplied by estimated compliance	× .80
Employee goal	$ 24,000

Table 19-3. Determining employee goal based on average hourly rate of pay and compliance.

Average hourly rate	$ 10.00
Multiplied by 12 (one hour's pay per month)	× 12
Suggested average pledge	$120.00
Multiplied by the number of employees	× 250
Goal potential	$30,000
Multiplied by estimated compliance	× .80
Employee goal	$24,000

in a special-gifts solicitation program and are contacted by a campaign volunteer from another company. When the solicitation takes place from outside the company through a separate executive division, the results are reported separately through that division. It is not possible to say which method is better—it depends to a great extent upon past results and the attitude of the CEO. If his or her cooperation is lukewarm at best, then an external solicitation often is the best approach. On the other hand, if the CEO is enthusiastic and cooperative, it is better to handle the executive solicitation from within the company.

Executive goals. In conducting the solicitation of executives, the CEO may be asked to estimate the potential to set as the goal. Provide the CEO with a schedule which shows guidelines for giving in different salary brackets and ask him or her to estimate the results if each executive responds according to that guide. Generally speaking, the computation is made confidentially, although the total amount is reported and the CEO agrees to a negotiated amount to be set as a goal. The computation is illustrated in Table 19-4.

Group Solicitation

Interrupting the work schedule of employees is often problematic. Also, it is often difficult for one individual to effectively communicate the ways in which the United

Table 19-4. Executive goals.

Position	Salary	Guide for giving	Suggested gift
President	$200,000	2%	$ 4,000
Executive vice president	150,000	2	3,000
Vice president	100,000	1½	1,500
Vice president	85,000	1	850
Vice president	75,000	1	750
Treasurer	70,000	1	700
Secretary	65,000	1	650
Total Potential			$11,450
Goal (80% of potential)			$ 9,160

Way serves the needs of the community. For these reasons soliciting employees in a group setting has gained popularity. A relatively short period of time is budgeted by each department in the company for a presentation of the United Way's needs. It can take only 15 minutes or, in some cases, as long as an hour.

A tight agenda is planned and adhered to so that the interruption of the work schedule is minimal. The department head or chairperson of the company campaign makes some preliminary remarks about the campaign, its goal and importance, and stresses that the company is endorsing it and lending its support. This is followed by a five to ten minute visual presentation—generally a film or a slide sound show that outlines the purpose, needs, and goals of the campaign. Frequently it will have a strong emotional appeal. Immediately afterward pledge cards are distributed and the company indicates how pledges may be paid. (It is generally done through payroll deduction.) If there is a recommended guide for giving, the employees are informed of it. They are asked to make their pledges and turn them in as they leave the room.

The advantages of group solicitation are:

1. Many individuals—from 25 to 100—can be solicited at the same time; thus the whole process is speeded up.
2. It provides a vehicle through which the institution can tell its story briefly and effectively. This could not be accomplished as easily through individual solicitation, particularly in a manufacturing plant where the production line cannot be interrupted.
3. A group setting provides a forum to anticipate and answer questions. This eliminates unfounded negative feelings and misinformation and gets the campaign off on a positive note.
4. It provides a setting to explain deferred-payment plans and to suggest the levels of giving necessary to make the campaign a success.

Pilot or Pace-Setting Campaigns

Employees can be motivated to give more generously through the example of generous giving by employees in other companies.

Early campaign planning should provide for the careful selection of a small number of companies to be asked to serve as campaign leaders in the employee divisions. They will conduct pilot campaigns well in advance of the regular employee solicitation. Basically they are intended to accomplish a number of things:

1. Focus staff and volunteer efforts on selected companies or government units where there is appreciable potential.
2. Demonstrate that higher levels of employee giving can be achieved both in companies where giving is already generous and where the giving is below par.
3. Test the campaign's acceptability under the social and economic conditions of the time, and determine whether substantially more money can be raised and whether the promotional campaign is effective.
4. Provide additional funds to make up losses the United Way may be suffering because other resources are no longer available, for example, if a major cor-

poration has left the community, or if losses have been sustained due to the deaths of major contributors.

5. Test new techniques in solicitation in different types of employee groups. A specific group may be targeted. For example, married women may be the focus to determine whether a particular approach will bring a response from supplementary wage earners whose husbands may also be asked to give at another place of employment. The construction industry might be selected to demonstrate that successful campaigns can be conducted even when employees are mobile and move from company to company.

The results of pilot campaigns should be widely publicized and used both at the campaign kickoff and in the bulletins that are issued as part of the campaign promotion. Newspaper publicity is also helpful. Publicizing the results of pilot campaigns can stimulate higher levels of giving among employees in other groups when the regular campaign is launched.

Pilot campaigns within a company. Just as a pilot campaign is helpful when conducted in specifically selected companies, the same principle can be adapted within a given company. In this situation, the company campaign committee selects a particular department for the pilot effort and the campaign among that department's employees is conducted in advance of the solicitation of other departments.

Provided the results are good, they should be widely publicized as part of the campaign promotion within the company and, again, can demonstrate that higher levels of giving can be achieved.

For pilot campaigns to be successful it is essential to follow all the proper procedures previously outlined: Obtain cooperation from top management, make arrangements for solicitor training, show the film to solicitors and employees, provide an adequate payroll deduction plan, get cooperation from the union, etc. Again, the pilot campaign can test an approach geared to a special interest. For example, in a firm that has many female employees, the promotion of services of particular interest to women might be used as a way of testing whether this approach is successful in bringing increased giving.

Continuing Pledge Plan

As noted, in some companies it is very difficult to interrupt the assembly line or manufacturing process in order to solicit employees. For this reason companies have sought to establish a system which would enable employees to give generously without an annual interruption of the work day. Over the years, some companies have solved this problem by developing of a continuing pledge plan.

The plan for continuing pledges is carried out by agreement between labor and management—if a union is involved—to conduct an all-out effort in a single year to enroll contributors by asking them to make a pledge which will be continued from year to year. There is no additional solicitation the following year, but the plan must provide that each employee has the right to discontinue his or her pledge at any time by notifying the payroll office.

The advantages of a continuing pledge plan are obvious. The company does not have to spend the time, money, and resources to conduct an annual campaign among its employees. However, a continuing plan, despite these advantages, may be fraught with problems for the future if certain safeguards are not followed:

1. Care must be exercised to ensure that giving is not taken for granted. Minimally, employees should be given literature about the campaign each year and thanked for their contributions. Otherwise, there is a loss of feeling of involvement.

2. Unless the continuing pledge is tied to a percentage of earnings rather than flat amounts, the results among employees over a period of years will be inadequate to meet changing economic conditions and community goals. For example, in the early days some plans suggested donations as small as 15 cents a week. Although this might have been adequate at that time, the ravages of inflation, the changing value of the dollar, and improved hourly rates of pay made this amount completely inadequate over a period of time. If, however, the plan is set up in such a way that employees are asked to give a percentage of earnings, say, six-tenths of one percent, then the results will increase as earnings escalate.

3. Promotions do occur and over a period of time some employees will move into the executive ranks. A plan needs to be adopted that recognizes that employees advance to more responsible positions and higher income levels. An employee who is promoted to an executive position can give much more generously.

4. Because there is considerable turnover in personnel, a plan needs to be adopted which will permit the enrollment of new employees either as they enter the company or shortly thereafter. Some companies prefer to enroll new employees immediately, while others prefer to defer this for a month or two so employees don't feel that the gift is a condition of employment.

5. Again, employees must be given the right to cancel pledges at any time.

Although continuing pledge plans do provide a convenient alternative to the annual campaign, there is much to be said in favor of continuing the annual campaign if it is not an undue burden for the company. The annual campaign gives the United Way an opportunity to restate its case every year and to better inform its giving constituency. It also allows for more flexibility—the amount requested of employees is not restricted by a formula. On the other hand, there are sometimes circumstances within a company which make it almost impossible to conduct a campaign at a particular time of year. If the company is on strike or has just had economic reverses and layoffs, the atmosphere might be very unreceptive to the usual annual campaign. Under these circumstances, the continuing plan permits charitable deductions to be resumed when the employees return to work. If layoffs have occurred, the deductions continue for those who are still working. In this way, the campaign will not sustain substantial losses.

On the other hand, it is interesting to note that in times of economic adversity, people often respond more generously than before because they identify with those who are in need. Frequently, an annual campaign, even under adverse circumstances, can raise substantially more money than before. A number of years ago I served as a United Way executive in a Midwestern community at a time when its major corporation was undergoing serious economic problems. A total of 25,000 employees were laid off at that company and the unemployment rate in the community rose to 20 percent. All of the supplier industries were also affected. Despite this situation, the United Way community goal was achieved every year by challenging those employee groups who were still working to give more generously. The selective use of pilot campaigns was a major factor in its success.

LOANED EXECUTIVES

A major factor in the success of United Way employee campaigns is the loaned executive program. A loaned executive is an employee—generally taken from the ranks of middle management—who is made available to the United Way for a specific period of time, generally two to three months, to work exclusively on the United Way campaign.

He or she is released by the firm, with its blessing, and is generally relieved of other work responsibilies during that period of time.

The loaned executive is generally assigned 25 to 30 companies in the United Way's employee division. In making the initial contact with the company, he or she may be accompanied by the top business executive who is soliciting the corporate gift and may be involved in making the preliminary arrangements for the employee campaign. Once these arrangements have been made, however, the loaned executive assumes the responsibility of working with the campaign committee and the campaign coordinator in the assigned companies. He or she helps the committee determine its timetable, makes plans for solicitor training and promotion, and plans for the actual solicitation. It is the loaned executives's job to see that all the proper steps are followed in each of the companies for which he or she is responsible.

In order to prepare the loaned executive, he or she is enrolled in a training course conducted by the United Way volunteers and staff. The course includes a detailed overview of the agencies supported by United Way, as well as an explanation of the United Way's budget policies and procedures and finances. The loaned executive is taken on a tour of a representative group of agencies, and given a concentrated course in all aspects of the United Way's solicitation method. The loaned executive learns how to deal with the top executives of major firms in making a sales presentation for the United Way and how to organize campaigns within the companies. A sample training program for loaned executives is shown in Figure 19-3. A program in a smaller city would use its most important features and adapt it by making the agenda shorter and more concentrated.

Corporations involved in the loaned executive program find that not only does the program contribute to the community, but it also brings important benefits to the company. The people selected to serve in this capacity have an opportunity to deal with and make presentations to the top executives of other corporations. This is invaluable in itself. They also gain considerable experience in organization and selling, which later can serve them in their corporate capacities. They return to the company more knowledgeable about community services and how to use them.

After the term of service has been completed, the United Way generally makes a formal evaluation of the loaned executive's performance which is sent to his or her superior and the corporate CEO. The evaluation format is generally reviewed beforehand with the loaned executives so that they are acquainted with what will be presented to their companies. If the loaned executives do well, it stands them in very good stead with their corporations and helps establish them as valuable members of the corporate

Figure 19-3. Training agenda for loaned executives.

Wednesday, August 1—United Way Office

8:00	Rolls and coffee
8:30	Welcome
8:45	Each loaned executive introduces himself or herself
	Movie: "The Winners" with John Madden and Lou Holtz
10:00	Break
10:15	The loaned executive job—overview of training
	Competency model review—loaned executive skills and job description
	Expectations/self-assessment/benchmarks
11:00	Agency tours
	(Lunch on the road)
3:00	Report by each loaned executive on tour observations
4:00	Social

Thursday, August 2

8:00	Rolls and coffee
	Loaned executive presentations of report on agency tours—observations
	Questions and answers
10:00	Break
10:15	Learning sales and negotiation skills
12:00	Lunch
1:00–	
4:00	Continuation of sales and negotiating skills

Friday, August 3

8:00	Rolls and coffee
8:30	General chairperson presentation
8:45	Questions/answers/impressions
10:00	Break
10:20	Admissions and allocations—how the money gets to the agencies
	Agency relations—how the United Way relates to the agencies
12:00	Lunch
1:00	Government relations—how the United Way works in the community
1:30	Steps to running a campaign (overview)
3:00	Break
3:20	Goal setting—personal and campaign goals
4:20	Movie—"Volunteer Report"
	Summary
5:00	Adjourn

Monday, August 6

8:00	Rolls and coffee
8:15	Presentation—loaned executive chairperson
8:30	Minicampaign—skit by former loaned executives
9:15	Goal setting/benchmarks—timetable, personal goals
9:45	CEO videotape—how to approach the CEO
10:00	Break
10:20	CEO presentation—what the CEO expects
10:45	Skills practice: CEO call/videotaping—practice calls
11:45	Lunch
12:45	Questions/answers—loaned executive's concerns and problems
1:00	CEO calls continued
2:45	Break
3:00	How to prepare for your calls
	Preview material
4:15	Review
4:30	Adjourn

Figure 19-3. (*Continued*)

Tuesday, August 7

8:00	Rolls and coffee
8:30	Review of previous day—questions
8:45	Campaign coordinator guest—how loaned executive works with the company coordinator
9:20	Discussion of campaign coordinator call
	How the loaned executive can have an impact on the employee campaign
10:00	Break
10:20	Film—"Solicitor Training"—loaned executive's part in solicitor training
11:45	Lunch
12:45	Skills practice: campaign coordinator call/videotaping
2:45	Break
3:00	Skills practice: campaign coordinator call/videotaping
3:30	Questions and answers
3:45	Committee meeting—role play by working with in-plant committee
4:00	Loaned executive skit (fun session)
4:30	Adjourn

Wednesday, August 8

8:00	Rolls and coffee
8:30	United Way president presentation
9:00	Communications/marketing division—services provided, plans
10:15	Break
10:30	Communications/marketing division (continued)
11:30	Lunch
12:30	Labor presentation—working with organized labor
1:30	Panel discussion
	Admissions and allocations
	Agencies
	Government relations
	Labor
	United Way management
3:00	Break
3:20	Review and catch-all
5:00	Adjourn

Thursday, August 9—Monday, August 13

Division meetings with volunteer staff

August 14—end of the campaign

The loaned executives work with the companies and their employee committees. The executives utilize their training to carry out the work of the campaign.

(Courtesy of United Way of St. Paul.)

team. The United Way, of course, is careful to see that both the corporation and the loaned executive are appropriately thanked for the services performed.

Although most are recruited from the corporate community, an increasing number of loaned executives are being drawn from government offices and the nonprofit sector. Regardless of where they are employed, the services loaned executives provide are essentially the same.

Loaned Executive Alumni Groups

Frequently the experience of serving as a loaned executive is so rewarding that many individuals can be persuaded to take on a continuing role in working on behalf of the United Way. A sort of camaraderie is often developed among loaned executives and they may form an alumni association to take on special projects in future years. These may include indoctrinating new loaned executives or conducting practice role-playing sessions to demonstrate the proper approach to a company. The alumni group might agree to assume the responsibility for a development program. This would involve working on an intensive basis with a limited number of organizations to find ways to tap their considerable giving potential. Some United Ways also develop a social calendar for these groups and hold parties to which husbands and wives are invited and outstanding work is recognized. Occasionally an event such as a golf tournament may be held.

PRECAMPAIGN CULTIVATION

An essential factor in keeping ongoing campaigns successful is developing new sources of income. Giving is never as generous in one company as in another. The large number of companies that must be contacted in a United Way campaign makes it difficult to perform a quality solicitation with each one.

The generous givers cannot be counted upon to continually increase their contributions. There comes a time when they want to be sure the United Way is doing its utmost to develop new sources of income. One way of accomplishing this is by making a careful analysis well in advance of the campaign to determine which corporations and employee groups could give substantially more.

Once the corporations and employee groups have been identified, a select group of experienced campaign leaders is recruited to assume responsibility for four or five accounts. Whenever possible the list should be reviewed in advance with business leaders to determine who is best qualified to make the call.

Information showing trends within a company, how the company compares with others, and the relationship among giving, inflation, and campaign goals is prepared for the campaign. Suggestions as to how the campaign might be strengthened are also made: Perhaps the CEO needs to be more involved, or the company chairperson needs more time to conduct the campaign. More effective use of the film and solicitor-training aids can be discussed. Since these calls are made well in advance of the campaign, management has an opportunity to review the situation and make plans for the campaign, or to seek early approval of an increase in the contribution budget for the corporate gift.

Precampaign cultivation should be continued from year to year to upgrade giving. A select group of companies may be asked to conduct pilot campaigns as a way to improve their results.

COMPANYWIDE CAMPAIGNS

In recent years, campaigns within large companies are being organized on a systemwide basis. When companies have many branches or manufacturing plants, the United Way has found it beneficial to organize the campaign on a companywide basis. In this situation, the company president generally makes a commitment to promote the United Way throughout the entire company and appoints a top executive for the purpose of implementing the campaign procedures.

By establishing the campaign on a companywide basis, company house organs and other materials are more efficiently used to promote the United Way. It is also possible to use a uniform and consistent approach to solicit employees instead of permitting decisions to be left to individual branches. A uniform payroll deduction and collection system can be arranged that is most beneficial to both the employees and the company. The backing of the campaign by the company president at headquarters is very helpful in encouraging the local management responsible for the campaign in the branches or plants.

Frequently, campaign results in each branch are publicized in the company newsletter, and this tends to create a sense of healthy competition, as well as enabling employees to feel a sense of accomplishment and pride in the results they obtained.

WORKING WITH EMPLOYEES ON A YEAR ROUND BASIS

One of the important challenges confronting United Ways is ensuring that employees are given the services they require when they are needed. Because United Ways support many agencies, it is not always possible for employees to know which agencies are available to assist them.

United Ways can take advantage of an important opportunity by developing an employee assistance program through which their staff can maintain contact with the employee committee in each company on a year round basis. By meeting periodically with the committee, the staff member has an opportunity to suggest services that might be useful to the employees and facilitate the use of agency services if problems arise. If there are any difficulties in obtaining needed services, the staff member can intercede with a particular agency and remedy the situation. Misunderstandings that may arise with regard to services also can be clarified.

If there are company layoffs, the United Way staff member can facilitate the referral of employees to appropriate public and private agencies. This not only ensures that the employees and their families will be adequately served, but also builds goodwill for the agencies and the United Way. After all, the main purpose of raising money is to ensure that people will receive the services they and their families require when they need them. An employee assistance program is one way of making sure it happens.

Many United Ways also conduct union-counselor training programs through which the stewards in various company unions are informed about the services public and private agencies in the community provide. Stewards may refer union members for service when there is a need. Frequently, the steward is the first person to learn about the problems of employees and their families, so the steward's ability to refer employees to the appropriate community resource may play a crucial role in resolving the problem.

The employee assistance program and the union counseling program can play a tremendous role in assuring both proper service to the employees and the continued support of the United Way. When employees can see that their peers are receiving essential services at crucial times they will respond to the campaign more generously.

20

BUILDING ENDOWMENT CAMPAIGNS

Over the course of time, most nonprofit institutions need to raise money for major renovations and to repair the buildings as they depreciate. Also, plans must be made for new buildings to meet expanding needs. Recently, the trend is not only to raise funds for building purposes, but to raise funds to create an endowment at the same time. As expenses increase and revenues decrease, the need for endowment income becomes even more important. Sometimes institutions can create endowments more quickly through a joint building endowment campaign than through a deferred-gifts program alone. Deferred gifts are often contingent upon the death of the donor or some other event. Expansion of physical facilities generally implies increased operating costs. Many nonprofit organizations may not be able to meet these expenses without income from an endowment.

THE APPEAL OF BUILDING CAMPAIGNS

Many fund raisers feel that, for a number of reasons, it is somewhat easier to raise substantial sums of money for building programs, that is, capital campaigns, than it is for operating campaigns: There is a tangibility to buildings that appeals to the donor. The donor can look at the building and say, "I helped create that." Also, capital campaigns generally ask for pledges over a period of time—one to five years—and then the obligation is over. In operating campaigns, donors know that they are going to be asked to give every year and possibly to increase their pledges annually. Therefore, they are frequently inclined to be more generous in giving for capital purposes than for operating programs.

Capital campaigns generally require much more substantial gifts and donors often respond positively to this challenge to their capacity and willingness to give. In operating campaigns gifts tend to reach certain levels and either remain constant or increase moderately.

THE MARKET FOR CAPITAL CAMPAIGNS

Few capital campaigns are directed to all members of the community. For the most part, they are a type of special-gifts campaign addressed to a number of select audiences.

The type of prospects approached in a capital campaign, of course, differs from institution to institution. A church must raise all of its funds from its own parishioners. Other institutions, such as hospitals, colleges, and certain types of human services organizations, may find that corporations represent a very substantial source of funds for their building programs.

Wealthy Individuals

In a capital campaign, nearly all institutions target wealthy prospects who can be expected to give much more generously than the average person. These individuals must be identified and should have some interest in the institution or they are not likely prospects. Although many wealthy individuals reside in a community, a substantial number may not be viable prospects because they have no special interest in the particular institution.

Foundations

Foundations can represent an important source of funds. Some foundations recognize the need for capital campaigns and give generously to them; others have policies which prohibit gifts for building purposes. Arts institutions, colleges and universities, and some human services organizations (including hospitals) may benefit from gifts by foundations. Capital campaign planners must carefully analyze the purposes and policies of the foundations before approaching them.

Corporations

Corporations are a major source of funds for capital and endowment campaigns. Some corporations will contribute to capital campaigns but won't donate money that will be used only for endowment purposes. When building and endowment campaigns are combined, most companies will rationalize that they are giving to the building campaign, and in this way the institution indirectly picks up endowment support it otherwise would not get.

General Support

In addition to corporations, wealthy individuals, and foundations, all institutions have potential contributors who might be described as being general supporters. They are members and patrons of the nonprofit institution, alumni, parents of participants, parents of students, clients, or parents of clients, and proprietors of small businesses. It is important for each institution to analyze its market carefully and organize its campaign accordingly.

Identification with the Institution

One of the advantages of the building endowment campaign is that it provides a ready opportunity for people to be directly associated with the institution in a tangible way or to remember others by making a gift in their name. Every capital campaign should seek to develop ways in which this kind of recognition can be given.

Tribute gifts. Some types of recognition pay tribute to certain individuals. These gifts can be categorized:

> *Honorials* are gifts made in honor of another individual, for example: In Honor of Dr. James Stewart.
> *Memorials* are gifts made in memory of another person, generally a loved one, such as a parent or a friend, for example: In Memory of Elizabeth Smith.
> *Personals* is a term I coined for the promotion of gifts to capital campaigns. The term is not widely used elsewhere. Basically, a personal provides an opportunity for a living person to give a gift in his or her own name and thus be identified with the institution in a tangible way during his or her lifetime.

Honorials, memorials, and personals—or tribute gifts—can be established within the campaign structure and they can be recognized in a number of ways. Frequently, a plaque is prepared and mounted in a conspicuous part of the building. The plaque may recognize donors according to the size of their gifts. A fairly common classification, for example, would be to recognize the donors of the ten largest gifts as major benefactors. The donors of the next largest gifts, perhaps those over $10,000, would be called benefactors; a third classification would be the $1,000 to $10,000 group and these donors could be listed as contributors. Within these classifications, the gift can be listed either in the name of the individual who made it (a personal) or as an honorial or memorial.

Sponsorship. Another feature of the capital campaign is that certain physical properties, such as particular buildings or equipment, may be offered for sponsorship to potential contributors. It is necessary to estimate the value of the property. An exact figure need not be provided, but there should be some relationship between its cost and the amount requested for sponsorship. A list of potential sponsorship projects is prepared and distributed as part of the campaign promotion. The donor is recognized by a small plaque placed in or near the facility.

Endowment gifts. In a capital campaign, recognition may also be given through the creation of endowment gifts. A symphony orchestra, for example, can seek a major gift which will be publicized as the John Jones Chair for First Violin. This denotes that the contributor has provided an endowment to support the position of first violin in the orchestra. Another such endowment might be for a scholarship. For example, The Oliver Smith Scholarship in Medicine would establish a source of income to assist a medical student. Yet another such gift might use its income for medical research and be called, for example, The Tom Watkins Medical Research Fund.

Payment Period

Traditionally, pledges to capital campaigns are payable over three to five years. The longer the payment period, the more generous contributors can be since they are able to make the payments in more manageable amounts over a longer period of time. Collecting pledges over a period of time, however, means that the money is not immediately available to pay for construction costs. This has to be taken into account in planning the budget.

BUDGET

The budget prepared for the capital campaign should be specific enough to provide the essential figures, but not so specific as to require tedious examination. Generally speaking, the major cost items to be covered should be:

- *Cost of the program or building.* This can be a flat amount, or it might be broken down according to the number of buildings or units involved.
- *Architect's fees.* The amount necessary to reimburse the architect for the plans is included.
- *Campaign and management expenses.* The money needed to conduct the campaign is included as well as the management fees needed to cover the expenses of accounting, disbursements, managing the program, and collecting the pledges over the three- to five-year period.
- *Debt service.* In view of the fact that construction may have to start before all pledges are paid, the institution may have to borrow money. The cost of the loan interest is the debt service, and should be charged to the budget.

In establishing the cost of the building program itself, it is also wise to anticipate that there may be some inflation over the construction period. If this is not taken into account, the organization may not have enough funds to complete the facility. The amount that should be considered depends upon the inflation rate at the time the budget is organized.

On the other hand, if the construction takes place over an extended period of time and the pledges are paid promptly, the institution may benefit from the short-term investment of its cash flow as payments on pledges are made. Even when construction has begun, it is seldom the case that payments have to be made immediately; rather, they will be phased in as construction progresses. Therefore, the cash on hand can be invested in short-term securities, and the income can be quite substantial.

SOURCE OF FUNDS

As a general rule, most campaigns expect that the 10 largest gifts will produce one-third of the funds required. The next 100 givers should provide the second third, and all other givers the final third of the goal. As a matter of practice, I always preferred to get 50 percent of the goal from the top 10 to 15 gifts, 30 percent from the next 100 gifts, and 20 percent from all others.

Top Gifts

A good way to start is to ask your campaign leaders to list 10 individuals and 10 corporations or foundations (whether or not they are current givers). Each might be asked to give 5 percent of the goal. This list should be augmented by a list of the 10 largest givers to the annual campaign. From this list of 30, the 10 to 15 major givers who should provide one-third to one-half the goal can be decided upon.

The needed gifts can then be categorized for promotion purposes, and presented in a chart to show the number of gifts required in each group. The chart can show the levels of gifts needed to achieve the goal:

Number of gifts	Amount	Total
1	$500,000	$ 500,000
3	250,000–500,000	1,000,000
10	100,000–250,000	1,750,000
Total		$3,250,000

The actual amounts required in these categories will, of course, depend upon the size of the capital campaign. In many campaigns, the amounts needed will be much smaller than those represented here; in others they will be larger.

A chart (see Chapter 8) gives the potential donors an idea of what is expected of them, and they can begin to think about their gifts in relation to the other top prospects. As I have already noted, the use of leadership or pacesetter gifts is a helpful way of getting the giving process started. It is important to build into this process campaign "askings" which are 25 to 50 percent higher than the minimum amount needed, since not all prospects will respond at the suggested levels.

Major gifts. Once the names of potential donors for the 10 to 15 largest gifts has been established, a list of potential donors for the next 100 to 200 largest gifts should be established. The potential gifts should be individually rated so that they will yield at least 33 percent of the goal.

The names of those donors and their assignment to campaign workers should be determined in accordance with the procedure described in Chapter 7. Basically, they will come from lists of prior givers and lists of carefully selected prospects gleaned from other sources.

Assignment

The assignment process described in Chapter 7 also determines who should approach the prospects expected to give the 10 largest gifts and the next 200 gifts.

Determining Gift Requests to Be Made of General Prospects

In determining what will be requested of individual prospects in the solicitation of medium-size and smaller gifts, several approaches can be taken.

Annual gift. One of the simplest approaches is to relate the capital campaign goal to the amount raised in annual giving. If, for example, the capital campaign goal was two and a half times the amount raised in the annual campaign, it would be possible to ask each prospect to give three times his or her annual gift, payable over a three- to five-year period. This provides a markup of about 20 percent above the minimum needed. Care should be exercised to individually rate and assign as many prospects as possible. Keep in mind that annual giving is not necessarily a true test of a person's capacity to give—rather, it reflects habit. Unless prospects are considered individually, the campaign may fall short.

Individual rating. In some cases, each prospect is rated on an individual basis. This is done by creating a formal rating or evaluation committee whose members know incomes and giving potential of the prospects—both corporations and individuals.

Standard of giving. For the general solicitation, some institutions use a standard of giving that they suggest as a guide to potential donors. This may be a graduated percentage of income, or it may be tied to other factors. Some educational institutions ask alumni to consider a gift based on the number of years that have passed since their graduation. The assumption is that their income levels have increased with age and experience.

Corporations. Corporations may be asked to give in accordance with one of the formulas (profitability, number of employees, and trade group averages) described in Chapter 11.

COMBINED BUILDING CAMPAIGNS

There are times when institutions may find it advantageous to band together in order to meet their capital requirements. Some communities conduct combined campaigns for their hospitals in order to build new facilities and update older ones. However, since reimbursement formulas used by the federal government and other third-party payers have recognized capital costs, hospitals have been less likely to raise funds through individual or combined capital campaigns. This situation may change.

In some communities, voluntary health, welfare, and recreation agencies also join together in a single campaign in order to raise capital funds under the auspices of the

United Way. These campaigns, although not widespread, are growing in importance. United Ways tend to view the development and financing of physical facilities as an important step in determining future agency programs. Such campaigns offer a variety of advantages to the community. Instead of having several fund-raising efforts, there need be only one, so campaign costs are reduced. Consequently, the number of appeals made to prospective givers is also reduced. When individual agencies do their own planning for physical facilities, they seldom know what other organizations are doing, so duplication of facilities can occur. But when citizens are involved in coordinating United Way plans for physical facilities they scrutinize each request carefully to ensure that additional facilities are actually needed.

The Process

Whether or not organizations should conduct a combined campaign is a top policy decision made by the major contributors in a community. They will decide on a combined campaign if they prefer to handle the financing of facilities in this way. Since the United Way already provides structure for a combined campaign, a meeting of major United Way contributors will provide a forum to get a consensus. As for getting a picture of the building requirements and future operating expenses for new facilities, that can be done by augmenting the regular budgeting process.

A few colleges and secondary schools use joint facilities when they are located in the same geographic areas. When this is the case, it is possible to plan and raise funds for a facility on a combined basis. Because of reduced federal reimbursement formulas, some hospitals may, in the future, find it advantageous to present a united front to the community for hospital needs rather than compete with one another for new facilities. Where this is the case, negotiations should be held between the boards of directors of the respective organizations in order to reach agreement on specific plans and arrangements. This is frequently done through the appointment of a joint committee representing each institution, and by adding a number of impartial major contributors who have an interest in the project, so that there will be objective participants in the decision-making process.

The combined building campaign is basically no different from the campaign an institution would conduct for itself. At one time it was thought that combined campaigns could not be successful because they lacked a defined constituency—that is, the constituency is too large and varied. Experience has proved this not to be true; a combined campaign is stronger because everyone involved has a stake in its success. More individuals, corporations, and foundations can be called upon for support, so the fund-raising market is broadened considerably.

A Combined Campaign Under the United Way

A combined campaign under the auspices of the United Way will generally be limited to two or three thousand prospects and, typically, will appeal to the major corporations, foundations, and individuals. A campaign chart of the successful combined capital campaign in St. Paul, Minnesota is shown in Figure 20-1.

In Figure 20-1, the *founders' division* represents approximately 200 major prospects—

Figure 20-1. The United Way combined building campaign.

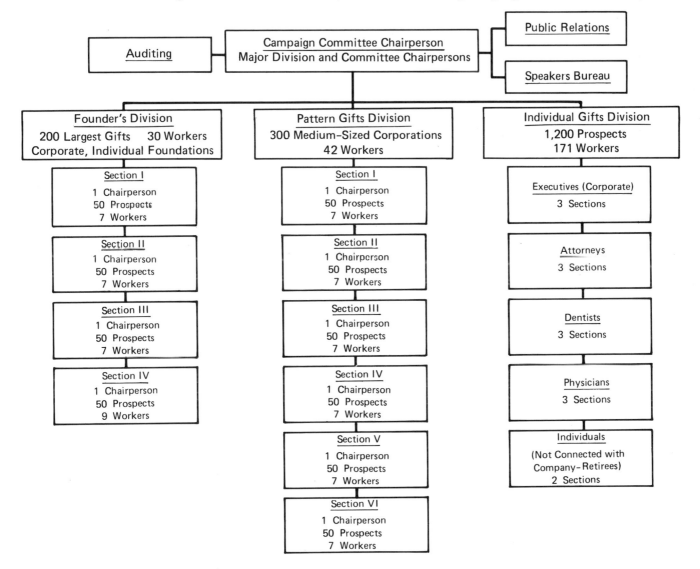

corporations, executives, and foundations—that could be expected to give $2,500 and over. The *pattern gifts* division solicits medium-size corporate gifts—approximately three hundred in this case. The *individual gifts* division covers the major executives in local corporations, as well as individuals who, though not connected with a company, can be expected to give $100 to $2,500. It also includes attorneys, physicians, and dentists.

Hospitals and Educational Institutions

Educational institutions or hospitals conducting combined campaigns should follow the same approach to prospects described in Chapters 16 and 17. A special campaign name should be adopted in order to indicate that the campaign is being made on behalf of more than one institution.

MAXIMIZING THE USE OF FUNDS IN CAPITAL CAMPAIGNS

A major consideration for nonprofit institutions conducting capital campaigns is the possibility of maximizing the use of its funds through financing opportunities which may be available. These opportunities may be available to individual and combined campaigns.

Government Funds

Sometimes federal or state funds are available on a matching basis if the nonprofit organization can provide donated funds. Community block grants can provide funds to augment private donations, thereby increasing the total amount available for building purposes. At one time, Hill Burton funds (provided by the federal government) were available for hospital construction on a matching basis, but that is no longer the case. However, from time to time, new federal funds do become available for a variety of purposes, and occasionally, federal funds can supplement the funds raised in a capital campaign.

The United Way in St. Paul was able to obtain a federal grant in a combined capital campaign to develop a multi-service agency in a low-income area of the city. This facility was planned to house a major settlement to include a city health department clinic, the city recreation department, legal-aid services, welfare department services, and family counseling. The United Way, through its capital fund campaign, provided $900,000 for this facility, and an application for funding was presented to the department of Housing and Urban Development (HUD) which resulted in a grant of $1,000,000. Thus $1,900,000 was made available to develop a facility to enhance services to residents of the area. Since HUD money could not be given to a private organization, the facility was deeded to the city, which in turn signed a contract guaranteeing use of the space to the agencies for a period of fifty years. The city also agreed to maintain the facility. A United Way agency was designated manager of the facility, and its operating costs were prorated among all the parties.

Tax-Exempt Revenue Bonds

Another system a nonprofit organization can use to maximize its voluntary funds is a program of tax-exempt revenue bonds. Through the use of such funding, an organization can meet its financial requirements at significantly lower interest than it could through commercial channels.

If properly arranged, an additional financial advantage can accrue to the institution through arbitrage. Basically, arbitrage is a system through which an institution invests its money at a higher rate of return than it has to pay in order to borrow money.

Arbitrage is a fairly complicated process, and any institution contemplating its use should be careful to get good legal counsel. For example, if the nonprofit institution makes traditional investments at the same time that it borrows other funds through the issuance of tax-exempt revenue bonds, the two actions must be considered incidental (and not purposeful). If available funds are invested along with some of the institution's other funds in investments that will yield 12 percent, that could be considered a normal financial transaction not directly related to the issuance of the revenue bonds. In some cases, it may be necessary to utilize a government agency to issue bonds—the city, county, or port authority, for example. Another requirement is that the institution not borrow more through revenue bonds than it actually needs to complete the project.

Although tax-exempt revenue bonds cannot be issued for more than the cost of the structure, allowance is made for architectural expenses, debt services, underwriters' discounts, insurance on the project, and issuance costs, thereby making possible a bond offering of 20 to 30 percent more than the building costs.

An institution, in order to get its building program started, issues revenue bonds for the total cost of the project plus estimated debt service of 15 percent and issuance costs. During the course of the bond period, paid pledges can be invested in short-term securities. The yield on these investments is higher than the amount that has to be paid to the bondholders. These campaign receipts can be held no longer than 13 months before they must be used to redeem the bonds. However, in the meantime, they can be arbitraged, giving the institution some additional funds that can be used toward the project.

Organizations contemplating use of revenue bonds should consult with government agencies authorized to issue bonds, and should seek the advice of knowledgeable investment bankers.

21

PLANNED GIVING: A DEFERRED-GIFTS PROGRAM

After annual giving and capital needs are taken care of, the third leg of a charitable organization's comprehensive giving program provides for the development of an endowment. The income from the endowment may be used for general operating support, special projects, or other programs stipulated by the giver. An endowment may be developed by raising money through a special capital endowment campaign or, more frequently, through the development of a deferred-gifts program.

Deferred gifts are charitable gifts made by an individual: Their benefits are not available to the organization until some future event occurs. The future event may be the death of the donor, but not necessarily. The deferred gift may involve the establishment of a temporary or permanent trust, the income from which is paid to the beneficiary organization. In other types of trusts, the income may go to the donor during his or her lifetime (or to others provided for in the trust instrument) with the residual amount after death going to the charitable organization.

The range of deferred-giving options available to potential contributors meet a great variety of needs, both for the donors themselves and for the charitable organizations. These include bequests, charitable remainder annuity trusts and unitrusts, lead trusts, gifts of life insurance, gifts of property, and pooled income funds.

Deferred gifts offer advantages both to the charitable organization and to the giver. To the charitable organization, they make possible the development of a corpus, or endowment. Its income helps to ensure the future stability of the organization and helps it further special programs. A deferred gift offers the giver the opportunity to be generous to an organization of his or her choice and to realize estate tax advantages and, in some cases, a substantial income tax deduction.

Because a fully developed deferred-giving program is rather complicated, it is best that institutions start in a simple way, and gradually build the program as time goes on. Time and circumstances will gradually lead the institution into more sophisticated types of deferred gifts to meet the needs of potential donors. If an institution attempts to launch its program in all directions, it may confuse potential givers and use staff time ineffectively. Therefore, a deferred-gifts program is best begun with the simplest approach, the development of bequests.

BEQUESTS

The easiest way for a donor to provide future support to an organization is to make provision in a will for a gift upon his or her death. This type of gift is referred to as a bequest. The donor's estate is reduced by the value of the gift, and the estate tax on the remaining value of the estate is lower. In computing the value of a gift, a deduction is allowed for the fair market value of the bequest. Generally speaking, there is no limitation on the amount that a donor can give to a charitable organization through a bequest, and no distinctions are made as to the types of organizations to which bequests can be made, provided they meet the Internal Revenue Code's charitable test.

A fairly simple paragraph incorporated in a donor's will can implement a bequest. Such a paragraph might read:

I bequeath the sum of $ _____ to _____ , a not-for-profit corporation located in the state of _____ .

(name of state)

An attorney should be consulted to ensure that the language is correct. It is extremely important that the proper name of the organization be incorporated in the bequest itself; otherwise, the intent of the donor and the organization designed to receive the gift may not be clear to the court.

Although bequests provide a decided advantage to the donor in reducing estate-tax liability, they have one disadvantage compared with other types of deferred gifts. Trusts, for example, not only provide estate tax benefits but also give the donor a sizable income tax deduction during his or her lifetime. The bequest does not. For this reason, donors contemplating a deferred gift may find their needs better met through the establishment of a charitable trust.

TRUSTS

As defined in Chapter 5, a trust is the vesting of legal ownership of property in a person or persons or trustees, for the benefit of another or others, or something committed to one's charge or care to be used for the benefit of another.

Basically there are two parts to a trust. First, there is the income or the right to receive income generated through the investment of the property. Second, the portion

of the trust that remains after the income has been received is referred to as the remainder interest. When a donor establishes a charitable trust, he gives property with
the provision that the income from its investment will be paid to him or his designee
for a period of time and the remainder of the trust will revert to the charitable organization after his death (or after the interest is terminated). In this way, the donor has
provided an income for himself during his life and has also provided for the beneficiary
organization upon his death. The trust may also be drawn to provide income to his
spouse after his death.

Charitable Remainder Unitrust

In a charitable remainder unitrust, the donor irrevocably creates a trust and transfers a principal sum to it (normally $50,000 or more), which is invested by the trustees
chosen by the donor.

The donor receives an income tax deduction the year the trust is established for
the present value of the trust's assets which the charity has a right to receive. This
amount is determined by Treasury Department tables and depends on the age and sex
of the donor. The trust instrument provides that a life income be paid to the donor or
some other person named by him. The donor (or other beneficiary) receives an annual
income in payments based on a fixed percentage (not less than 5 percent) of the fair
market value of the trust assets. (Their value is reassessed each year and the income—
5% of assets—changes with the changing value of the assets.) The donor may also elect
to receive the actual trust income only if such "accounting" income is less than the
stated percentage. The shortfall can be made up in later years. That is, the accounting
income can be a larger amount than the stated percentage of fair market value.

Quite obviously, when the income is related to the net value of the assets, the
income can fluctuate, depending upon the type of property and the way in which the
assets change in value.

If, for example, the assets are principally stocks, the value of the stocks will vary
according to fluctuations in the stock market. If the investments fail to realize the percent
income provided for in the trust, the difference must be taken from the trust assets to
ensure that the donor will receive the amount that is stipulated. If dividends received
from the investment of stocks are reduced and the trust is unable to meet the 5 percent
income requirement, funds have to be taken from the corpus. This reduces the remainder that the charity will receive upon the death of the donor. However, the value
of the donor's estate will still be reduced on the basis of the value of the assets at death
so that estate taxes will be correspondingly lower.

Charitable Remainder Annuity Trust

In a charitable remainder annuity trust, the donor irrevocably creates a trust and
transfers a principal sum to it (normally $50,000 or more) which is invested by the
trustee. As in the case of the unitrust, the donor receives a charitable income tax deduction and, on the same basis, the donor or other life-income beneficiary receives
annual payments of a fixed-dollar amount. The annual payments must be at least 5
percent of the initial net market value of the contributed principal, but may be more.

The amount the donor receives remains constant throughout the term of the trust. Upon termination of the trust, the assets are turned over to the nonprofit organization.

For example, if the donor contributes $50,000 to a charitable remainder annuity trust, he might provide that he receive $5,000 a year for life. The trustees would have to invest the money in a way that would ensure that the donor receives that amount annually. If the investments do not realize enough to pay the donor, the additional funds have to be taken from the principal. That reduces the remainder available to the charity upon the termination of the trust.

In both the charitable remainder unitrust and the charitable remainder annuity trust, the donor benefits because he has removed from his estate a principal sum that cannot be taxed upon his death. He also receives credit for a charitable contribution deduction dependent upon the donor's sex and age at the time the gift is made.

Unitrust versus annuity trust. If a stable income is the donor's most important consideration, the annuity trust is better. A stable income may well be the prime consideration if the beneficiary is an elderly parent or a child who will be going to college. For this reason, gifts of municipal or corporate bonds are a good security to choose. In addition to assuring a fixed income to the trust, their asset value at maturity is already known. If tax-exempt bonds are contributed, the annuity is paid to the donor tax free.

In a period of inflation, a donor may wish to assure himself of increased income to offset inflation as much as possible. In this case, a charitable unitrust may be the best vehicle. Its payments to the donor are based on the changing value of the assets, which normally increases with inflation. Another advantage of the unitrust is that the donor may make additional contributions to the trust and increase his income (since the income fluctuates according to the net value of the assets). This is not possible with an annuity trust, because its income is fixed.

Life Insurance in the Charitable Remainder Trust

Life insurance can easily be incorporated into the charitable remainder trust: The donor transfers appreciated property to the trust. The trust sells the property (recognizing no capital gain) and invests the proceeds. The trust uses the annuity to meet its annual obligations to the trust beneficiary, typically the donor, his spouse, or their children. The beneficiary takes part or all of the charity's annual payment and uses it to pay the premium on a life insurance policy on the donor's life. At the donor's death, the proceeds are paid to the beneficiary of the policy. If properly arranged, the life insurance can be removed from the estate of the trust beneficiary. This is usually accomplished by creating an irrevocable life insurance trust. Through life insurance, the donor can guarantee the policy beneficiaries a substantial tax-free gift at his death. The donor can also choose to make the charity the beneficiary of his policy and thereby increase the amount of his gift.

Here is an example of how life insurance can be used to maximize the effectiveness of a charitable remainder trust: Donor owns land in which he has a basis of $75,000, but has appreciated to a fair market value of $300,000. He wants to make a substantial donation to his university but also wants to maximize benefits for himself and his family. These objectives can be accomplished by establishing a charitable remainder annuity trust. (A unitrust or a pooled income fund could also be used.) The donor transfers the land to the trust, which sells it for $300,000. The trust does not have to pay capital gains tax because the asset is to be used for charitable purposes. The trust takes the $300,000 and purchases a single-premium annuity currently yielding 12 percent annually. The donor receives an income tax deduction for the present value of the remainder interest to the university. The terms of the trust require it to pay a fixed amount (valued at 12 percent of the original trust assets) to the income beneficiaries. The beneficiaries could include the donor, his spouse, their children, or others.

If the donor is the beneficiary, there is no gift tax. If the spouse is the trust beneficiary, there should be no gift tax because of the marital deduction and the annual exclusion. Other beneficiaries would be taxed subject to the availability of an annual exclusion. The income received by the beneficiaries could be used to pay life insurance premiums on the donor's life. If the donor is the beneficiary of the income, then the life insurance can be kept out of his estate through an irrevocable trust with Crummey provisions. Crummey provisions can qualify the annual premiums to the trust as "present interest" gifts, which averts gift tax through the $10,000 annual exclusion. Generally, the Crummey provisions allow the trust beneficiary the right to demand payment of the annual gift (premiums) to the trust for a limited period of 30 to 60 days and before the trustee pays the premiums to the insurance company. The donor's estate receives an estate tax charitable deduction for the remainder value, which is transferred to the university upon the trust's termination. The interest income lasts as long as the trust provisions require. With this planning, the donor has made a substantial gift to the university, obtained significant tax benefits for himself and his family, and created additional funds for his beneficiaries through the use of life insurance.

Advantages of a charitable remainder trust. In summary, a donor who makes a substantial gift to a charitable remainder trust realizes a number of significant advantages:

1. He obtains an income tax charitable deduction on the basis of the present value of the assets that the charity has a right to receive when the donor dies.
2. He reduces the size of his taxable estate because the remainder interest passing to the charity qualifies for the estate tax charitable deduction.
3. He provides a stream of income to his beneficiaries or himself.
4. He makes a substantial gift to a charity. This approach combines both income tax and estate tax deductions to minimize the expense to the donor and maximize the charity's gift.
5. By using life insurance, he can make a substantial gift to charity and restore the value of the gift to his spouse or family upon his death.

POOLED INCOME FUND

The pooled income fund accommodates donors of small amounts. It might be likened to a mutual fund where the earnings on the fund are paid in units. A donor transfers money or securities in the amount of $5,000 or more to the charitable organization's pooled income fund. The fund includes not only the donor's contribution but those of several or many other donors. Each gift is assigned a value at the time it is received. The income from the investment of the pooled income fund assets is then distributed to the donors (or other beneficiaries) according to the number of units that gift represents in relation to the total. The donor receives an income tax charitable deduction equal to the charity's remainder interest in that gift.

When the donor (or other beneficiary) dies, no further payments are made and the prorated value of the gift in the fund is used by the charitable organization. (The organization already has the gift, but at the donor's death it has unrestricted rights to the property and the income.) As with the charitable remainder trust and unitrust, the donor receives a life income and reduces the size of his estate for tax purposes.

Constraints. There are some cautionary measures which should be kept in mind with regard to charitable remainder trusts:

- Be very sensitive to the particular provisions of the trust. Make sure all the requirements of the unitrust, annuity trust, or pooled income fund are met.
- The donor should never engage in negotiations with a buyer of the trust's assets. If he does, the IRS may attribute the gain from the sale to him. The name of an income beneficiary other than the donor may constitute a taxable gift. The donor avoids the gift tax only if he retains the power to revoke or terminate the income interest.

The charitable remainder trust is a valuable tool to have in your estate planning arsenal. It combines income and estate tax deductions, and eliminates capital gains taxes on appreciated property while getting part of the value of that property out of the estate. At the same time, it provides a sizable gift to the charity of the donor's choice. It provides money which the beneficiaries can use to purchase life insurance on the donor. At his death, the insurance proceeds are income tax free, and may be estate tax free. This technique is not simple, but the benefits are such that every philanthropist who has a large estate should be aware of it.

CHARITABLE LEAD TRUST

The charitable lead trust is less well known but can be used in the development of a deferred-gifts program. In the lead trust, the charity and the beneficiaries switch places. As in the case of a remainder trust, the property is transferred by the donor to a trust. However, in this case, the income received from the property is paid to the charity for a specified number of years, and at the end of that time period, the trust principal reverts to the donor or a member of his family.

A gift of property is transferred to the trustees who invest the funds, and the charity receives the investment income on a yearly basis. The income must be in the form of a guaranteed annuity or represent a fixed percentage of the fair market value of the trust property as determined yearly.

Although the charitable remainder trust cannot pay less than a certain amount to the income beneficiary—generally 5 percent—there are no such restrictions in the lead trust, and the donor may select any percentage of income level he chooses. Additionally, a charitable remainder trust's income payment period cannot exceed 20 years, whereas there is no such limitation in the case of a charitable lead trust. If the period of payment to the charity is less than ten years, the donor is taxed on the income received from the trust each year. However, he gets a sizable up-front charitable deduction based upon the income interest (as defined by the Treasury Department) which the charity will receive. If the period of the lead trust is 10 years or more, the donor does not have to report the trust income received by the charity.

Let's look at how a less-than-10-year trust works: A donor transfers $200,000 to a lead trust, and provides that a qualified charitable organization be paid a guaranteed annuity of $10,000 for a period of five years. The remainder at the end of that period reverts to the donor. Assuming a discount rate of 10 percent, annuity tables prescribe a factor of 3.7908 for valuing the worth of an annual annuity of a dollar for five years. In this case, the IRS permits the donor a charitable deduction of $37,908 (3.7908 × 10,000) representing the income the charity would receive. This is partially offset by the fact that he must report the trust payments to the charity each year for five years, and pay taxes on them. The owner may claim an income tax deduction of up to 50 percent of adjusted gross income unless the gift is made to a charity where the deduction limit is 20 percent.

A less-than-10-year lead trust is most valuable in the situation where a donor has an unusually high income in a particular year and wants to assist a nonprofit organization and take advantage of a major charitable tax deduction that year. The more-than-10-year-lead trust is valuable in the situation where a donor wants to reduce his taxable income and desires to continue an income stream to a charity of his choice but cannot, because of the tax deduction limitations—that is, he is in danger of exceeding the 50 percent allowable deduction. In the charitable lead trust, the cost of the gift tax to family members can be appreciably reduced by the value of the charity's income interest.

If the donor decides later that he wishes to contribute the corpus to the charity, he may do so through his will. In this case, the gift is a bequest and the donor thereby reduces his estate for tax purposes.

Life Insurance in the Charitable Lead Trust

Life insurance can help maximize the charity's ultimate benefit through the charitable lead trust. The charity can use part or all of the income paid to the charitable beneficiary to pay premiums for insurance on the donor's life. If the trust's term ends before the donor dies, the charity can elect to take a paid-up policy, borrow the cash value to pay the premium, or continue to pay premiums from other contributions. When the donor dies, the insurance company pays the proceeds to the charity. The result is that the charity receives a substantial "gift" through the insurance proceeds.

Consider the example of a corporate executive whose income can sustain his family's standard of living. He also accumulates securities valued in excess of $500,000. Fifty percent of the dividend income these securities generate is gobbled up by income taxes. The executive would like to see a charity to benefit from this income. He executes a charitable lead trust and transfers his securities to it for a period of 15 years. The trust is drawn to make annual payments of 6 percent of the trust's original value (an annuity trust) to the charity. This means the charity will receive $30,000 per year for the 15-year period. The charity uses $8,000 of its $30,000 annual contribution to purchase $200,000 of life insurance on the donor's life. This leaves $22,000 to the charity for operating purposes. If the donor dies within the 15-year period, the charity will realize $200,000 in tax-free insurance proceeds. If the donor is alive at the end of 15 years, the charity can take the cash value of the life insurance. The securities held by the trust would be paid to the donor's survivors according to the trust's terms. The donor has:

1. Reduced his personal income taxes.
2. Reduced the size of his estate and his estate taxes by giving away the additional income the securities would have produced.
3. Made annual gifts to the charity for 15 years.
4. Made possible the contribution of $200,000 to the charity through the insurance proceeds the charitable lead trust has paid for with its annual income.

Thus the donor can keep substantial property in the family on a very favorable tax basis while still making a substantial charitable contribution.

Advantages of the Lead Trust

A donor who creates a charitable lead trust enjoys some important benefits:

- For a 10-year-or-more lead trust, the donor's taxable income is reduced by the income the contributed assets would normally earn.
- For a less-than-10-year trust, the donor receives a substantial up-front income tax deduction.
- The trust may be drafted to direct the corpus to one or more charities as a bequest through the donor's will at his death.
- The trust allows the donor to make a substantial gift to a charity with reduced gift-tax results to the family.

Lead trusts should be used only for large estates where neither the surviving spouse nor the donor's heirs need the income. The trust can be established either during the donor's life, using assets that are expected to appreciate substantially, or at his death. Assets which ultimately pass to the family will receive a stepped-up tax basis; this will allow them to be sold without capital gains taxes.

GIFTS OF LIFE INSURANCE

Philanthropic individuals are often reluctant to contribute current income or assets because of concerns about inflation and taxes. At the same time, charitable institutions seek regular contributions from highly motivated donors. Charities want to generate deferred gifts without losing their annual gifts. A potentially attractive opportunity for both donors and charities to achieve their objectives can be accomplished through gifts of life insurance.

Life insurance allows the individual to donate substantial property or cash, but requires a minimal outlay. The charity can either continue the annual premiums or receive a paid-up policy. The death benefit will always be more than has been paid in insurance premiums. Therefore, the gift can appreciate substantially with a minimal cash outlay. Taking a paid-up policy will not require any cash outlay on the part of the charity and will still give it a sizable gift upon the death of a donor.

The donor can get tax benefits from gifts without significantly reducing his income. This is particularly appealing to the individual who does not have the necessary assets to make a substantial gift outright, but wants to be generous and has arrived at a position in life where he can dispose of some of his life insurance without impairing the future income of his dependents. In other cases, life insurance offers the donor an opportunity to be generous to a charity with a minimal outlay of cash.

Existing Policies

In order to get an income tax deduction for an existing policy's value, the existing policy must be irrevocably assigned to the charitable organization so that the insured maintains no "incidents of ownership," such as the ability to change the beneficiary or borrow against the cash value.

The donor may continue to make cash payments to the charity equal to the premium payments. He can take these contributions as income tax deductions. He can also give the policy to the organization without making any additional contributions for the premiums. In this case the cash value of the insurance may be taken as a deduction.

The benefits to both the donor and the charity of the gift of an existing life insurance policy is illustrated in Figure 21-1.

New Policies

If a new policy is needed on the donor's life, the preferable procedure is for the institution to apply for it and be its owner and beneficiary. The donor merely makes a cash gift each year so the charity can pay the premiums. This is the safest approach to take if the donor wishes to maximize his charitable contributions.

Life insurance policies made within three years of the insured's death may be drawn back into the insured's taxable estate but can qualify for an estate tax deduction if the charity has been named beneficiary.

Assuming that ownership arrangements and "incidents of ownership" problems are satisfied, the donor can enjoy significant income and estate tax benefits. The annual premium will be deductible to the donor and he will not be taxed on the increased cash value of the policy (as he would if he were to cash it in and make a charitable contribution from the proceeds). Also, the face value of the policy is not included in his estate.

From the charity's point of view, it is receiving a regular donation through the regular premium payment which increases the cash value of the policy each year. The loan value as well as the potential for a substantial gift if the donor dies are also increased. By taking the donation as premium payments, the charity is not necessarily

Figure 21-1. Using life insurance as a charitable gift.

OBJECTIVE: To provide a substantial charitable bequest with an annual contribution of approximately one to four percent of the amount of the bequest.

At all times, the estate of the donor remains intact for the family's benefit in the event of death; the charity receives at least the full value of the bequest.

Step 1. Donor has a life insurance policy in the amount of the bequest desired.

$100,000 whole life policy with waiver of premium. Male—age 40. $1,906 premium.

Step 2. Donor transfers all ownership of the policy to the charity, making the charity the irrevocable beneficiary of the policy on the donor's life.

$1,906   contribution—50 percent
   953   Tax savings
$ 953   Net cost of contribution

Step 3. Policy builds values during insured's life.

Living values:
10 years—$19,266
20 years—$62,140

Death benefit:
10 years—$109,856
20 years—$144,317

These values built through annual deposits. After the sixteenth year dividends could be used to fund the future premiums, if a limited payment period is desired. (This could also be accomplished on newer universal life or adjustable life policies by invoking the "premium stop" provision after 10 or 15 years.)

Step 4. Upon the donor's death, the charity receives a substantial gift which could be reinvested to provide income.

Example: Death occurs in twentieth year— $144,317 received as death proceeds. (Base $100,000 policy plus $44,317 of additional paid-up insurance from dividends.) If the $144,317 was invested at 10 percent interest, the charity would receive a perpetual annual income of $14,317.

SUMMARY

Annual contribution of $1,906 for 20 years of premiums provides an aftertax cost of $953 multiplied by 20 = $19,060 created gift of approximately $144,000.

Original bequest	$100,000
Bequest at death in twentieth year	144,000
Total contribution	38,120
Less tax saving at 50 percent	19,060
Net contribution to create $144,000 bequest	$ 19,060

NOTE: This illustration is based upon current insurance company dividend projections which are not guaranteed. If a level bequest of $100,000 is desired, dividends could be used to reduce premiums immediately, or after the sixteenth year, to fund all future premiums.

NOTE: If a new policy is needed, the charity will apply for and be its beneficiary. Therefore, Step 2 is unnecessary. However, the benefits illustrated would be the same.

Source: Integrated Equity Management Inc.

---

losing the benefit of a cash donation it would have received since it can borrow the cash value each year. (The face value will always be higher than the loans against the policy.)

Recently developed life insurance products provide that cash values grow or earn current market interest rate. Some new policies allow for cash withdrawals instead of borrowing against the policy. In any event, a tax-exempt organization does not benefit from the tax deduction another beneficiary would receive on loan interest paid when borrowing against the policy. However, when it withdraws cash values, the charity receives funds tax free even if the cash value withdrawn exceeds the cumulative premiums paid on the policy. Thus, they do not have to pay interest for the use of the funds. The annual gift is sustained and the potential for a deferred gift is still present upon the death of the donor.

If an individual holds a policy which is nearly or completely paid up, he can elect to contribute the policy to a nonprofit organization. The donor is permitted to claim an income tax deduction equal to the value of the policy or its cost, whichever is lower. In addition to the income tax deduction, the face amount of the policy is removed from his estate, thereby reducing the portion of the estate subject to federal estate tax. The cost of the policy would represent the total premiums the donor has paid over the years, plus any accumulated dividends. If, for example, the cash value of his policy is $17,500, the donor could use that amount as an income tax deduction and reduce his income taxes by as much as $8,750, if he is in the 50 percent tax bracket, and $7,000 if he is in the 40 percent bracket the year he makes the gift.

A younger person who has not built up the cash value of his policy could purchase a second policy and contribute it to the charity of his choice. The advantage to the younger donor is that the cost of such a policy is not high because of his age. He assigns the policy and all its rights to the institution. He is permitted to claim an income tax deduction for the amount of the premium payment made each year. Upon his death, the institution receives the face value of the policy. If the donor had to discontinue payment on the policy, the institution could choose either to pay the premium itself and eventually collect the full face value or to convert the policy into paid-up insurance and later collect the reduced face value.

GIFTS OF REAL ESTATE

Prospective donors may have real estate which has appreciated substantially in value over the years. The real estate may be a farm that no family member is interested in farming, or it may be income property which has appreciated in value but is not considered a vital part of the family's holdings. In situations like these, the donor may make the real estate an outright gift to a nonprofit organization and gain an income tax deduction equal to the fair market value of the property. He also can consider making a gift to the institution through a bequest. In that case, he gets no income tax deduction, but removes a substantial asset from his estate and reduces his estate taxes.

In the case of an outright gift, the charity may sell the property. Since the charity does not have to pay taxes, it can use the total amount of the gift either for a specific purpose or for reinvestment to bring additional income.

Gifts of property have substantial benefits to the donor because they remove the property and the worry of its management from his care. They also reduce the assets that will be taxable in his estate. The donor is relieved of the real estate taxes on the property and does not have to pay any capital gains tax when the charity sells the property since it is an outright gift. The donor reduces his income taxes by virtue of the deduction he may take for the charitable gift.

Bargain Sales

Bargain sales represent the sale of property to a charitable organization for an amount considerably lower than its market value. The bargain sale permits the donor to escape a substantial amount of capital gain he normally realizes on the sale of the property while still making a substantial charitable gift and realizing an income tax deduction.

Say a donor has property worth $100,000 that cost only $30,000 at the time of purchase. He wants to sell it to a charity for $50,000 but retain the additional $50,000 for his own personal use. Since the donor sells the property to the charity for half of its fair market value, only half of the basis ($30,000 × 50 percent = $15,000) offsets the cash proceeds ($50,000). The charity, in turn, may sell the property for $100,000, reimburse itself for the purchase price ($50,000), and still have a contribution of the remainder ($50,000). The donor has the receipts from the sale of the property for his own use and an income tax deduction of $50,000 representing the difference between the value of the property and its sale price.

By making this gift, the donor has a reportable gain of $35,000 ($50,000 less $15,000) on which he is taxed. The capital gains tax, however, is much lower than regular income tax rates. This is substantially offset by the fact that he has a $50,000 contribution to the charity which he can deduct over a five-year period up to the 30 percent limit of adjusted gross income permitted for appreciated capital gain property. And the donor still has $50,000 available to him to invest as he sees fit.

ESTABLISHING POLICIES FOR A DEFERRED-GIFTS PROGRAM

The first step an institution must take to start a deferred-gifts program is to authorize the appointment of a deferred-giving committee.

The committee's purpose should be to recommend policy to the board of directors, give overall direction to the program, help plan its promotion, and assist the staff in making contacts with potential donors. The size of the committee will depend upon the size of the institution itself. It should be large enough to permit the necessary representation, but not so large as to make decision making difficult. The people best qualified to serve on this committee are: past campaign chairpersons and presidents (the old guard), top businesspeople, technical experts who are CPAs, trust officers from major banks, and insurance agents. The financial professionals provide technical expertise, while the lay members may have contacts with prospective donors and will also help judge what is best for the institution and the donor.

One of the first things the committee should do is to recommend policies to the board of directors. Some policy considerations to be decided include formalizing the goals of the deferred-gifts program. A board statement outlining the general purposes of the deferred-giving program should be made. Second, the continuation of the committee, its purpose, size, and scope should be authorized. Third, a decision should be made about the type of gifts which will be sought, that is, whether bequests, charitable remainder trusts, life insurance, or other deferred gifts should be emphasized in presentations to potential donors.

As noted earlier in this chapter, it might be decided that initially the program should emphasize obtaining bequests. This is the simplest way to get started, involves less staff work, and is most easily explained to potential donors. As time goes on, individual circumstances of donors may require other kinds of deferred-giving programs such as unitrusts and gifts of life insurance and property. This way, the institution can gradually phase in other more complicated forms of deferred gifts.

Restricted and Unrestricted Gifts

Another issue to be decided is whether the program will stress the need for unrestricted gifts whenever possible, but respect the wishes of the donor if he wishes to restrict them. Some organizations may have member agencies or units—separate colleges or agencies—that the donor might wish to endow and the policy will need to make provision for this.

Who Will Be Trustee?

Where trusts are part of the program, the institution must decide whether it will serve as its own trustee or whether it will use the services of a trust department of a bank. The policy should probably encourage the donor to name his own trustee—either the trust department of a bank, an attorney, or a responsible individual.

The nonprofit organization may, of course, serve as its own trustee, but when it does so it takes on considerable responsibility with respect to the guardianship and investment of funds. The administration of trusts can be a complicated affair. Furthermore, the laws concerning trusts are constantly changing and this puts an additional burden upon the staff responsible for the program. Serving as one's own trustee also involves fiduciary responsibility to manage trust assets properly.

Legal Counsel

The policy should provide that legal counsel will be consulted regarding any matters affecting the deferred-gifts program that are unclear or require legal interpretation. The policy should also provide that the institution will advise the prospective donor to use the attorney of his choice to draw up a will, provide for a bequest, establish a trust, or make other deferred gifts.

Some institutions provide copies of suggested legal instruments for this purpose to the donors' attorneys, but seldom give them to the donors themselves. This ensures that the donor will obtain legal counsel.

Budget

The board must provide a budget for the execution of the progam. The budget should include provisions for staff and funds to promote the program and cover the usual overhead expenses.

Staff

The board should authorize specific staff persons to represent the institution in the conduct of the deferred-gifts program. Only those who understand the program and have a thorough knowledge of the policies of the organization should discuss deferred gifts with potential donors. Those qualified individuals generally include the top executive of the organization and the development director of the deferred-gifts program.

Avoid Conflict with the Annual Campaign

If an institution conducts an annual campaign it is advisable for it to emphasize that support of the annual campaign always takes precedence over the deferred-gifts program. This, of course, is not always possible because a donor may establish a trust rather than give to the annual campaign. However, exceptions aside, the major emphasis should be on maintaining sustaining support for the institution through its annual campaign. As a matter of fact, a deferred-gifts program can sometimes be implemented by selecting a limited number of prospects during the annual campaign: After soliciting—and obtaining—their annual gifts, the staff member or volunteer should remind them of their importance to the institution, how much it needs their continued support, and suggest that they consider some form of deferred gift.

Primary Interests of Donor

Policy should clearly indicate that the interests of the donor always supersede the interests of the organization. When seeking out potential donors whose gifts may bring in a substantial income, this important consideration may be overlooked. An institution should never accept a deferred gift when it would work to the detriment of either the donor or his family.

Member Institutions

When there are member colleges or agencies in a federation the policy should clearly delineate the activities of the deferred-gifts program in relation to the other parts of the institution. It is not a good idea for member units or organizations to solicit deferred gifts as well. Potential donors will be confused and overwhelmed. On the other hand, the policy should permit the donor to designate gifts to a particular division of the institution or the member agency of his choice.

Financial Reporting

The policy should provide the kind and amount of financial reporting that will be made to the board of directors each year. The report should include the progress made, the total amount of deferred gifts received, the income generated, and the purposes to which it will be applied.

Deferred Gifts and Community Foundations

Because community foundations are so broad in scope and make grants to meet many varied needs, they too are interested in receiving bequests, trusts, and other forms of deferred gifts. In some communities, individual institutions and community foundations become competitive, especially since community foundations are now required to raise additional funds each year in order to maintain their classification as community foundations or public charities. Rather than create conflict or competition, charitable organizations should work cooperatively with the community foundation.

The nonprofit institution can promote its own deferred-giving program among its donors, but suggest that they can also make their gift through the community foundation. Of course, donors must specify that their gifts be restricted to the nonprofit organization of their choice. This solves two problems: It helps the community foundation obtain the additional funds it needs and it permits the individual institution to receive endowments from its donors either directly or through the community foundation.

Marketing

Once it has established its policies, the deferred-gifts committee should draft a marketing plan. It is essential to define the prospects to whom the deferred-gifts program will be directed. Although an occasional broad promotion is worthwhile, most institutions find their best market to be those prospects over age 50 who have advanced both in years and financial well-being, whose family responsibilities are minimal, and who have demonstrated an interest in the institution.

Prospect identification. The staff, with the help of volunteers, must identify the best prospects. They are usually readily identified from lists of givers to the annual and capital campaigns. Other lists, including prior patients, alumni, etc., should also be reviewed. Single people over age 50 or couples who do not have major responsibilities to dependents are the best source of deferred gifts. But, as pointed out previously, the deferred-gifts options are so broad that almost anyone can be a prospect.

Direct mail. The marketing plan should include selected mailings to prospective donors. These mailings should be made at least once a year, but preferably three or four times annually. They should stress the institution's need for continuing support and the potential income and estate tax savings that can be realized by donors through deferred gifts. Generally these mailings invite interested persons to inquire further about the opportunities for planned gifts.

Personal calls. The marketing plan should also make provision for personal visits by both staff and top volunteers to those prospects who have indicated an interest in the program, as well as those who represent potential givers and have indicated past support. People seldom take action to make major gifts on their own unless there is a selective personal approach to ignite their interest.

Professional groups. Letters should be mailed to CPAs, attorneys, and trust officers, advising them of the deferred-gifts program. The number of gifts likely to be received from tapping these sources depends on their clientele. If they deal with clients who would derive tax benefits from a deferred gift, they will be in a position to suggest making a major gift to a nonprofit organization.

Publications The marketing plan should also include articles in the institution's house organ as well as any other publications. The annual report is an excellent place to list donors who have made deferred gifts and to promote the program among future donors. Newsletter announcements of new gifts and special recognition of these gifts are important facets of the program.

Tribute gifts. Since many donors like to be associated with tangible programs, the creation of tribute gift opportunities—memorials, honorials, and personals—are an extremely important part of a deferred-giving program. This permits the donor not only to make a meaningful gift, but also to associate his name with a program of special importance, or remember others who have special meaning in a tangible way.

Estate planning seminars. Estate planning seminars are frequently used to promote deferred-gifts programs. These are generally developed with the assistance of trust officers and attorneys who frequently lend their services free of charge. These seminars include discussions of the necessity of adequate estate planning, current tax provisions, savings that can be realized on income and estate taxes through estate planning, and the services that can be provided by attorneys and trust departments.

The seminar also presents the opportunity to discuss the deferred-gifts program. The way in which deferred gifts become a part of overall estate planning can be described. Potential donors can be advised that they can preserve capital and provide income and at the same time help the nonprofit institution of their choice. (See Figure 21-2 for a sample agenda for an estate planning seminar.)

A number of commercial organizations offer professional counsel to institutions in organizing and conducting deferred-gifts programs. These services include orientation and refresher seminars in deferred giving. In addition, they usually provide brochures and pamphlets imprinted with the name of the charitable organization. Generally these will cover the importance of estate planning, promote bequests, and explain the benefits of the various types of deferred gifts to the donor and the charitable institution. They also explain the income and estate tax savings realizable through deferred gifts.

Staffing a Deferred-Gifts Program

To be successful, most organizations will need a deferred-gifts specialist on staff. Many institutions contemplating a deferred-gifts program have trouble finding the funds to staff and implement the program. Because of their nature, deferred-gifts programs may not bring any income for several years. Many must await the deaths of the donors. More deferred-gifts programs fall by the wayside for lack of funding than for any other reason.

An organization may be successful in getting start-up money from a foundation. Since the grant is for a relatively short time—one to five years it frequently allows for initial staff funding under a foundation's policies of short-term funding. Foundations frequently show an interest in helping an organization start a deferred-giving program because it has the longer-range goal of helping the organization increase its level of self-support.

Effect of Foundation Funding

The effect that foundation grants may have on the establishment and success of a deferred-gifts program is well illustrated by the Deferred Gifts Project of the Northwest Area Foundation. Grants made to 30 colleges and universities helped them develop over $118 million in deferred gifts between 1974 and 1982. See Figure 21-3 for the foundation's own report on the success of the project.

Figure 21-2. Sample agenda for an estate planning seminar.

   I Definition of estate planning
  II Estate planning objectives
      a. Costs of transferring estate
 III Methods of minimizing transfer costs of estate
      a. Marital deduction
      b. Gifts to family members
 IV What comprises your estate?
  V The importance of wills: the advantages and disadvantages of simple and complex wills
      a. Joint tenancy and right of survival
      b. Gift taxes
      c. Probate
      d. Law of intestacy
      e. Tax advantages
 VI Trusts—definitions, types, purposes
      a. Living trusts; funded and unfunded
      b. Life insurance trusts
      c. Totten trusts
      d. Irrevocable trusts
VII Charitable gifts
      a. Bequests
      b. Charitable trusts
      c. Life Insurance
      d. Stock
      e. Other property
VIII Handling the family business
      a. Private annuity
      b. Installment purchases
      c. Recapitalization
      d. Buy-sell agreements
 IX Structuring life insurance arrangements
      a. Ownership by spouse
      b. Ownership by Community Trust
      c. 501(c)(9) trust
  X Making things easier for survivors after death
      a. Keep the spouse informed
      b. Safekeeping of valuable records
      c. Joint tenancy for checking and savings accounts
      d. Maintenance of income tax records
      e. Use of competent estate planner

When there is a central fund-raising organization, a deferred-gifts specialist may be hired at the central organizational level. It would be less expensive for churches to hire staff at the diocesan level. Likewise, it would be more practical for a United Way or United Arts Fund to hire its own personnel to work on behalf of all of its member agencies. Multi-hospital systems may find it advantageous to hire staff at the corporate level rather than in each individual hospital. This depends upon the hospital budget as well as geographic considerations.

If a decision is made to emphasize bequests, the program may be started in a small organization with a minimum budget and staff. Certainly a well-prepared brochure mailed to members can be effective. This can frequently be followed by a few selective calls on donors able to make substantial gifts. I know of one pastor who makes regular home visits to his parishioners each year. In the course of conversation, he has an

Figure 21-3. Results of Northwest Area Foundation's start-up grants for deferred-gifts programs in 30 colleges.

The Deferred Gifts Project initiated by the Foundation in 1974 illustrates the Foundation's intention of distributing "seeds, not apples" in making grants. Incentive grants were made to participating colleges to help underwrite the cost of establishing deferred gifts programs. The Foundation also provided a program model, formal training of deferred gifts officers from each institution, and specific guidance in monitoring program development over an initial two-year period.

Foundation grants from the inception of the project to date (approximately $1,000,000) have leveraged more than $118,774,000 in recorded and confirmed gift provisions in force, and $44,386,000 in cash flow from matured gifts for 30 colleges participating in the project. Though not all of these can be considered a direct result of the project, the acceleration in deferred gift activity at participating colleges was remarkable.

Eighteen colleges participating in the first round of the Deferred Gifts Project in 1974 reported 3,264 confirmed gift provisions during a seven-year period ending in the fiscal year 1981–82, at a value of $82,331,695, and actual cash receipts from 839 matured gifts for $35,939,414. (Values at maturity generally exceed initial recorded values.) Eleven colleges were selected to participate in a second round of the project in 1977, with one institution participating as an auditor. This group reported 957 confirmed gift provisions from the inception of the project (four years) at a value of $36,442,579 and 243 matured gifts for $8,447,469. Project totals to date are 4,221 deferred gift provisions at a value of $118,774,274, an average of $28,139 per recorded gift, and 1,082 gifts matured for $44,386,883, an average of $41,023 cash value per gift matured. For a breakdown by institution of recorded and completed gifts, see the tables that follow.

A number of institutional variables affected performance. Staff turnover and attrition have seriously impaired achievement at several colleges. However, those colleges that have been able to sustain marketing and prospect development activity through the efforts of a designated staff officer consistently deployed in deferred gift development have done well. Deferred gifts are not numerous, about 20 to 26 new gifts have been confirmed, disclosed, and recorded at each institution per year, but many of these gifts are large enough to significantly enhance an institution's future.

NORTHWEST AREA FOUNDATION
DEFERRED GIVING PROJECT
Recorded Deferred Gift Provisions
and Matured, Completed Gifts
(from inception of project only)

Institu-tion	GROUP I Gifts Recorded Number of Gifts	Dollar Value	Gifts Completed Number of Gifts	Cash Dollars	Institu-tion	GROUP II Gifts Recorded Number of Gifts	Dollar Value	Gifts Completed Number of Gifts	Cash Dollars
1.	345	$13,024,400	75	$ 5,330,830	19.	41	$10,297,464	7	$ 282,041
2.	219	10,371,933	67	3,144,491	20.	95	8,740,174	27	1,925,922
3.	185	9,682,773	61	4,670,996	21.	68	3,929,600	22	1,630,793
4.	294	7,742,900	59	4,678,790	22.	207	3,885,638	42	641,437
5.	273	6,405,730	50	379,790	23.	36	3,541,000	29	1,508,850
6.	184	5,721,510	32	2,153,817	24.	207	2,578,000	35	514,645
7.	287	4,718,013	42	251,163	25.	137	1,282,779	33	220,532
8.	249	4,672,528	29	2,549,027	26.	na	650,000	3	202,000
9.	90	3,444,492	15	1,685,466	27.	27	546,150	2	17,390
10.	375	3,299,888	100	1,414,670	28.	27	349,824	5	234,860
11.	65	2,900,397	36	1,552,351	29.	30	344,950	8	536,739
12.	114	2,675,027	4	415,988	TOTALS	875	$36,145,579	213	$7,715,209
13.	222	1,998,112	183	1,364,676	Auditor	82	297,000	30	732,260
14.	144	1,741,424	52	2,760,305	TOTALS	957	$36,442,579	243	$8,447,469
15.	65	1,435,643	8	28,505					
16.	40	1,273,270	na	na					
17.	50	991,689	22	3,509,834					
18.	63	231,966	4	48,715					
TOTALS	3,264	$82,331,695	839	$35,939,414					

Average Per Institution Per Year: 26 gifts for $653,426—average gift, $25,224; 6.7 gifts matured for $285,233.

Average Per Institution Per Year: 20 gifts for $821,490—average gift, $41,309; five matured gifts for $175,989.

Figure 21-4. Sample letter of intent.

Letter of Intent

AS AN EXPRESSION OF MY CONCERN AND COMMITMENT TO

NORMAL UNIVERSITY

I AM MAKING PROVISION

TO SUPPORT THE SCHOOL OR COLLEGE OF

_____

(please specify)

THROUGH

_____ My will   _____ A trust agreement
_____ A life insurance policy   _____ Other *(please specify)*
                                                          _____

In the Approximate amount of $ _____
(indication of amount optional)

This Letter of Intent is an expression of my present plans, is subject to revocation or modification by me, and is not legally binding on me or my estate.

_____   _____

DATE   SIGNATURE

☐ Check here to permit the use of your name as participating in this program,
☐ with or ☐ without disclosure of amount. Thank you.
(use of names is motivating and exemplary to others)

GRATEFULLY ACKNOWLEDGED THIS DATE

_____

Acknowledging Official   (Date)

Normal University will be able to continue its fine
educational programs with the help of your long–range commitment.
Thank you on behalf of the University Community,
students and faculty of future years.

opportunity to talk to them about the future needs of the church or special building requirements. Frequently the parishioner will ask how he might help and this often leads to a special gift or a provision for one in the donor's will. The pastor has had remarkable success with minimum expense, utilizing his regular visits as an indirect means of prompting interest in a gift which might otherwise not have been made.

Of course this approach won't work for most organizations. In these cases, there is no substitute for biting the bullet and making the financial investment for full or part-time staff necessary to get the program rolling.

If no other option is available, another way to at least get a start is to integrate the deferred-gifts program into the regular campaign. Regular campaign workers who solicit wealthy individuals are trained in deferred-gifts philosophy. After they have asked for and received the donor's pledge to the annual campaign, they talk about the future needs of the institution and the necessity for creating an endowment. They ask the donor to give some thought to including the organization in his estate planning and give him material summarizing the options available. In this approach, it is essential that the need for annual support is emphasized, so the donor does not reason that a bequest in his will takes the place of a gift to the annual campaign.

It is important to remember that even if an organization does not have the staff and budget to undertake a full-scale deferred-gifts program, it is better to get a start than to do nothing.

Letter of Intent

A letter of intent is useful to finalize the gifts. (See Figure 21-4.) One of the problems inherent in the conduct of a deferred-gifts program is that it is frequently difficult for the nonprofit organization to find out whether bequests have been made or trusts established. For this reason, it is often difficult to measure the success of the program.

The letter of intent (or a form) given to the donor either at the time he is approached or later by mail gives him an easy way of informing the organization that he intends to make a gift to the organization. The form permits the donor to indicate the type of gift—bequest, insurance, trust—and the approximate amount. A tactful way to approach the donor is to point out that the letter of intent helps the institution plan for the future because it will know what resources and income it is likely to have in succeeding years.

APPENDIXES

APPENDIX A

Sample visual case presentation for the Children's Heart Fund. (Courtesy of the Children's Heart Fund and Ernhart and Associates.)

Our | PURPOSES | Are:

to provide an international program of humanitarian concern offering surgical correction for indigent children with heart defects; and to expand knowledge of heart disease in the young through education and research by:

- Diagnosing children with heart defects
- Providing life-giving surgery
- Securing transportation of heart-crippled children to the Twin Cities
- Providing educational programs for health-care personnel
- Providing supplemental training programs for health-care personnel
- Disseminating knowledge of diagnosis and treatment of children's heart diseases
- Continued research

Children's
Heart Fund

OBJECTIVES

To assist in identifying, diagnosing, and curing children with defective hearts in the United States and around the world

---

To broaden the areas of the world where services for heart-crippled children and the benefits of Children's Heart Fund educational programs are available

---

To enhance the educational components of the program in diagnosis, heart catheterization, heart surgery, and all-around operative care

---

To facilitate on an international basis free exchange of current concepts in cardiac medicine among physicians, nurses, and other professionals

---

To improve existing, and create new, cardiovascular centers in developing countries

---

To utilize effectively the case material generated by patient treatment programs for research studies

---

COMMON CHILDREN'S HEART DEFECTS

VENTRICULAR SEPTAL DEFECT:

"Hole in the heart"-anomalous communication between the main pumping chambers of the heart

TETRALOGY OF FALLOT:

"Blue Baby"-anomalous communication between the main pumping chambers of the heart plus restricted flow of blood from heart to lungs

RHEUMATIC VALVULAR DISEASE:

Acquired damage to heart valves resulting from rheumatic fever

EFFECTS

—Marked growth retardation

—Shortness of breath

—Impaired physical endurance

—Over-worked heart—weakened heart muscles—heart failure

—Susceptibility to infections and decreased ability to withstand other illnesses

RESULT

Without corrective surgery—death before age 25

---

1 IN EVERY 300 CHILDREN BORN HAS A HEART DEFECT WHICH WILL RESULT IN DEATH AT AN EARLY AGE

Heart Fund

NUMBER OF CHILDREN RECEIVING TREATMENT HAS INCREASED BY 800% IN THE PAST 10 YEARS

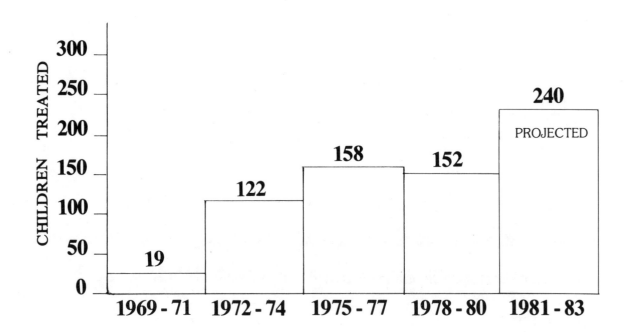

CARDIOVASCULAR SURGERY COSTS

—Current average cost of open heart surgery is $15,000 PER CHILD

—Children's Heart Fund provides heart surgery at no cost to the indigent family

DEDICATED PROFESSIONALS

---

38 DIFFERENT PROFESSIONALS CONTRIBUTE THEIR SKILLS DURING SURGERY AND ALL-AROUND OPERATIVE STAGES

Cardiovascular surgeon
Pediatric cardiologist
Anesthesiologist
Nurse anesthetist
Pathologist
Radiologist
Dentist
Radiology technician
Operating room nurses
Lab technician
Heart lung bypass technician
Escort nurse/interpreters
Social workers
Administrator-voluntary agencies
Intensive care unit nurses
Electrocardiogram technician
Pediatric nurse
Pediatric aide
Post anesthesia room nurse
Out-patient nurse
Pharmacist
Dietician
Medical records clerk
Chaplain
Heart catheterization lab tech.

OVER $5,500,000 OF GOODS AND SERVICES HAVE BEEN DONATED WITHIN THE PAST DECADE

THANKS FROM AROUND THE WORLD

---

451 CHILDREN FROM THESE COUNTRIES HAVE RECEIVED TREATMENT

Egypt
Greece
Ethiopia
Honduras
Hong Kong
India
Kenya
Korea
Malaysia
South Vietnam
Sudan
Uganda
United States
Zaire

ADDITIONAL REQUESTS FOR HELP

Liberia
Malawi
Thailand
Guatemala
Nigeria
Nicaragua
Philippines
Algeria

WITH PROPER FACILITIES AND ADEQUATE FUNDING, HUNDREDS OF ADDITIONAL CHILDREN COULD HAVE BEEN GIVEN LIFE-SAVING SURGERY

A GROWING BASE OF SUPPORT

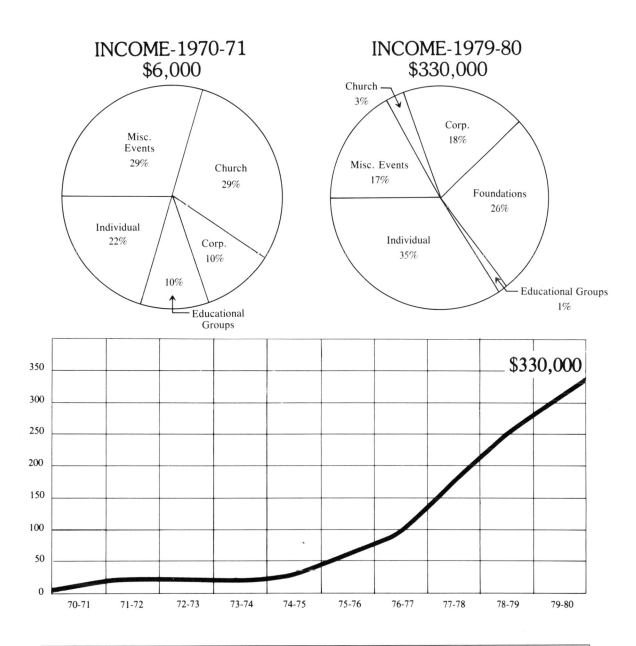

INCOME-1970-71
$6,000

Misc. Events 29%

Church 29%

Individual 22%

Corp. 10%

10%

Educational Groups

INCOME-1979-80
$330,000

Church 3%

Corp. 18%

Misc. Events 17%

Foundations 26%

Individual 35%

Educational Groups 1%

$330,000

| 350 |
| 300 |
| 250 |
| 200 |
| 150 |
| 100 |
| 50 |
| 0 |

70-71 71-72 72-73 73-74 74-75 75-76 76-77 77-78 78-79 79-80

982% INCREASE IN PRIVATE SUPPORT IN THE PAST TEN YEARS

438% INCREASE IN CORPORATE SUPPORT IN THE PAST TEN YEARS

EDUCATION

Teaching of physicians around the world by surgeons and specialists of the Children's Heart Fund

Case presentations of classic, advanced, and extraordinary lesions at lectures, continuing education meetings, and seminars

Exchange programs for training of key medical personnel in cardiovascular medicine

Training of nurses, interns, and residents in appropriate techniques in care and treatment of cardiac patients

---

THE CHILDREN'S HEART FUND VOLUME OF 60 TO 70 PATIENTS A YEAR PROVIDES AN EXPANDED FORUM FOR EDUCATION AND RESEARCH

RESEARCH

The Children's Heart Fund is the first program in the United States providing an on-going service of free treatment for indigent heart-crippled children worldwide.

It has one of the largest case loads of pediatric and adolescent valvular disease.

It generates data for study of over 22% of congenital and acquired heart disease case histories in the young in the Twin Cities.

THREE-YEAR PROGRAM NEEDS

REFERRAL AND ASSESSMENT $75,000

For collection of medical history and physical,
x-rays, electrocardiogram and other data, review
and assessment of operability and urgency,
scheduling for admittance, securing transport and
medical escort/interpreter, completing international
travel arrangements.

PRE-OPERATIVE CARE AND DIAGNOSIS 150,000

For housing and food, screening for infections and
other diseases, initial testing and diagnostic
examinations, heart catheterization including
hospitalization as required, definition of lesion,
surgical-cardiology conference, plan for surgery.

SURGICAL SUPPORT 275,000

For hospital selection and admittance, pre-surgical
testing, anesthesia, drugs, operating room supplies
and supplementary costs, operating room personnel,
heart-lung bypass supplies, monitoring blood.

POST-OPERATIVE CARE 425,000

For one-to-one intensive care nursing, monitoring,
drugs and intravenous solutions, respiratory support,
supplementary testing, supplies and equipment;
pediatric unit or surgical unit care, equipment and
supplies; housing and food during post-discharge
recovery period; final examination and testing;
collection of discharge, operative, and other medical
reports and take-home medications; arrangements
for departure and travel.

EDUCATION AND RESEARCH 325,000

For training of nurses, interns, and residents in
appropriate techniques in care and treatment of
cardiac patients; and continued research in pediatric
and adolescent valvular diseases.

TOTAL PROGRAM NEEDS $1,250,000

PROPOSED FACILITY

12,000 SQUARE FEET

SPACE PLANNED FOR:
-Patient rooms
-Student rooms
-Recreation area
-Children's playroom
-Kitchen facilities
-Dining room
-Storage

-Laundry
-Administrative offices
-Conference room
-Volunteer workroom
-Resident manager quarters
-Medical records storage
-Classrooms
-Research library

CAPITAL EQUIPMENT

Kitchen and food storage equipment
Housekeeping equipment
Laundry equipment
Indoor/outdoor recreational equipment
Furniture
Office equipment

ENDOWMENT/PLANNED GIVING

Provides added stability to the on-going operation of the Children's Heart Fund.
Enables donors of modest means to make a major gift.
Provides opportunity for donor to perpetuate a family name.
Insures an investment that lives on forever.
Provides opportunity for memorial gifts.

Children's
Heart Fund

THREE-YEAR NEEDS

1981-82   1982-83   1983-84

PROGRAM NEEDS	$1,250,000	
PROPOSED FACILITIES	1,100,000	
CAPITAL EQUIPMENT	150,000	
TOTAL THREE-YEAR NEEDS		$2,500,000
ENDOWMENT/PLANNED GIVING		500,000
COMBINED TOTAL		$3,000,000

Investment in Children's Advancement Fund

We need			*We have*	
Number of Gifts	*In the Range of*	*Total*	*Number of Gifts*	*Total Pledges*
1	$500,000	$ 500,000	—	—
2	250,000	500,000	1	$ 250,000
2	100,000	200,000	1	100,000
4	75,000	300,000	3	215,000
6	50,000	300,000	5	246,631
15 gifts of $50,000 or more		$1,800,000	10	$ 811,631
10	$ 25,000	$ 250,000	9	$ 236,550
15	15,000	225,000	9	140,000
20	10,000	200,000	5	48,625
25	5,000	125,000	17	88,800
75	1,000–3,000	100,000	41	$ 74,800
145 gifts of $1,000 or more		$ 900,000	81	$ 588,775
Many gifts of $1,000 or under		$ 300,000	152	$ 130,103
TOTAL		$3,000,000	243	$1,530,509

APPENDIX B

AT&T's contributions policy outlined in its foundation guidelines.

Programs and Eligibility

■■■■■■■■

AT&T Foundation is the principal source of philanthropy for AT&T and its subsidiaries.

The Foundation's scope is national, emphasizing support of private higher education and institutions and projects in the areas of health care, social action and the arts. Its aid to local communities is provided primarily through the United Way.

In each of its program areas, the Foundation seeks institutions, organizations and projects whose aim is to advance the full participation of women and minorities in our society.

Contributions by AT&T employees to educational and cultural institutions throughout the country are matched equally by AT&T Foundation. These matching gift programs are independent of other grants and also provide a way for the Foundation to extend its giving to some institutions that might otherwise be ineligible for Foundation funding.

AT&T Foundation does *not* award grants to individuals, buy advertisements, or donate equipment. Except in rare instances, it does *not* fund conferences or contribute to the creation of new organizations. Other excluded organizations and purposes are:

■ organizations not classified as tax exempt under Section 501(c)(3) of the Internal Revenue Code

■ organizations that discriminate by race, color, creed, gender or national origin

■ organizations whose chief purpose is to influence legislation

■ political organizations or campaigns

■ religious organizations when denominational or sectarian in purpose

■ operating expenses or capital campaigns of local health and human service agencies other than hospitals

■ local chapters of national organizations

■ sports teams or athletic competitions

■ banquets or other fund raising events

Higher Education

■■■■■■■■

Support of higher education was the nucleus of AT&T's original corporate contributions program and is central to the future direction of AT&T Foundation.

It reflects the conviction that developing and maintaining excellence in our institutions of higher learning are essential to the economic health of our nation and to the future leadership of institutions in all sectors of our society.

Recognizing that business supports public education through tax dollars and believing that diversity is

255

important to the American educational system, AT&T Foundation concentrates its support primarily on independent colleges and universities. It also provides financial assistance to national organizations serving the academic community.

AT&T Foundation seeks to:

■ advance research and teaching and promote excellence in curricula important to the development of physical sciences, communications and information sciences

■ provide opportunity for minority youth and women in the study of science and engineering

■ advance excellence in liberal arts education

The Education program centers around Special Purpose Grants in Science and Engineering awarded to both public and private institutions to strengthen disciplines viewed as vital to the future of information management and communications.

These grants are designated for research, curriculum development and enhancement, or other departmental needs in such areas as electrical engineering, computer science, materials science, chemistry and physics. This component of the Education program is *not* open to application.

Independent colleges and universities may apply for grants for special development programs or improvement of facilities. Although the Foundation is particularly interested in research universities of national stature, support is considered for smaller universities and colleges if they are located in areas where AT&T has a major presence.

In development campaigns, the Foundation has special interest in support of junior faculty in the sciences and humanities, development of curricula in telecommunications and management information systems, and programs incorporating international studies into the professional education of business and engineering students.

The Foundation's program to further educational opportunity for minorities includes support of the United Negro College Fund, an Aid to Black Colleges Program directed primarily to schools with engineering curricula, and support of national organizations helping minorities pursue careers in engineering and business.

Operating support for colleges and universities is provided only through the Independent College Funds of America and the United Negro College Fund.

In addition to the excluded purposes shown on page 1, the Education program does *not* consider proposals for:

■ named academic chairs
■ elementary and secondary schools
■ social sciences or health sciences programs
■ medical and nursing schools
■ junior and community colleges
■ industrial affiliate programs
■ technical trade associations

Health

AT&T Foundation supports institutions and projects that improve the resources available to the medical profession to treat physical and mental health problems. It also seeks to increase the presence of minorities in the medical profession and to improve the quality of health services in disadvantaged communities.

Provided with a government certificate of need, AT&T Foundation will consider support for major development campaigns of:

■ national medical centers with reputations for excellence in teaching, research and specialized services
■ local hospitals
   – if they serve as emergency care facilities in communities where AT&T has a major concentration of employees or
   – serve a substantial proportion of the underprivileged in their patient population

Projects of national application will be considered in the areas of health care cost-containment and substance abuse.

AT&T Foundation Medical Scholarships provide financial assistance to promising medical students at minority colleges. These scholarship programs are administered by the colleges and are *not* open by application to the Foundation.

In addition to the excluded purposes shown on page 1, the Health program does *not* provide operating support or fund:

■ programs to reduce deficits
■ organizations formed to combat specific diseases
■ medical research

Social Action

AT&T Foundation supports social action projects with national application and national institutions addressing socio-economic problems. It also provides annual operating grants to United Ways throughout the country to help maintain and improve the health and welfare of communities where AT&T employees live and work.

Projects of special interest are those that advance one or more of the following objectives:

■ foster the progress of equal opportunity throughout our society for:
  – minorities and women
  – the physically and mentally disabled
  – young people and the elderly
■ improve the quality of life in America by undertaking initiatives in:
  – community development
  – job training and employment
  – conservation of energy and the environment
■ enhance the effectiveness of the not-for-profit and public sectors

Projects should serve as models for other organizations and lend themselves to evaluation of results that can be disseminated to a wide audience.

Arts and Culture

AT&T Foundation supports nationally-known cultural organizations and projects of national or regional scope in areas where AT&T has a major presence. Its primary interest is in the performing arts.

To qualify for consideration, organizations must have been professionally managed for at least five years and compensate both artistic and managerial personnel.

Eligible organizations include symphony orchestras, dance, theatre and opera companies, performing arts centers, museums and private non-academic libraries.

The Arts and Culture program also funds arts service organizations whose primary function is to offer technical assistance or professional services to Foundation-eligible institutions.

The Foundation has particular interest in projects including:

■ special performances
■ new productions
■ presentations or commissions of new work
■ special exhibitions
■ major institutional development or expansion programs for which there is a demonstrated need

The Arts and Culture program will *not* consider annual operating support above $2,500 unless the request is from a consolidated fund representing a consortium of arts groups.

The Foundation will underwrite selected projects in a program *not* open to application. These initiatives include domestic tours by nationally-recognized classical and modern dance companies, performances of 20th century American music by major symphony orchestras, and films of rare and unusual artistic interest.

In addition to the excluded purposes shown on page 1, the Foundation does *not* fund:

■ student groups
■ arts education and therapy
■ chamber groups
■ competitions
■ training or scholarships
■ restorations or historic villages
■ endowment campaigns for unrestricted purposes
■ public radio and television stations for unrestricted purposes

Grant Application Procedures

To determine AT&T Foundation interest in receiving a proposal, please submit a letter of inquiry, preferably of no more than three pages, with the following information:

■ a description of the institution or organization and a statement relating its purpose to the general interests and specific priorities of the Foundation
■ a summary of the purpose for which the grant is being sought and evidence of need for the activity
■ an overall operating budget for the current fiscal year showing anticipated sources of revenue and expenses and (if project support is sought) a detailed budget for the project

Representatives of institutions and organizations of *national* import should write to:

Secretary
AT&T Foundation
550 Madison Avenue
Room 2400
New York, N.Y. 10022

Others should direct their inquiries to the AT&T office shown in the enclosure.

APPENDIX C

Sample foundation policy.
(Courtesy of the Bush Foundation.)

GRANTMAKING POLICIES AND PROCEDURES

MAJOR CURRENT INTERESTS

1. The Bush Foundation is predominantly a regional grantmaking foundation, with broad interests in education, human services, health, arts and humanities, and in the development of leadership.
2. The Foundation is interested in education at all levels, with major emphasis in higher education. In recent years, most of the Foundation's grantmaking in higher education has been in particular, pre-defined areas of emphasis. These include assisting private colleges with matching grants to complete capital fund drives, grants for faculty development, and for training in the joint fields of child development and social policy.
3. The Foundation seeks to support projects which may help demonstrate and evaluate ways to lessen, prevent or resolve contemporary social problems. Those projects which involve the elements of relatively early intervention and reasonable cost are of particular interest.
4. The Foundation seeks to encourage the delivery of good health care, at reasonable cost to recipients and to society. The Foundation wishes to consider proposals for programs that will improve the quality, accessibility, and efficiency of health care services within the Foundation's geographic region. Recently, grants have been approved for programs that seek to develop more information about the provision of health services within the region, to improve the clinical and leadership skills of rural physicians.
5. Within its geographic region of major interest, the Foundation supports the arts and humanities, including music, theater, dance, visual arts, and the general preservation of our cultural heritage. Since 1975 the Foundation also has provided fellowships for individual artists in Minnesota.
6. The development of leadership potential was of particular interest to the founder of The Bush Foundation, and will continue to command its interest and resources.
7. In several of the program areas discussed above, the Foundation has also sought to promote minority opportunity. This represents a continuing interest.

8. The Foundation has supported programs of interest to women, sometimes in separate programs (such as assisting shelters for battered women), and sometimes in programs which are available to men and women on an equal basis (such as the Bush Leadership Fellows Program). The Foundation's interest in this general area is to support regional programs which improve the quantity and quality of options available to women. The Foundation also hopes to encourage educational programs at several age levels which might help achieve this result.

Restrictions and Areas of High Selectivity

1. The Foundation will concentrate its major interest on projects originating in, or of special value to Minnesota, North Dakota and South Dakota. The Bush Leadership Fellows Program and the Bush Clinical Fellows Program include coverage of these states plus the counties of western Wisconsin which are part of the Ninth Federal Reserve District. A limited number of major non-regional programs have been approved, such as grants in child development and public policy, or support for historically black private colleges. In each such case, the program outlines are discussed and approved by the Foundation Board prior to making the related initial grants. Proposals for projects outside the United States ordinarily will not be approved.
2. The Bush Foundation ordinarily will not contribute to other private foundations, but this shall not preclude its joining with one or more foundations in a common effort of special interest.
3. The Foundation does not make direct grants to individuals except through established, defined programs such as the Bush Leadership Fellows Program, the Fellowship for Artists Program, and the Bush Clinical Fellows Program. Ordinarily the Foundation's grants are made only to non-profit, tax-exempt organizations.
4. Although the Foundation seeks to appraise each grant proposal on its merits, the following kinds of grant proposals are less likely to be approved than others:
   a. Proposals for building construction in medicine.
   b. Proposals requesting support to cover past operating deficits.
   c. Proposals seeking general and continuing operating support.
5. The Foundation for some time has been reluctant to provide funds for basic research within established academic disciplines. In September, 1974 the Board of Directors voted to cease granting funds for project research in the biomedical and health sciences.

Grantmaking Procedures

Responsibility of Decisions
All commitments of grant funds are made by the Board of Directors. The Board usually meets quarterly. The Grants Committee, a six-member subcommittee of the Board, discusses all grants prior to final Board action, and makes recommendations of final action to the Board.

All grant proposals to be considered by the Grants Committee and the Board are first investigated by the Foundation's staff. The results of these investigations are made available to the Grants Committee and the Board.

Time Required for Decisions
Grant proposals should be submitted to the President of the Foundation three months prior to the Board meeting at which consideration of the proposal is desired. This normally is a

minimum time needed to complete the steps required for consideration. But if the proposal is highly specialized, if it requires the review of outside consultants, the process of consideration usually takes longer.

The Board has approved additional preliminary screening procedures for University of Minnesota proposals, and for requests seeking construction funds for major hospitals and medical centers. The Foundation staff will explain these steps to anyone wishing further information about them.

Ordinarily one member of the Foundation's program staff is assigned to work on a specific proposal when it is received by the Foundation. This staff member will suggest further discussion with the author of the proposal if it seems necessary, and may also seek other opinions and background information. This staff member will also be responsible for presenting the proposal, the results of the related investigation, and the staff's composite recommendation to the Grants Committee and to the Board.

Preliminary Inquiries

The Foundation staff welcomes brief preliminary letters inquiring about possible interest of the Foundation in providing funds for a particular project. The staff also is pleased to answer written or telephone inquiries concerning application procedures, desired documentation, timing problems, and so on.

In answering questions about the possible future Foundation action on a proposal idea, the staff replies usually will range from "possible" to "unlikely." These staff appraisals never signal quick, optimistic encouragement as to final outcome. At the same time, they rarely are so discouraging as to prohibit finally any further consideration. However, recent staff estimates suggesting that proposal ideas seemed "unlikely" to command board interest and final approval have almost always proven correct, even though the estimates in no way commit or limit later Board action.

Exploration of Other Sources of Support

Grant applications ordinarily should explore all other possible sources of support in addition to The Bush Foundation. This exploration does not hurt the chances for a favorable decision by The Bush Foundation, but may improve the chances that the project will find support somewhere. In the event other sources do provide partial or full support, The Bush Foundation should be notified promptly, so that the staff may revise the amount requested in line with up-to-date and realistic needs.

Grant Proposals

Form of Presentation

There is no special form for applying for a grant. The proposals made to the Foundation vary widely as to purpose, and hence vary also as to the documentation needed for fair consideration. Plans which have been worked out thoughtfully and described concisely are always welcomed. Expensive brochures and extra packaging generally seem wasteful.

Desired Contents

A detailed list of "Application Requirements" is available at the Foundation office, and should be requested before drafting a final proposal. Following is a summary of the information which ordinarily should be provided in a completed proposal for a new project:

1. A clear description of the project, what it may be expected to achieve, and why it is important to undertake.

2. A detailed expense budget for the project, showing how the requested funds would be spent and during what time periods and showing where the income is expected to come from. The budget should make clear how the major elements of income and expenses were estimated. Applicants should specify when payment of funds is desired from the Foundation, and in what amount. If more than one payment is requested under the grant, a suggested schedule of payments should be provided.
3. A statement of other possible sources of support, public or private, which have been or will be solicited concerning the project, including a statement of funds which have been received or pledged.
4. If the project is to be continued after the period for which support has been requested, an explanation of how continuation of the project is to be financed. This explanation should include an income and expense projection for the program through one year beyond the last year for which Bush support is requested.
5. The procedure and criteria by which effectiveness of the grant should be judged after the grant funds have been expended.
6. Information concerning the organization and the responsible officers who intend to carry out the project:
   a. A brief description of the organization making the proposal.
   b. The names and primary affiliations of the organization's directors or trustees.
   c. The name(s) and qualifications of the person(s) who would administer the grant.
   d. An audited balance sheet and income statement, if available, for the organization's previous fiscal year.
7. A copy of the organization's most recent tax-exempt ruling from the Internal Revenue Service, along with either a statement as to any revisions which may be pending, or a statement that there has been no change and none is pending.
8. If the request comes from a department or individual in an organization, the request also should be endorsed by the administrative head of the organization. If possible, the endorsement also should comment upon the relative priority of the request compared with other needs which The Bush Foundation may be asked to support.
9. For demonstration projects, research studies, and experiments, a description of similar work which has been carried out previously by other agencies would be helpful, along with an estimate of the significance of this prior work to the proposed project.
10. Proposals seeking funds for basic research should be written so that the project and its importance may be understood by non-specialists, and also so that the specific work plan may be understood and reviewed by consultants in the specific discipline involved. The Foundation has been extremely selective in approving grants for basic research of all kinds.

Approved Grants

Notification of Approval
The Bush Foundation will send written notice to applicants concerning all Board decisions to approve or deny grant proposals, usually within ten days following the Board meeting involved. During this period, the Foundation notifies newspapers in Minnesota and the Dakotas and radio and television stations of grants which have been approved. The Foundation Center in New York City is also notified of approved grants so that its central data file may be kept current.

Reports to the Foundation
The Foundation will require progress reports at least annually stating what has been accomplished by expenditures of the grant funds, along with appropriate financial reports as to

how the funds were spent. Grant funds may be spent only for the purposes granted. Uncommitted funds at the end of the grant period must be returned to the Foundation unless other arrangements have been proposed beforehand and approved formally by the Foundation's Board of Directors. Following the end of the period for which funds were granted, the grantee must provide the Foundation with a final financial accounting for the grant funds and an evaluation and summary of the results obtained.

Disposition of Foundation Papers

In October, 1980, The Bush Foundation Board approved an archive agreement with the Minnesota Historical Society which provides that Foundation papers of potential historical interest will be catalogued and stored by the Society, and eventually will be available to scholars and other interested persons. The files of approved and denied grant applications and of fellowship applications will not be given public access, however, until fifty years following the date when those files were created. Other items such as annual reports or clipping files, which are either immediately publishable or already published, will be given immediate public access by the Society.

Summary Statistics for Recent Grants

The following tables summarize The Bush Foundation's recent grants, classified by the purpose for which funds were granted, by size and duration of grants, and by the geographic location of the grantees.

Summary of Grants Approved in Fiscal Year 1984 Classified by Size, Duration, Geographic Location of Grants

Classification of Grants		Number of Grants Approved
I. Size	$0– 9,999	5
	10,000– 24,999	17
	25,000– 49,999	22
	50,000– 99,999	17
	100,000– 199,999	27
	200,000– 499,999	14
	500,000–1,500,000	4
	Total	106
II. Duration	1 year	50
	2 years	26
	3 years	26
	4 years	4
	Total	106
III. Geographic Location	Minnesota	83
	North Dakota	5
	South Dakota	12
	Other	6
	Total	106

Summary of Grants Approved in Fiscal Years 1982, 1983, 1984 Classified by Purpose for Which Funds Were Granted[1]

Program Area	1982	1983	1984	3-Year Total
A. Arts & Humanities	$ 3,967,793 (11) 23.0%	$ 1,145,050 (15) 8.0%	$ 1,248,178 (14) 8.8%	$ 6,361,021 (40) 13.9%
B. Education	8,446,855 (39) 49.1%	6,845,520 (35) 47.6%	5,933,096 (35) 42.0%	21,225,471 (109) 46.4%
C. Health	746,265 (6) 4.3%	1,443,140 (10) 10.0%	1,612,253 (8) 11.4%	3,801,658 (24) 8.3%
D. Human Services	2,182,366 (34) 12.7%	1,628,528 (29) 11.3%	2,032,844 (34) 14.4%	5,843,738 (97) 12.9%
E. Miscellaneous	630,000 (9) 3.7%	1,905,190 (20) 13.3%	1,825,200 (12) 12.9%	4,360,390 (41) 9.5%
F. Fellowship Program Stipends	1,236,000 (3) 7.2%	1,406,000 (3) 9.8%	1,477,000 (3) 10.5%	4,119,000 (9) 9.0%
Totals	$17,209,279 (102) 100%	$14,373,428 (112) 100%	$14,128,571 (106) 100%	$45,711,278 (320) 100%

[1] In each cell, the dollar figure represents the total amount granted, the figure next below in parenthesis shows the number of grants made, and the bottom figure shows the percentage of all grant dollars awarded during that fiscal year.

Index

accountants
  institute of, 173
  as prospects, 145
account-by-account listings, 93–94
account management, 90–92
acquisitions, as affecting contributions policy,
    107–108
administration
  strengthening of, 20
  volunteers, 49
advanced gifts, 58
advertising, *see* promotion
affiliated organizations
  policy needs for, 18
  for United Arts Fund, 155
age, as determining factor in contribution
    status, 11–12
alumni
  advertising appeal to, 77
  college campaigns aided by, 164
  loaned executive, 207–208
  as prospects, 60
American Association of Fund-Raising
    Counsel, 9–10
American Cancer Society
  general information on, 190
  residential campaigns by, 140
American Council for the Arts, art council
    funding study by, 156, 157
American Heart Associations, residential
    campaigns by, 140
American Institute of Certified Public
    Accountants, 173
American Red Cross
  Community Chests and, 17
  general information on, 190
  policy problems of, 14–15
  slogan of, 74
  theme of, 74
Annual Appeal Sunday, 184

annual campaigns
  for arts organizations, 149
  in colleges, 161
  deferred-gifts program in, 233
  results of, 92
  soundings in, 19
annual diocesan appeal, 182–183
  payment period for, 184
  promotion of, 186
  timing of, 186
annual giving, 177
annual reports
  for foundation presentations, 129
  as prospect list information source, 60
  see also reports
annuity trusts, 222–223
answers and questions, in cultivation
    meetings, 99
appeals
  annual diocesan, 182–183
  Annual Sunday, 184
appointments
  corporate campaign, 100
  see also assignments
architects, as prospects, 145
art campaigns
  contributions in, 10, 12
  councils for, *see* art council campaigns
  credibility of, 28
  deferred giving in, 150
  fund-raising in, 149–150
  fund sources for, 153
  leadership in, 152
  of Minnesota Orchestra Association, 150–
    152
  package deals offered by, 139, 159
  prospects for, 57, 59, 153
  structure for, 150–153
  tax support for, 4–5
  timing of, 152

art council campaigns
fund allocation by, 159
fund sources for, 156
general discussion of, 153
markets for, 153–155
package deals offered by, 139, 159
prospects for, 156
timing of, 156
art gifts, 48
articles
for deferred-gifts program, 234
see also newspapers; press
Asking Corporations for Money (Murphy), 103
assignments
account, 90–92
appointments and, 100
campaign, 90–92
as campaign function, 65
group, 66
associations, as prospect list information
source, 60
AT&T, contributions policy of, 104, 255–257
athletic clubs, as prospect list information
source, 60
attorneys
deferred-giving aided by, 232
as prospects, 143–144
audience identification, 77–80
auditing committee, 198
automation, as affecting small business
campaigns, 139
awards
foundation campaign, 132
see also recognition

balls, charity, 180
banks
as information source, 126
prospect identification through, 61
Bar Associations, as aiding in professional
solicitation, 144
bargain sales, 230–231
bazaars, 180
bellwether gifts, 89, 90
bequests, 221
benefits, fringe, 18
billboards, 85
Blue Cross/Blue Shield, 15
board of directors
in corporations, 39
feasibility studies aided by, 19–20
of Minnesota Orchestra Association, 150
policy needs for, 18
as prospects, 122
responsibilities of, 14
see also development directors; executive
directors
boards
affiliate, 155
see also committee

bond gifts, 48
branch operations, 109
breakfasts, campaign kickoff, 86
brochures
for case presentations, 100
print materials and, 84
see also promotion
budget
of deferred-gifts program, 232
requirements, 101
versus goals, 67
building corporations, as prospects, 41
buildings, small business campaigns in office,
137
bulletins, 35
church, 186
in follow-through program, 37
pacing results in, 89
see also newsletters
Bush Foundation, 42
sample foundation policy of, 258–263
business, small
future trends in, 139
identification of, 136–137
solicitation of, 136–140, 152
United Way campaigns aided by, 193
business associations, as prospect list
information source, 60
Business Week, 118–119

calls, *see* telephone calls
campaigns
annual, *see* annual campaigns
art, *see* art campaigns
assignments, 90–92
bulletins, 37, 89
capital, *see* capital campaigns
case, 74, 78, 79
college, *see* college campaigns
combined, 215–218
conflicting, 34, 35
corporate, *see* corporate campaigns
councils, 19
credibility of, 28
endowment, *see* endowment campaigns
failure of, 8
feasibility studies for, 19–20
follow through in, 27, 37, 198
foundation, *see* foundation campaigns
hospital, *see* hospital campaigns
kickoff, 86–87, 89
leadership in, *see* leadership
mail, *see* mail campaigns
management of, *see* management, campaign
nonannual, 96–97
operating, *see* operating campaigns
organizational charts for, 62–63, 169, 178,
184
over-the-top, 4
pace-setting, 202–203

pilot, 89, 202, 203
policies for, 19
political, 35
primary school, 168–170
professional, 143–146
promotion of, *see* promotion
prospects, *see* prospects
recognition within, *see* recognition
renovation, 7, 8
reports, *see* reports
residential, 140–143
result projections in, 92–94
saturation, 56
sectarian, *see* Catholic institutions
    campaigns; Jewish federation campaigns
status analysis, 94–95
structures, 57–58
teaser, 75–77, 84
telephone, *see* telemarketing
timetables for, *see* timetables
timing of, *see* timing, campaign
training for, *see* training
United Way, *see* United Way campaigns
candor, avoidance of, in foundation
    campaigns, 132
capital campaigns
    assignments in, 215
    budget for, 213
    combined, 215–218
    endowment gifts in, 212–213
    fund sources for, 214–215, 218–219
    goal establishment for, 70–71
    market for, 211–213
    sponsorship in, 212
    top gifts in, 58, 64
    tribute gifts in, 212
    versus operating campaigns, 210–211
    see also campaigns; endowment campaigns
capital gifts, 180
card-by-card analysis, 96
card calling meeting, 188
cards
    prospect, 92
    stop, 137
card value
    as funding base, 68–69
    results projection and, 93–94
case presentations
    Children's Heart Fund, 103
    corporate, 100–102
    general discussion on, 74, 78–79
Catholic institutions campaigns
    annual diocesan appeal in, 182–184
    funding for, 182–183, 184
    goal setting in, 186
    organizational groupings in, 184–186
    parish assessment in, 182–183
census tract
    data, 140–141
    as geographic division, 137, 142

certificates, as means of recognition, 35
CFAE, *see* Council for Financial Aid to
    Education (CFAE)
chairpersons
    in corporate campaigns, 98, 108
    as leadership positions, 29
    in professional campaigns, 144, 145
    recruitment of, 64–65
    in residential campaigns, 98, 108
challenge, in goal achievement, 68
challenge gifts, 110, 134
chamber of commerce, as prospect list
    information source, 59
charitable lead trust, 225–226
    life insurance in, 226–227
charitable remainder annuity trust, 222–223
charitable remainder unitrust, 222
charity balls, 180
Children's Heart Fund
    case presentation of, 103
    visual presentation for, 243–254
churches
    contributions to, 9, 10
    displays used by, 85
    promotion for, 72
    prospects for, 38, 57–58, 62
    speakers' bureaus in, 84
civic organizations
    contributions to, 10
    rosters of, 60, 122
classification, trade, 114–115
clientele
    advertising appeal to, 79
    policy needs for, 18
    see also prospects
Clifford trusts, 40–41, 44–45
closely held corporations, 40, 41
closing out reports, 92, 96
clubs
    athletic, 60
    country, 60, 122
    giving, 145, 167
    private membership, 60
    rotary, 60
    service, 60
college campaigns
    alumni as aiding, 164–165
    building endowments in, 165–168
    contributions to, 9, 10
    corporate gifts for, 161–162
    credibility of, 28
    displays in, 85
    faculty gifts for, 162, 164
    foundation gifts for, 162
    general information on, 160–161
    giving clubs in, 167
    individual gifts for, 161
    matching gifts for, 162, 163
    parents as aiding, 164
    promotion for, 80

college campaigns (*continued*)
  prospects for, 57, 62
  timing of, 167–168
  see also education
combined campaigns, 215–218
commitment requests, 99
committee
  auditing, 198
  corporate contributions, 103–104
  prospect evaluation, 112–113
  rating evaluation, 112–113
Community Chests
  background information on, 190
  policy problems of, 17
  promotion of, 75–77
community foundations, 45–46
Community Fund, 190
community obligation, 50
company prospects, 59–60
compensation policy, 18
competition
  contributions affected by, 107–108
  goal division for, 71
  pacing results for, 89
computers
  in letter campaigns, 179–180
  for result projections, 93
Conference Board, The
  corporate contributions study by, 108
  corporate contributions survey by, 10
conflicts
  with additional campaigns, 34
  with community events, 35
conservatism, in campaign projections, 96–97
consumers appeal, 79
  see also prospects
contests, 86
continuing pledge plan, 203–205
contributions, 5
  age as determining, 11–12
  data, 9–10
  manager, 103
  policy, 104, 107–108
  see also gifts
Coolidge, Calvin, on gifts, 99
cooperatives, as campaign prospects, 41
corporate campaigns
  calls for, 100–103
  contributions committee in, 103–104
  cultivation program in, 98–99
  general information on, 108–111
  as major source of income, 98
  presentation techniques for, 103
  reasons for, 105–108
  request size for, 111–120
corporate foundations, as campaign
    prospects, 42
corporate gifts, 9, 10
  for capital campaigns, 211
  for college campaigns, 161–162

  for United Arts Funds, 155
  for United Way campaigns, 191
  see also corporations
corporations
  building, 41
  campaigns for, *see* corporate campaigns
  closely held, 40
  mutual companies as, 40–41
  as prospects, 39, 57
  publicly held, 40
  real estate, 41
  see also corporate gifts
cost efficiency, 104
Council for Financial Aid to Education
    (CFAE)
  college support and, 160
  hospital contribution study by, 110
  matching gifts study by, 110
  national corporations survey by, 168
Council on Foundations, as information
    source, 108
counselor training programs, 209
country clubs, as prospect list information
    source, 60, 122
CPAs, as prospects, 145
credibility
  campaign, 28
  goal achievement as affecting, 68
criticism, as affecting contributions policy, 106
cultivation meeting, 98–99
cultural organizations
  corporate contributions to, 110–111
  private organizations aided by, 7

deanery, as geographic division of diocese,
    184
decision-making process, 130–131
deductions, tax
  contributions affected by, 105–106
  see also government
Defense Department, 14–15
deferred-giving program
  in art organizations, 150
  bequests in, 221
  budgets for, 232
  for colleges, 160
  endowments and, 210, 220–221
  foundation funding as affecting, 235–239
  in hospital campaigns, 180, 181
  legal council for, 232
  letters of intent in, 239
  life insurance in, 227–230
  marketing of, 234–235
  policies for, 231–239
  pooled income fund in, 224–225
  real estate in, 230–231
  staff for, 232, 235
  trustees for, 232
  trusts in, 221–224, 225–227
dentists, as prospects, 145

Department of Commerce, 116
Department of Health and Human Services, 175
Department of Labor, 113, 136
development directors
    account management by, 92
    importance of, 52–53
    prospect identification aided by, 59
    see also board of directors; executive directors
dinners
    campaign kickoff, 86
    for college campaigns, 168
    for corporate campaigns, 98
    by Jewish federations, 188
    for percent clubs, 106
diocesan appeal, 182–183
direct mail
    in deferred-gifts program, 234
    see also mail campaign
directories, foundation, 126, 129
disappointments, management of, 88
displays, 85
divisions
    goals, 69–70
    kickoffs, 89
    leaders, 90
    promotional strategy of, 80
    results analysis, 93–94
documentaries, 84
dollar objectives, 67, 90
donor-advised funds, 45
donor interests, 233
Dun & Bradstreet, on small business, 136

economy
    campaign timing affected by, 34–35
    goal establishment affected by, 68
education
    combined campaigns in, 217–218
    corporate contributions to, 10
    prospects for, 38
    tax support for, 4–5
    see also college campaigns
electonic media, 84
emotions
    promotion appeals to, 77
    satisfaction of, 50
Employee Retirement Income Security Act (ERISA), 171
employees
    contributions formula for, 113–114
    as group identification, 47
    policy needs for, 18
    as prospects, 57
    see also personnel
endowment campaigns
    appeal of, 210–211
    building, 165–168
    capital campaigns and, 161

general discussion of, 210
    goal establishment for, 70–71
engineers, as prospects, 145
enthusiasm, 68
equity, return on, 118–119
ERISA (Employee Retirement Income Security Act), 171
essay contests, 86
estate planning seminars, 235
executive directors
    importance of, 52
    responsibilities of, 14
    see also board of directors; development directors
executives
    advertising appeal to, 77, 78–79
    loan program, 205–208
    solicitation of, 200–201
exemption letter, 127
expenses
    control of, 7
    see also budget

faculty
    advertising appeal to, 79
    gifts, 162
    as prospects, 57
family foundations 42–43
Family Service of Greater St. Paul, community group questionnaire of, 22
fashion shows, 180
federations
    Jewish, *see* Jewish federation campaigns
    policy needs for, 18
    policy problems of, 16
feasibility studies, 19–20
films
    in promotional campaigns, 84–85
    in small business campaigns, 137
    see also slide sound presentations
final reports
    closing out in, 96
    outstanding gift estimates in, 92
financial objectives, 67, 90
financial reporting, 233
financial resources, 18–19
5 percent clubs, 106
follow-the-leader principle, 99
follow-through
    campaign, 37
    in United Way campaigns, 198
    visits, 27
Ford Foundation, 42
Fortune 500 companies, 41
foundation campaigns
    approaching, 129–130
    of Bush Foundation, 258–263
    considerations for, 133
    decision-making process in, 130–131
    evaluation of, 135

foundation campaigns (*continued*)
  factors involved in, 131–132
  identification of, 126–127
  information sources for, 126–127
  presentations to, 127–129
  types of, 133–135
  see also foundations
Foundation Center, 127
Foundation Directory, The, 46
foundations
  campaigns, see foundation campaigns
  for capital campaigns, 211
  community, 45–46, 233–234, 235–239
  corporate, 42
  council on, 108
  family, 42–43
  general-purpose, 43
  gifts, 10, 162
  hospital, 173–177
  independent, 42–43, 175
  Minnesota Orchestra Association, 151
  National Council of, 126–127
  operating, 46–47
  special-purpose, 43
  united, 17
  for United Arts Fund, 153
  for United Way campaigns, 191–192
  see also trusts
fringe benefits, 18
Fund-Raising Council, American Association
      of, 9–10
future leadership planning, 53, 55
future trends, in small business campaigns,
      139

Gallup Organization survey, 8–9
gender, as affecting contributions, 11–12
general partnerships, 39
general public, 7
general-purpose foundations, 43
general supports, 211–212
generosity, as characteristic of chairperson, 29
geographic organization
  of alumni, 164
  in Catholic institutions, 184
  in residential campaigns, 142
  in small business campaigns, 137
gifts
  advanced, 58
  art as, 48
  bellwether, 89, 90
  bonds as, 48
  capital, 180
  challenging, 110, 134
  corporate, *see* corporate gifts
  deferred, *see* deferred-giving program
  faculty, 162
  foundation, 162
  funding base determined by, 68–69
  individual, 9, 10, 152, 161, 193

in-kind, 48
  life insurance as, 48, 227–230
  major, 150, 214
  matching of, 110, 133
  of Minnesota Orchestra Association, 150
  real estate, 48, 124, 125, 230–231
  restricted, 232
  securities as, 124, 125
  size of, *see* request size
  stock, 48
  top, 58–59, 61, 64, 214
  tribute, 212, 235
  types of, 47–48
  unrestricted, 232
  see also contributions
giving
  annual, 177
  clubs, 145, 164, 167–168
  guides, 125
  patterns, 8–9, 11
  satisfaction in, 5
goals
  achievement challenge, 68
  annual, 69
  basic funding base and, 68–69
  breakdown, 71
  campaign, 35–36
  in Catholic institution campaigns, 186
  definition, 36
  determination, 114
  division, 69–70
  employee, 199–201
  executive, 201
  high versus moderate, 67–68
  in United Way campaigns, 198
government
  absence of, 5
  contributions policy and, 106–107
  funds, 218
  policy needs for, 18
graduating class organization, for college
      campaigns, 164–165
grants
  in art organizations, 149
  matching, 133
  see also foundations
graphics, in promotional materials, 84
grievances, 18
group assignments, 66
  see also assignments
group solicitation, 201–202

health, as concern of chairperson, 29
health and human services
  contributions to, 11–12
  corporate aid to, 10
  residential campaigns by, 140
  tax support for, 4–5
  see also hospital campaigns

Health Maintenance Organization (HMO),
172
holidays, as affecting campaign timing, 35
honorials, 212
hospital campaigns
combined, 217–218
contributions to, 9, 10, 12, 110–111
credibility of, 28
foundations in, *see* hospital foundations
fund raising for, 177–181
general discussion of, 171
hospital expenses and, 171–173
implementation of, 181
prospects for, 57
hospital foundations
advantages of, 173, 175
characteristics of 173, 174, 176–177
policy decisions for, 175–176
Housing and Urban Development (HUD), 218

income, 7, 9, 11
incompetence, as hindering campaign
progress, 37, 52
independent foundations, 175
as prospects, 42–43
independently wealthy, *see* wealthy prospects
Independent Sector survey, 8–9
individual gifts, 9, 10
for college campaigns, 161
for Minnesota Orchestra Association, 152
for United Way campaign, 193
individuals
as prospects, 38, 47–48, 60–61
solicitation of, 198–201
industrial development department, as
prospect list information source, 60
in-kind gifts, 48
insurance, *see* life insurance
intercampaign cultivation, 109
interests, appealing to, 102
Internal Revenue Service, *see* IRS
interviews
feasibility study for, 19–20
in promotional campaigns, 84
introductory remarks, in cultivation meetings,
98
investments, program-related, 134–135
IRS
foundation designation by, 45 126, 134, 173
tax forms of, 8
trust approval by, 44–45

Jewish federation campaigns
follow-up in, 188
leadership development in, 189
promotion in, 189
solicitation for, 187–188
techniques for, 188
timing of, 189
training for, 188–189
job descriptions, 64

kickoff, campaign, 86–87
gift announcement at, 89
Kiwanis clubs, as information sources, 60

law suits, as expense, 172
lawyers, as prospects, 143–144
leadership
in arts campaign, 152
campaign, 28–30
managing, 53
planning for, 53–55
recruitment of, 64–65
role of, 51–55
for United Jewish fund, 189
as volunteer motivation, 50
lead trust, 225, 227
legal council, in deferred-gifts program, 232
letters
in Arts Fund campaign, 155
in college campaigns, 164
in deferred-gifts program, 234
exemption, 127
in hospital campaigns, 177, 179–180
of intent, 238, 239
of recognition, 35
of request, 100
small business campaigns aided by, 137
see also mail campaign
life insurance
in charitable lead trusts, 226–227
in charitable remainder trusts, 223–224
as gift, 48, 227–230
limited partnership, as prospect, 39
line solicitation, 199
Lions clubs, as information sources, 60
lists, prospect, 59
long-distance runs, in promotion campaigns,
86
long-term plans, 69
luncheons
campaign kickoff, 86
contributor, 20, 27
in corporate campaigns, 98
in hospital campaigns, 181

ma-and-pa small business, 137
mail campaign
general discussion on, 143
in hospital campaigns, 177, 179–180
in professional campaigns, 144, 145
in residential campaigns, 142
small business campaigns aided by, 137,
139
see also direct mail; letters
major gifts, 150
in capital campaign, 214
management
account, 90–92
funds, 155
as group identification, 47

management, campaign
  account management in, 90–92
  bellwether gifts for, 89
  pilot campaigns for, 89
  pacing results in, 89–90
  result projection in, 92–94
  solicitation in, 90
manufacturers, as prospect list information
  source, 60
marathons, in promotional campaigns, 86
mass-mailing programs, 179
matching grants, 133
media
  blitz, 34
  electronic, 84
  policy needs for, 18
  policy versus, 14
  in promotion campaign, 72
  techniques, 84–86
medicard legislation, 172
medicare legislation, 172
meetings
  card calling, 188
  cultivation, 99
member institutions, 233
memorials, 212
mergers, as affecting contributions policy,
  107–108
Minnesota Literacy Council, promotional
  campaign of, 76–77
Minnesota Orchestra's Annual Guaranty
  Fund, 150, 151
money
  asking for, 102
  see also gifts
motion picture films
  in promotional campaigns, 85
  see also films
motivation
  in campaigns, 36–37
  in kickoff, 86
motives of volunteers, 49–51
Murphy, Dennis (*Asking Corporations for
  Money*), 103
mutual companies, as prospects, 40–41

National Association of Independent Schools,
  gift report by, 110
National Council of Foundations, as
  information source, 126–127
natural neighborhood, as geographic division,
  137, 142
newsletters
  pacing results in, 89
  in promotional campaigns, 85, 87
  see also bulletins
newspapers
  Catholic, 186
  prospect list aided by, 59
  see also articles
nonsupervisory solicitation, 199

objectives, dollar, 67, 90
objectivity, in fund raising, 13
obligation, as volunteer motivation, 50
office buildings, as location for small business
  campaigns, 137
operating campaigns, 7, 8
  top gifts in, 58, 64
  versus capital campaigns, 210–211
operating foundations, as prospect, 46–47
opinion poll, 21
orchestras, as beneficiaries, 159
organizational policies, *see* policy
organization chart, 62–63, 169, 178, 184
oversell, avoidance of, in promotional
  campaign, 80
over-the-top results, 4

pace-setting campaigns, 202–203
pacing of results, 89
package deals, 139, 159
parents, as aiding in college campaigns, 164
parish assessment, 182–183
partnerships
  as prospects, 39
  small businesses as, 136
payment period
  in annual appeals program, 184
  in capital campaigns, 213
  in United Ways campaigns, 198
peer influence, 51
personals, as tribute gift, 212
personnel
  advertising appeal to, 77
  breakdown of, 61–63
  competency of, 37, 52
  goal establishment for, 35–36
  importance of, 52–53
  motivation of, 36–37
  policies, 18
  projections, 96
  recognition of, 35–36
  recruitment of, 29–30, 33, 64–65
  role of, 51–55
  trade classification of, 114–115
  training of, 30, 31, 36–37
  see also employees; volunteers
phonathon
  in college campaigns, 165
  in residential campaigns, 142
  see also telemarketing
phone campaigns, *see* telemarketing
physicians, as prospects, 144–145
pilot campaigns
  in campaign start-up, 89
  in United Way campaigns 202–203
planning
  fund-raising, 10
  leadership, 8, 53–55
  long-term, 69
  pledge, 203–205
  short-term, 69

plaques
    in capital campaigns, 212
    as recognition, 35, 36
    see also recognition
pledge plan, 203–205
policy
    areas requiring, 18–19
    problems caused by lack of, 14–17
    public identification for, 17
    public relations as, 14
    revision of, 20
political campaigns, 35
polls, opinion, 21
pooled income fund, 224–225
posters, as recognition aid, 35
potential, campaigning by, 200
preassignment of prospects, 65–66
presentations
    case, 100–102
    in corporate campaigns, 100, 103
    visual, 98, 142
    written, 103, 109, 127, 130
press, 14
    pacing results through, 89
    in promotional campaigns, 85
    see also articles; newspapers
primary schools
    campaigns for, 168–170
    corporate contributions for, 110
print materials, 84
    brochures and, 100
    see also promotion
PRIs (program-related investments), 134–135
private membership, as prospect list
        information source, 60
problem summary, 100
professional campaigns, 143–146
professional development staffs, 56
    prospect identification aided by, 59
professional fund-raising counsels, 19–20
professionals
    campaign for, 143–146
    in deferred gifts program, 234
    as prospects, 57
    in United Arts Funds, 155
    in United Way campaigns, 192–193
profit
    as corporate request basis, 117–118
    trade groups and, 115–117
program proposals, 98
program-related investments (PRIs), 134–135
program requirements, 101
projections
    conclusions based on, 95
    employee, 96
    general information on, 92–93
    methods of, 93–94
    nonannual campaign, 96–97
promotion
    of annual diocesan appeal, 186
    audience identification for, 77–80

committee, 72–73
    by Community Chest, 75–77
    divisional strategy in, 80, 81, 82
    elements of, 74–75
    kickoff, 86–87
    media techniques for, 84–86
    by Minnesota Literacy Council, 76–77
    objectives of, 30–31
    public relations and, 14, 18, 30–31
    purpose of, 72
    of United Jewish Fund, 189
    of United Way campaign, 198
property
    as gifts, 48, 124, 125, 230–231
    policy needs for, 18–19
proposals, program, 98
proprietorships
    as prospects, 38–39
    small businesses as, 136
prospect cards, 92
prospects
    accountants as, 145
    account-by-account listing of, 93–94
    alumni as, 60
    architects as, 145
    for arts organizations, 57, 59
    assignment of, 65–66
    attorneys as, 143–144
    business, 38–41
    for churches, 38, 57–58, 59
    for college campaigns, 57, 62
    company, 59–60
    cooperatives as, 41
    corporations as, 39–41
    dentists as, 145
    directors as, 122
    engineers as, 145
    foundation, *see* foundations
    grouping of, 61–63
    for hospital campaigns, 57
    identification, 57–58, 59–61, 234
    individually owned enterprises as, 38–39
    individuals as, 38, 47–48, 60–61
    information sources for, 59–60
    lists, 59
    mutual companies as, 40–41
    partnerships as, 39
    physicians as, 144–145
    preassignment of, 65–66
    principal, 58–59
    proprietorships as, 38–39
    rosters for, 60, 122
    small businesses as, 57, 121
    solicitation of, *see* solicitation
    sponsors as, 57
    trusts as, 38, 43–45
    users as, 57
    value, 68–69
    wealthy, *see* wealthy prospects
psychological atmosphere, of campaign, 88

publications
    in deferred-gifts program, 234
    in promotional campaign, 85
public institutions
    community relationships within, 14
    versus private organizations, 40
publicly held corporations, 40, 41
public relations, 14
    employees as source for, 18
    objectives of, 30–31
    see also promotion
public support test, 45–46

questionnaires, 20–26
    as luncheon follow-up, 27
questions and answers, in cultivation
    meetings, 99
quota system, 139–140

radio, 14
    in promotional campaign, 84
ratings
    methods for, 112
    projection, 96–97
    small business campaigns aided by, 139
real estate
    as gifts, 48, 124, 125, 230–231
    prospects within, 41
receipts, as recognition aid, 35
recognition
    campaign, 35–36
    in corporate campaigns, 102–103
    explanation of, 37
    as volunteer motivation, 51
    of wealthy prospects, 124–125
records, in United Way campaign, 198
recruitment
    for leadership positions, 29–30, 64–65
    planning, 53, 55
    strategy for, 30
    time allowances for, 31
Red Cross, *see* American Red Cross
relationships
    group, 14
    policy as affected by, 17–19
religious holidays, as element of campaign
    timing, 35
renovations campaigns, 7, 8
reports
    annual, 60, 129
    closing out, 92, 96
    Dun & Bradstreet, 136
    foundation, 135
    as information source, 60
    meeting, 37
    problems with, 92
    as recognition, 35–36
request size
    basis of, 102
    corporate campaigns as avoiding, 100

corporate responsibility as affecting, 111–
    112
    employee quotas and, 139–140
    giving ability as affecting, 112
    giving propensity as affecting, 112
    rating method for, 112–113
requirements, program, 101
residential campaigns
    approaches to, 140–143
    general information on, 140
restricted gifts, 232
restricted trusts, 45
results
    over-the-top, 4
    pacing of, 89
    projection of, 92–94
return on equity, 118–119
review boards, 172–173
robotics, 139
Rockefeller Foundation, 42
rosters
    as aiding in prospect preassignment, 66
    as prospect list information source, 60
Rotary clubs, as information source, 60

St. Joseph's Hospital, patient opinion poll of,
    21
St. Paul Ramsey United Arts Council, 154
    corporate benefits program of, 158
satisfaction motivation, 50
saturation campaigns, 56
saturation solicitation, 137
schools
    corporate contributions to, 110
    see also education
seasons, as consideration in campaign timing,
    34
secondary school campaigns, 168–170
    corporate contributions to, 110
    see also education
sectarian campaigns, *see* Catholic institutions
    campaigns; Jewish federation campaigns
securities gifts, 124, 125
seminars, estate planning, 235
separate corporate-employee campaign, 194–
    196
service, as concern in corporate campaign,
    104
service clubs, 60
service volunteers, 49
7/7 principle
    in prospect grouping, 61–62, 64
    in small business campaigns, 137
shopping centers, as location of small
    business campaigns, 137, 139
short-term plans, 69
sick leave policy, 18
single corporate-employee approach, 193–194,
    195

slide sound presentations
  in annual diocesan appeal, 184
  in promotional campaign, 85
  see also films
slogans
  promotional, 74
  see also theme
social agencies
  contributions to, 10
  credibility of, 28
  private organizations aided by, 7
Social Security, 171
Social Security Amendment Act, 172
solicitation
  as element of successful campaign, 90
  of individuals, 198–201
  for Jewish federation campaigns, 187–188
  line, 199
  nonsupervisory, 199
  of professionals, 144
  saturation, 137
soundings, 19
  personal interviews for, 19–20
  questionnaires for, 20–26
speaking
  bureaus, 84
  chairperson's responsibility of, 29
special gifts, 58, 124–125
special interest services, 101
special-purpose foundations, 43
sponsors
  in capital campaigns, 212
  as prospects, 57
sports promotion, in promotional campaign, 86
staff, *see* personnel
Standard Industrialization Classification, 116
statement of purpose, 127
stock
  gifts, 48
  policy needs for, 18–19
stockholders, 107
stop cards, 137
strategy
  explanation of, 36
  goals within, 67
  organizational, 30
studies, feasibility, 19–20
suggestion policy, 18
summary
  in cultivation meetings, 98
  statement, 100–102
support
  case presentation requirement for, 102
  public, 45–46
symbols, in promotional campaigns, 76

tax(es)
  advantages, 220–221
  deductions, 105–106

exempt revenue bonds, 218–219
  forms, 8
teaser campaign, 75–77, 84
  Community Chests' use of, 76
telemarketing
  in arts campaign, 156
  in college campaigns, 165
  general discussion on, 143
  by Minnesota Orchestra Association, 152
  phonathons and, 142, 165
  in residential campaigns, 142
  small business campaigns as aided by, 137
  see also telephone calls
telephone calls
  in arts campaigns, 156
  in corporate campaigns, 100, 109
  in deferred-gifts program, 234
  in professional campaigns, 144
  see also telemarketing
telephone directory, as prospect list
  information source, 59
television, 14
  in promotional campaign, 84
termination policy, 18
term of office policy, 18
test, public support, 45–46
theme
  audience identification and, 79
  in print materials, 84
  in promotional campaigns, 74
  slogans and, 64
third-party payers policy, 18
timetables, 31–33
  dollar objectives in, 90
  organization charts and, 62
  in promotional campaign, 80, 83
  in residential campaigns, 142
  as responsibility of development staff, 52
  top management, 53, 54
timing, campaign
  of annual diocesan appeal, 186
  of arts campaign, 152
  of college campaigns, 167
  in corporate campaigns, 129
  in foundation campaigns, 129
  general information on, 31–35
  of Jewish federation campaign, 189
  in United Way campaigns, 197
top gifts, 58–59, 61, 64, 214
top leadership management, 53
  see also leadership
tours, in promotional campaigns, 84
tracts, as geographic divisions, 137, 142
trade classification
  employee, 114–115
  of group average, 115
  profitability and, 115–117
training
  counselor, 209
  elements of, 36–37

training (*continued*)
    by Jewish federations, 188
    for loaned executives, 206–207
    sessions, 139
    in United Way campaigns, 198
tribute gifts, 212
    in deferred-giving program, 235
trustees, 232
trusts
    Clifford, 40–41, 44–45
    charitable lead, 225–226
    charitable remainder, 222–223
    general discussion of, 221–222
    life insurance and, 223–224
    as prospects, 41, 43–45
    restricted, 45
    unrestricted, 45
2 percent clubs, 106

United Arts Funds
    art councils and, 153
    slogan of, 75
    theme of, 75
United Foundation, 17
United Fund, 190
United Jewish Fund, 187
United Negro College Fund
    corporate gifts to, 161
    slogan of, 74
    theme of, 74
United Way
    campaigns, *see* United Way campaigns(s)
    contribution study by, 11
    corporate support of, 108, 111
    example survey from, 23–27
    as information source, 119
    policy problems of, 17
    slogan of, 75
    theme of, 75
    United Jewish Fund and, 186–187
United Way campaign(s)
    background information on, 190–191
    case, 78–79
    combined, 216–217
    companywide, 208–209
    conflicts, 34
    employee campaigns within, 193–198, 209
    loaned executive program in, 205–208
    precampaign cultivation in, 208
    for professionals, 144
    prospects for, 57, 191–193
    saturation, 56
    for small business, 137, 139

solicitation for, 198–205
unitrusts, 222
universities, *see* college campaigns
unrestricted gifts, 232
unrestricted trusts, 45
users, as prospects, 57

vacation policy, 18
Vatican approved programs, 182
vendor policy, 18
visits, follow-up, 27
visual case presentation, 243–254
visual presentation
    in corporate campaigns, 103
    in cultivation meetings, 98
    in training sessions, 142
volunteers
    account management by, 92
    administrative, 49
    goal achievement affecting, 68
    in hospital campaigns, 181
    motives for, 49–51
    policy needs for, 18
    recruitment of, 30, 34
    role of, 51–55
    service, 49
    training, 36–37
    see also personnel

ward, as geographic division, 137, 142
War Fund, 190
wealthy prospects
    assignment of, 122
    campaign presentation to, 123–124
    college funding aided by, 161
    as group identification, 47
    hospital funding aided by, 171, 177
    identification of, 121–122
    as prospects, 57, 211
    United Arts Fund aided by, 155
    United Way campaigns aided by, 192
welfare, as concern in corporate campaign, 104
widely held corporations, 41
women's activities, 149
worker's compensation, 171
written presentations
    for branch operations, 109
    in corporate campaigns, 103
    in foundation presentations, 127, 130

youth programs contributions, 12

About the Author

William J. Smith is a renowned expert in the field of fund raising. He has had over 40 years of experience in coordinating grants programs for various organizations and has directed campaigns to raise money even during periods of social unrest, war, or depression, when the public tended to be either preoccupied or simply unable to afford much in the way of donations.

After working his way through Case Western Reserve and Ohio State Universities, Smith spent the major portion of his professional career as an executive for the United Way movement. Starting out in local United Ways, he later joined the United Way of America as Director of Campaign Services for the entire country. During the time he served in that capacity the United Way movement raised an average of approximately $1 billion a year. Smith then decided to return to local community service, and he became Chief Executive of the United Way in St. Paul, Minnesota, where he served for 16 years. During his administration, the St. Paul United Way ranked, proportional to its size, among the top three in the country in the amount of support received from individuals, foundations, and corporations. One of his major accomplishments in that position was to conduct a joint building campaign for 12 United Way agencies that was oversubscribed by $1,800,000.

Taking an early retirement in 1977, Smith has since been a consultant in matters of finance and fund raising to a diverse range of clients, from hospitals to the Catholic Archdiocese of St. Paul/Minneapolis to the St. Paul United Arts Fund. He helped the Ordway Music Theatre locate funds to build a new $45-million facility. Most recently Smith has served as a consultant on corporate contributions to the Minnesota Mutual Life Insurance Company, one of the nation's largest insurance firms. In this connection, he drafted a grants program whose proceeds went toward retraining the unemployed, and for this Minnesota Mutual received an award from the National Alliance of Business. Smith himself has received special recognition for his services from such groups as the American Red Cross, the American Heart Association, the Boy Scouts, and the Salvation Army. In addition, he received the highly coveted Capital City Award from the St. Paul Chamber of Commerce for his outstanding service to the community.